Film *as* Philosophy

Also by Rupert Read

THE NEW WITTGENSTEIN (*editor*)

THE NEW HUME DEBATE (*editor*)

THOMAS KUHN: The Philosopher of Scientific Revolution

RECENT WORK IN PHILOSOPHY AND LITERATURE

Film *as* Philosophy

Essays in Cinema After Wittgenstein and Cavell

Edited by Rupert Read and Jerry Goodenough
University of East Anglia

First published 2005 by
PALGRAVE MACMILLAN
Houndmills, Basingstoke, Hampshire RG21 6XS and
175 Fifth Avenue, New York, N. Y. 10010
Companies and representatives throughout the world

PALGRAVE MACMILLAN is the global academic imprint of the Palgrave
Macmillan division of St. Martin's Press, LLC and of Palgrave Macmillan Ltd.
Macmillan® is a registered trademark in the United States, United Kingdom
and other countries. Palgrave is a registered trademark in the European
Union and other countries.

ISBN-13: 978–1–4039–4900–4   hardback
ISBN-10: 1–4039–4900–X   hardback
ISBN-13: 978–1–4039–9795–1   paperback
ISBN-10: 1–4039–9795–0   paperback

This book is printed on paper suitable for recycling and made from fully
managed and sustained forest sources.

A catalogue record for this book is available from the British Library.

Library of Congress Cataloging-in-Publication Data
Film as philosophy : essays on cinema after Wittgenstein and Cavell /
edited by Jerry
    Goodenough & Rupert Read.
       p. cm.
    Includes bibliographical references and index.
    ISBN 1–4039–4900–X (cloth) – ISBN 1–4039–9795–0 (pbk.)
    1. Motion pictures–Philosophy. I. Goodenough, Jerry. II. Read, Rupert J.,
1966–

PN1995.F45755 2005   2005047530
791.43′01–dc22

10   9   8   7   6   5   4   3
14   13   12   11   10   09   08   07

Printed and bound in Great Britain by
Antony Rowe Ltd, Chippenham and Eastbourne

Contents

Preface

The origins of this book lie in the joint interests of its editors in both philosophy and the cinema. Some years ago we came together to teach an undergraduate unit entitled 'Film and Literature as Philosophy', an experience that over time has clarified our belief that going to the cinema could do more than just provide nice illustrative examples for brightening up philosophy seminars, that film and watching film could actually *be* philosophy. We have been delighted to find that we are not the only ones who feel this way, and this book contains some fine examples of thoughts on and around this theme from some of the most interesting contemporary philosophers.

The book is crowned by a substantial new interview with Stanley Cavell, whose eminent work in the (post-?)analytical philosophy involved in Wittgenstein studies and in 'film analysis' has increasingly come together: here he gives an enlightening and detailed – dialogical – description of what *philosophical* reasons there are for watching films. We are grateful to him for this interview and to Andrew Klevan for all his work on that project.

We would also like to express our thanks to all of those students of ours who have forced us to sharpen up our ideas about film as philosophy over the years, to the many participants in our *Philosophers at the Cinema* film series, and to our fellow teacher, film theorist and philosopher, Emma Bell. Thanks also to Nick Bunnin and Michael Grant for early help in imagining this book. Rupert would also like to thank Juliette Harkin, for helping him to watch the films about 'madness' which lie close to the core of this collection, whether they are explicitly discussed in it or not. Finally, we are most grateful to Luciana and Daniel, our editors at Palgrave Macmillan, for all the sterling work they have put in to help make this project a reality.

Notes on Contributors

Nancy Bauer is an Associate Professor of Philosophy at Tufts University, in Boston, where she teaches courses in feminism, modern European philosophy, and philosophy and film. She is the author of *Simone de Beauvoir, Philosophy, and Feminism* (2001) and is currently writing a book called *How to Do Things With Pornography*.

Simon Critchley is Professor of Philosophy at the New School for Social Research, New York and at the University of Essex. He is author and editor of numerous books, most recently *On Humour* (2002) *Very Little...Almost Nothing* (revised edition, 2004) and *Things Merely Are* (2005).

Simon Glendinning is Fellow in European Philosophy at the European Institute at the LSE. He obtained his PhD at Oxford and has taught in the Philosophy Departments at the Universities of Kent and Reading. His research has often engaged with figures and ideas from so-called 'continental philosophy' but he has always sought to address his writing to an English-speaking (and reading) audience. He is the author of *On Being With Others: Heidegger-Derrida-Wittgenstein* (1998) and is currently completing a book on 20th Century philosophy in Europe. He has published widely on issues in the philosophy of mind and the philosophy of animal life.

Jerry Goodenough is Tutor in Philosophy at the University of East Anglia, researches and publishes in the field of personal identity and mind, and has a keen interest in philosophy, science fiction and the cinema. With Rupert Read he has been teaching an undergraduate unit on film and literature as philosophy at UEA for some years, and helps organise UEA's philosophical film society 'Philosophers at the Cinema'.

Phil Hutchinson is Lecturer in Philosophy at Manchester Metropolitan University UK. His philosophical interests include (first) Wittgenstein, (then) film, Philosophical Method, and Ethics (virtue, character and personhood). Any spare time is spent seeing and listening to music, which for about 60% of the time will be the John Coltrane Quartet. He's convinced that there must be some profound philosophical significance to

Elvin Jones's drumming but has yet to discern it (don't hold your breath).

Stuart Klawans has been the film critic for *The Nation* since 1988 and contributes articles on film to the 'Arts & Leisure' section of *The New York Times*. He is the author of *Film Follies: The Cinema Out of Order* (a finalist for the National Book Critics Circle Awards, 1999) and *Left in the Dark: Film Reviews and Essays, 1988–2001*. His articles and essays have appeared in publications including *Film Comment, Newsweek, The Village Voice, Grand Street, Parnassus: Poetry in Review*, the book review sections of *Newsday* and *The Chicago Tribune*, and the *TLS* (for which he was the 'American Notes' columnist, 1989–91). He was a recipient of a John Simon Guggenheim Memorial Foundation grant (2003–04) for a critical study of the films of Preston Sturges.

Andrew Klevan is Lecturer in Film Studies at the University of Kent where he teaches courses entitled *Female Performance in Hollywood* and *Film Style, Interpretation and Evaluation*. His essay 'Guessing the Unseen from the Seen: Stanley Cavell and Film Interpretation' appears in *Contending with Stanley Cavell* (ed. Russell Goodman 2005). He is author of two books on film: *Disclosure of the Everyday: Undramatic Achievement in Narrative Film* (2000) and *Film Performance: From Achievement to Appreciation* (2005).

Stephen Mulhall is Fellow and Tutor in Philosophy at New College, Oxford. His research presently focuses on Wittgenstein, Heidegger, Kierkegaard and Nietzsche, and so on the relations between politics, ethics and religion, as well as on the connections between philosophy and literature. His recent publications include: *Inheritance and Originality* (2001), *On Film* (2002) and *Philosophical Myths of the Fall* (2005).

Rupert Read is Senior Lecturer in the School of Philosophy at the University of East Anglia (Norwich). His publications include *The New Wittgenstein* (2000) and *Kuhn* (2002), and papers in *Philosophy, Philosophical Investigations, Philosophical Papers, Philosophical Forum, Proceedings of the Aristotelian Society, Philosophical Psychology*, and *Philosophy Psychology Psychiatry*. He enjoys debating in print with the likes of Michael Dummett, Noam Chomsky, Louis Sass and J.M. Coetzee. He is currently working on issues in the philosophy of maths, on Wittgenstein and Zen Buddhism, and on a manuscript on psychosis in film and philosophy.

David Rudrum teaches at London Metropolitan University. His work explores the relationship between philosophy, literature, and film. He has edited a collection of essays on *Literature and Philosophy: A Guide to Contemporary Debates* (forthcoming 2005) and is currently preparing a monograph on *Wittgenstein and the Theory of Narrative*.

Introduction I: A Philosopher Goes to the Cinema

Jerry Goodenough

> Film is made for philosophy; it shifts or puts different light on whatever philosophy has said about appearance and reality, about actors and characters, about scepticism and dogmatism, about presence and absence. – Stanley Cavell[1]

Introduction

Why might a philosopher want to go to the cinema? One reason, of course, could be just to watch the film, to be entertained, etc. Wittgenstein is alleged to have spent many happy hours in the Cambridge fleapits of the 1930s where his choice of viewing was often the most banal of Hollywood fare: 'oater' cowboy movies, Busby Berkeley musicals, and so on. We might see film here as a relief from the pressures of thinking philosophically.[2] In this sense, film is philosophically no more significant than reading detective novels, going fishing, or indulging in any other pastime that distracts one or stimulates other aspects of oneself than the purely intellectual.

But a philosopher *qua* philosopher has, I think, at least four different reasons for going to the cinema. Firstly, a philosopher may care about the cinema itself, about the technology and processes and social meanings of watching films. Parallels may be drawn between the masses immersed in the darkness and the chained inhabitants of Plato's cave in *The Republic*. The social and psychological aspects of film-going may be explored.[3] The philosopher may have an interest in the nature of film as a perceptual experience, a process whereby a series of slightly different still pictures are projected onto a surface in the darkness with sufficient rapidity to be understood by human minds as a single moving picture.[4] This raises interesting questions about human perception, and the psychological as well as social conventions involved in the cinematic experience. Such a philosopher might enjoy performances of films that are quite open about their own nature *as* film.[5] Or perhaps those avant-garde movies that play with the technology, where cartoon or abstract designs are drawn straight on to the celluloid, etc. One might even point to the film that raises the greatest challenge to the whole concept of motion pictures, Derek Jarman's *Blue*.[6] We might call this approach Philosophy and the Cinematic Experience.

A second reason for taking an interest in film is that a film may *illustrate* philosophical themes and issues. Watching such a film may provide the philosopher with illustrative examples, and this is particularly important for the philosopher – most of them, these days – who must also *teach* philosophy. Such films may be part of the common cultural currency of their students. Using examples extracted from films for pedagogical purposes may increase students' engagement with the topic, brighten seminar discussions with dramatic examples from a medium with which most students will be familiar.[7]

A popular example of film for this purpose is the Wachowski brothers' *Matrix* trilogy. This set of dark science-fiction fantasies provides a graphic illustration of a number of philosophical issues. Our hero, Neo, is awakened from his everyday life to discover that *that* life was in fact a computer programme; in reality, his body – together with those of almost all other human beings in the world – was being kept unconscious by the machines that have now taken over the world. The Matrix is a shared life-programme generated by the machines and fed to these bodies, giving them a consistent dream that they take to be everyday life.

Such a film appeals to some long-standing philosophical problems: to the difference between appearance and reality, to questions of solipsism, the nature of dreaming, and so on. It illustrates certain moves in Descartes' methodological scepticism in the *Meditations*, adapts Putnam's brain-in-a-vat case, and relates to Nozick's experience-machine.[8] But *The Matrix* avoids approaching these issues in a very philosophical way. (A philosophical discussion would get in the way of the action![9])

A third reason for a philosopher to enter into the darkness with pop-corn and soft drink might be to watch a film in which philosophical issues *are* mentioned in a serious and central way. This is a much smaller category of film, film *about* philosophy. Perhaps the only serious attempt at producing a feature film *about* a philosopher is Derek Jarman's *Wittgenstein* (1993). Made on a low budget, it is a peculiar and sometimes obscure portrayal of scenes in the life of the philosopher.

But it is imaginative in its visualisations and makes a serious effort at communicating something of Wittgenstein's thought, and of what Jarman takes to be the link between the thought and the man's life.

Jarman's film may be the only important biographical film about philosophy in the analytical style.[10] However, philosophy as an activity, a way of life, a way of thinking, still occurs in film outside of the Anglo-Saxon tradition; in cultures such as the French, philosophy has more of a public profile. And here at least, one can find films that don't just *illustrate* philosophical themes but incorporate them into the action or discuss them explicitly.

The final reason for luring the philosopher into the cinema is the one at the core of this book: to see film *as* philosophy, as in some sense *doing* philosophy. I don't claim that these reasons are mutually exclusive, more areas along a spectrum of increasing philosophical interest. A film need not occupy a single narrowly-defined place on this spectrum: a particularly rich film might spread itself along from illustration to film *as* philosophy. In the next three sections of this introduction, I want to look at these last three notions of philosophical film in more detail, in each case examining it through an analysis of films that seem to me to illustrate it well.

Film as illustrating philosophy – *Total Recall*

The Matrix is presently a paradigm instance of a film that *illustrates* philosophical issues, but I want to examine instead another, earlier Hollywood science-fiction blockbuster, Paul Verhoeven's 1990 film *Total Recall*, starring Arnold Schwartzenegger. This was a considerable success – though never a cult in the way that *The Matrix* has become. It has many of the characteristics of a mainstream Hollywood feature – big-name stars, expensive sets and special effects, a considerable emphasis upon violence and action. Yet it also makes reference to a number of philosophical issues, and often in a quite interesting way. (This isn't the deliberate aim of its producers – my co-editor calls it 'a work of accidental genius'.)

The film began life as a short story by Philip K. Dick, 'We Can Remember It For You Wholesale', one of his many stories and novels that dealt with discrepancies between our experiences and some underlying reality. In a late interview Dick said:

I studied philosophy during my brief career at the University of California at Berkley. I'm what they call an 'acosmic pan-entheist', which means that I don't believe that the universe exists. I believe that the only thing that exists is God and he is more than the universe. The universe is an extension of God into space and time. That's the premise I start from in my work, that so-called 'reality' is a mass delusion that we've all been required to believe for reasons totally obscure... I've always had this funny feeling about reality. It just seems very feeble to me sometimes. It doesn't seem to have the substantiality that it's supposed to have.[11]

Dick's work can have a surprisingly philosophical content. This is not a problem for the sort of popular action movie that the producers of *Total Recall* had in mind. What *is* is that 'We Can Remember...' is very short indeed, and the central character, Douglas Quayle, doesn't do much: most of the story is about what has already happened to him, rather than about what he does.

Quayle, a mild-mannered nobody in the future, goes to have implanted memories of an exciting trip to Mars as a special-agent. But the implant process doesn't work; technicians discover that he already possesses a set of suppressed memories with this content, which are now brought to the surface. The agency that sent Quayle on his mission intends to kill him, but he persuades them instead to implant a fantasy that will block his memories of the mission. The fantasy is that, after a childhood encounter with aliens, Quayle is the only person who, through his continued existence alone, protects Earth from alien invasion. But the implant technicians have trouble here too, for they discover he already has suppressed memories of *this* fantasy. Perhaps Quayle really is the one person standing between the world and alien destruction after all.[12]

This storyline is unsuitable for a Schwarzenegger movie, but the twist at the end aligns it with the short SF stories dramatised in television series like *The Twilight Zone* or *The Outer Limits*. For a Hollywood action movie, certain genre commitments must be fulfilled. The leading character must be a figure of action rather than someone to whom things just happen. (In the early parts of *Total Recall* Arnold is precisely such a passive character, but he soon turns into the appropriate action figure.) More importantly, in order to be a financial success – and in order to justify its vast budget – such a film must appeal to the widest possible audience. This entails making its philosophical content not particularly cerebral, emphasising action and visual spectacle. What is slightly surprising is just how much philosophical content remains.

There are three key philosophical issues that the film addresses. The first of these is the nature of experience and the importance of the cause of *our* experiences. The activities of the Total Recall company, inserting false holiday 'memories', remind us of Nozick's thought experiment, where it is argued that, if we are both moral and rational, we want not just good experiences but experiences that have the right cause. If a machine could give us any apparently real experience we like, would we be prepared to live in it? If it made it seem as though we were having the best life imaginable? If it were arranged so that we forgot that we were in such a machine? To the extent that we believe that this situation is inferior to real life, to that extent we deny the importance merely of *having* experiences, and insist upon their being caused in the right way. Quade (notice the name change away from the ornithological overtones of the original story!) does not feel this way.[13]

The second issue concerns the nature of personal identity across time. For it turns out that Quade used to be Hauser, a government agent on Mars. Hauser's psychology was deleted and a new personality, that of Quade, was inserted into the same body. Using Locke's criterion of personal memory, since Quade remembers nothing of Hauser's life, he is a different person from Hauser, although the same human being (body) and therefore sometimes taken for Hauser. Where the film is particularly ingenious is in having Hauser record video messages for Quade: thus one person is able to talk to another, later person who will subsequently inhabit his body! If the conspirators succeed in restoring Hauser to his body, has Quade been murdered? (Can one murder a person without murdering a human being?) It is important for Quade to resist the return of Hauser, to embrace his 'new' identity through his choices and actions. (The bizarre Kuato, a spiritual leader who turns out to be a wizened head attached to another man's chest, provides another test case for theories of personal identity.)

Thirdly there is the question of external-world scepticism. Could the whole of my experience be a dream/nightmare? At one point in the film this is the doctor's message to Quade, who refutes the doctor by killing him! But this leaves open the possibility that some or all of Quade's experiences are indeed unreal, part of the artificial dream-world created by Total Recall. (The subterranean and paranoiac way in which this thought is sustained is rather more subtle than the direct presentation of the issue in *The Matrix*.) Though the central part of the narrative leads us to reject this interpretation, some of my students[14] have raised the possibility of whether the ambiguous 'awakening' opening and closing shots indicate that it has all been just a dream. (Quade's last line: 'I just had a terrible thought…What if this is all a dream?') There is also the question of the nature of limited sensory doubt: here Quade's use of the holographic image projector deliberately raises problems of what is real and what is not for his enemies.

What we have, then, is a considerable amount of philosophical material being presented in the unlikely form of a Hollywood action movie. If this form restricts the depth of exploration of any of these matters, it still allows their distribution to the film-going public. On the surface these issues, particularly the questions of memory, reality versus appearance, and the real nature of the self, are presented merely as plot-devices and so run the risk of being overwhelmed by both the high-speed action and the special effects. This, then, is philosophical difficulties as entertainment; but we can hope that some of these issues stay in the mind of the viewer long enough to be recalled and discussed in the pub afterwards.

Film about philosophy – *Ma Nuit Chez Maud*

Our second category is films *about* philosophy, and these – as noted above – are a much rarer item. There have been few films dedicated to philosophers, at least *as* philosophers.[15] There have been documentary films about philosophers, e.g. the Quine series of videos mentioned earlier, though few of these are of cinematic interest. An exception here may be Kirkby Dick and Amy Ziering Kofman's 2002 film, *Derrida*, a stylish documentary that both depicts Derrida's public activities as a philosopher, his speeches and meetings, and yet at the same time deconstructs them. It is thus rather more than a mere documentary.

In an interview about the making of the film, Derrida put his finger on the problem of making films about philosophers:

Q. *How can you separate a philosopher's writing from his life?*
A. I don't know if you can, but most classical philosophers did try to separate them, and some of them succeeded. If you read philosophical texts of the tradition, you'll notice they almost never said 'I,' and didn't speak in the first person. From Aristotle to Heidegger, they try to consider their own lives as something marginal or accidental. What was essential was their teaching and their thinking. Biography is something empirical and outside, and is considered an accident that isn't necessarily or essentially linked to the philosophical activity or system.[16]

Many classical philosophers have indeed seen themselves in this way.[17] An interesting attempt to make a non-documentary film that precisely tried to illuminate the man through the philosophy and *vice versa* was Jarman's *Wittgenstein* mentioned earlier.

However, I want to concentrate upon another film, for Eric Rohmer's *Ma Nuit Chez Maud* is consciously about philosophy, about the roles and limitations of philosophical thinking in everyday life. (Rohmer's films are always in some sense philosophical.) Needless to say, it is a French film and so comes from a culture in which philosophy has not been completely marginalised as an academic discipline but still plays some role within mainstream culture. French philosophers appear on TV chat-shows and often possess charisma and popularity, even if they sometimes lack the clarity and rigour of their Anglo-American cousins.[18] Much of French life has been dominated by Catholicism, an intellectually rigorous religion, and Rohmer's film is about, among other things, the interplay between philosophy and religion. Indeed, when it came out in 1969 one critic said of it that it was little more than a skeleton upon which to hang Rohmer's philosophical observations. But it is not a stodgy or over-intellectual film, for Rohmer has a light hand: the debate here is carried out with considerable charm and humour.

The film's unnamed protagonist and narrator (played by Jean-Louis Trintignant) is a Frenchman of about 30, an engineer with interests in mathematics who, after working abroad, has returned to the central French industrial town of Clermont-Ferrand. He is also a Catholic of a sort, with perhaps more of an intellectual interest in religion than a genuine spiritual commitment. His dual nature is symbolised by the purchase he makes in a bookshop at the beginning of the film, a volume on mathematical probability, and a copy of Pascal, who embodies the triumph of faith or unreason over mathematics or reason. The narrator is to meet two characters who represent this duality. First he runs into an old friend, Vidal, a Marxist with a strong belief in the rationality of history. Vidal introduces him to Maud, an attractive brunette divorcée living with her little daughter; Maud is a creature of desire and appetite rather than reason. But our hero also keeps running into an unknown blonde woman (Françoise), on the streets or coming out of church, a woman who represents his heart's desire: this, he decides irrationally, is the woman he must marry. (A Pascalian leap of faith?) Black and white, brunette and blonde, desire for its own sake or desire in accordance with reason: the struggle is on.

The film, then, plays with the Wager from Pascal's *Pensées*. Bet on the existence of God: if you are wrong you lose nothing, but if you are right you gain eternal bliss. Bet against God (or refuse to bet, which comes to the same thing) and you stand to win nothing if you are right, but lose eternal bliss in favour of infinite darkness if you are wrong. The balance of the returns seems obvious. And this is the very limit of reason, says Pascal; when the moment comes to embrace God you cannot do this rationally, but must cast aside reason and make the leap of faith. The question is whether our hero can make a similar leap.

He is unreliable in a number of ways. He claims to be a Catholic, but obviously hasn't practised much. He is plainly uncomfortable in church. He lacks self-discipline, is made uncomfortable by the rigour of Pascal. (The moral, not the mathematical rigour: he is, after all, a mathematician too!) Sometimes he pleads predestination, that life is in some way preordained for him. At other times he worries about free will, about the necessity of making the right moral choices. The decision in the middle of the film whether or not to sleep with Maud[19] is presented in terms of such a free moral choice.

Yet his life *is* in a sense preordained. Rohmer shamelessly uses coincidence to keep bringing the narrator into contact with the unknown Françoise through a series of accidental meetings.[20] We may say that the film director 'plays God' with their characters, and here this is literally true. Rohmer's manipulation of Françoise and our hero, bringing them together, taking them apart, can be seen as standing in for the way that God plans and manipulates our lives. God and his role in life and thought are central to this film, which opens with a long sequence in church, the Christmas service after which our hero first glimpses Françoise. And, lest we think these meetings are an accident, the very last sequence of the film reveals that Françoise has already been connected to the action, is the character unnamed but described by Maud during *her* night with us.

The narrator seems doomed to failure, yet the coincidental meetings with Françoise keep occurring. 'What are the probabilities of two people meeting randomly?' he asks Vidal early in the film. Probability is an underlying theme here. If the improbable keeps happening, is that a mere expected symptom of randomness? Or evidence that events are being directed? That there really is a God working in the world? These coincidences may be outrageous, but they don't strike us like that, for Rohmer embeds them in a realistic framework of natural action and setting.[21]

The setting of the film is important: we are, as characters keep insisting, in the provinces, not Paris. The action takes place in Clermont-Ferrand in winter, the dead of the year and yet also the time of Christmas and re-birth, the time – as Eliot's *Little Gidding* reminds us – when wonderful things happen. The film is deliberately made in black and white, and these two colours are another theme. Outside and inside. The white glare of the snow, the cosy darkness of the interiors, particularly of the church. Maud the brunette and Françoise the blonde. Maud lives down in the middle of town, Françoise up in the purity of the mountains. Maud is really only happy at night, Françoise is a day-person, comfortable outside. All the issues are clear, as ultimately there are no grey areas for Pascal: either you bet or you do not. The narrator seeks to escape from the artificial – Maud – to the natural – Françoise: a night at *her* house has an entirely different character. And this theme of the triumph of nature is emphasised in the film's coda (when the link between Maud and Françoise is made clear) in the final move of our hero away from Maud and down towards Françoise, the sea and the light.

There is a Catholic reading of values here. Maud, the creature of appetites and sensuality, is regarded as unnatural, urban, societal, living in a world ruled by mechanistic logic. It is Françoise's world – the world of marriage, the bet on God – which comes to represent 'the natural fluent order of things, attained through a grace that passeth all understanding'. Thus Rohmer presents a reversal of the values that we have become used to in the modern world, not least in the industrial world of France a few months after the revolutionary events of May 1968. He teases us with the possibility that free will may not exist, and with the certainty that, like our hero, we must believe in it anyway. This is perhaps a reactionary philosophy we are being offered; critics described Rohmer's cinema as going 'against the stream' – the stream of French cinema (Truffaut, Godard, etc.) but perhaps of modernity too. But it is presented with great elegance.

To spend a night with Maud, then, involves spending our days in a world where philosophy and theology are real, are talked about in bars, and structure the thinking of the protagonists. Has there ever been a movie whose central theme was the *refusal* of the hero to have sex with a beautiful woman? Possibly so, but a movie where the decision was based upon moral and philosophical principles? Here to refrain, not to act, is to make a bet, to take up one side of Pascal's wager, so the ultimate *in*action of the movie is at the same time the beginning of its most important action, the choice of the light over the dark. Pascal was right: doing nothing, not choosing, is itself a choice. These issues themselves, the dry logic of Pascal, the working-out of free will and predestination, are brought alive when seen in the dramatic context of people making decisions about their lives, in the cinematic context of the constant play of light and dark within the dark of the cinema, until we emerge into the light of the world outside the cinema just as our protagonist began the film by emerging into the light outside the church, and ends it by moving towards the light and Françoise. Cinema and philosophy are gently woven together. One could sit through *Total Recall* and emerge untainted by any philosophical thought at all: but one cannot understand the evening *chez* Maud without grasping something of the moral and theological themes working themselves out in the background.

Film *as* Philosophy – *Blade Runner* and *L'Année Dernière à Marienbad*

It is the contention of this book that it is possible to understand watching a film as itself engaging in philosophy. I want to illustrate this by looking at two very different films, Ridley Scott's cult science-fiction classic *Blade Runner* (1982, re-released in a significantly different director's cut in 1992) and Alain Resnais' 1961 *L'Année Dernière à Marienbad*.

Scott's film fits nicely into our category of films illustrating significant philosophical issues. It derives from Philip K. Dick's 1968 novel *Do Androids Dream of Electric Sheep?*, though Scott's screenplay, which had several contributing script-writers, differs in significant ways from Dick's book. The story is set in the 21st century in an America that has survived a great disaster that has completely eliminated almost all animals. Yet animals and the animal motif can be seen throughout the film: the owl, snake, unicorn, dove and others.[22]

Two technological advances together drive the plot. Firstly, we are now capable of creating artificial entities that look and behave like the originals. Neither the owl nor the snake in the film, for instance, is a 'real' animal – they're clever fakes, moving replications of creatures. And secondly, we have started the difficult and dangerous job of colonising the other planets, an obviously unattractive proposition since, despite the overcrowding, pollution and non-stop rain on Earth, the colonising companies have to work hard to attract people to work off-earth. A solution is the creation of artificial human beings, replicants as they are called in the movie, that possess thought and language and rationality. Depending upon the particular job they are designed for, they possess great strength or intelligence or attractiveness. The replicants do the *work* work: they *labour*. (They can thus be seen as yet another representative in science-fiction of the mistreated working classes, a theme that goes back to H.G. Wells and beyond.)

By virtue of these qualities replicants are dangerous to 'real' human beings, and so are forbidden to come to earth. The companies and the law together employ special detectives, blade-runners as they are known,[23] to hunt down and 'retire' such runaway machines, though to the audience 'retirement' looks just like killing. Our hero, Deckard (Harrison Ford), is one such blade runner, and we follow him as he tracks down four particularly dangerous replicants – Roy, Pris, Leon and Zhora – who have rebelled and come to earth. They seek life from their creator, Tyrell, for, in recognition of their special dangerousness, all replicants have a built-in limited lifespan, so their existence will terminate after just four years.

Replicants seem to be in many ways persons like ourselves. So the film from the outset raises the issue of what we mean by personhood. Daniel Dennett argues (in a famous and much re-printed paper, 'Conditions of Personhood') for six necessary conditions that something must fulfil in order to be a person. The first of these is rationality: a person is essentially a rational thinking being. The second is intentionality: a person is the kind of thing to which intentional states like belief and desire can rationally or usefully be ascribed. The third is possession of a particular relational property, that of being able to be treated as a person.[24] A person must be the kind of thing that others can treat as a person. And this is entwined with a condition of mutuality: a person is the kind of thing that treats others as persons. Fifthly a person must possess linguistic ability. And sixthly, a person is conscious.[25]

We satisfy these conditions, while dogs and cats don't: they aren't linguistic, have a limited rationality, and – most importantly – we can't (rationally) treat them as persons and they don't treat us like persons either. (Though they may treat us as particularly dim specimens of doghood or catness.) Of course, on this reading babies aren't persons either, though we may treat them as potential persons. Notice that Dennett says nothing about being made of carbon-based cells, in fact nothing about being human. His analysis leaves open the possibility that there could be non-human or even non-biological persons provided that they could satisfy these conditions, gods, robots or Martians. Or replicants. Our problem, as viewers of *Blade Runner*, is that these replicants seem to fulfil almost all of Dennett's conditions for personhood. They look like human beings, act like us, seem to possess rationality and language and intentionality and so on. But society refuses to treat them as persons; instead they are runaway machines that must be decommissioned. This discrepancy between *our* intuitive feelings about replicants and this future society's provides much of the film's philosophical tension.

Why, then, a film? What philosophically can a film do here that a book cannot? This can be answered via reference to some remarks of Wittgenstein's. In discussing the philosophical problem of other minds, Wittgenstein makes the point that you have to absorb an awful lot of philosophy before you can seriously doubt that other people might be conscious. In part he saw his writing as a kind of inoculation or therapy against this effect of philosophy. We do not often, he says, reason to the conclusion that other people are conscious.[26] It is an inevitable concomitant of our dealings with them. We do not philosophise to the conclusion that dogs and cats probably feel pain – we cannot avoid that belief if we live with them. They share a form of life with us, not sufficiently to enable us to think of them as proper persons but certainly enough for us to see them as feeling creatures like ourselves. We are, if you like, persuaded at a deeper and more fundamental level than the merely rational.

Blade Runner does not just make us intellectually aware that the replicants satisfy many possible conditions for personhood. Rather, by sharing this portion of their lives, by seeing their quest for life, the way they relate to each other, by comparing it with Deckard's job of termination, we must inevitably come to *feel* for them, anger, fear, lust at one particular point, and, at the end, perhaps a profound pity and admiration. How could anyone *not* treat these replicants as persons? Society has somehow gone terribly wrong here. The film allows us to perceive and to feel, to experience what is happening at a deeper and more persuasive level than any mere written account could manage. Engaging with the film forces us to recognise that we largely share a Wittgensteinian 'form of life' with these replicants.

The 1992 director's cut differs significantly from the 1982 film. Scott was persuaded to re-cut the film so that it more closely resembled his original intentions, and in particular the ending has been significantly altered. (One really needs to have seen both versions of the film in order to understand the full implications of this discussion.) Scott removed the happy ending that the original studio cut had imposed, with its sudden declaration that Tyrell's secretary, Rachel – unlike the other replicants – had a normal lifespan, something that makes a liar of Tyrell in his confrontation with Roy. (If it could be done for Rachel, it could presumably be done for the other replicants.) What is left is Rachel's status as an advanced replicant who does not know she is not human until she learns it from Deckard.

Scott also removed the 1980 version's intrusive voice-over, a narration which put you inside Deckard's mind but which tended to point out what you ought to be thinking or feeling at key moments such as the death of Roy, rather than allowing the picture to speak for itself. By withdrawing us from Deckard's first-person viewpoint in this way, Scott allows the picture to be considerably more ambiguous on the question of whether or not Deckard is himself an unknowing replicant like Rachel. There is much to be said for either side of this debate: Deckard might, for instance, be a much better blade-runner as a replicant, on the 'set a thief to catch a thief' principle, stronger, smarter, able to take the incredible amount of physical punishment dealt out to him by Roy at the end. And he would suffer less from moral qualms if he didn't know that he was a replicant – on the assumption here that replicants are capable of *having* moral qualms! On the other hand, the scenes with Tyrell would have to be re-interpreted, as he would have known about Deckard all along if he were a replicant, and the absolute moral and legal prohibition on replicants on Earth would have to be revised.

But the very fact that the film *is* ambiguous about Deckard's humanity is philosophically relevant. Personhood is not an all-or-nothing business. Candidates can more or less approximate to the required conditions, be more or less like a person. The official ideology of *Blade Runner*'s world is that replicants are mere machines, incapable of feelings, incapable of seeing themselves as persons, or of seeing *us* as persons. But Scott allows us to eavesdrop on the relationship between the replicants, between Leon and Zhora, and especially between Roy and Pris. Roy's response to the death of Pris is presented as one of grief pure and simple, a wrenching physical grief in no way different to the response that a similarly situated human being would have.

On the other hand, Scott maintains the ambiguity of the film with some subtle touches. In two cases we have reports of events that have happened off-screen, a device that helps to minimise their tremendous emotional charge. At the beginning of the film we are told that the escaping replicants killed the crew and passengers of a space-ship in order to get to Earth. At the end, we overhear a radio report that Sebastian, the only human friend the replicants had, a sweet unworldly man who, like them, suffers from a drastically restricted life-span, has been found murdered. The implication is that Roy is responsible, that Sebastian was disposable once he had served his purpose of enabling Roy to get access to Tyrell. These two examples of cold-bloodedness would indicate that the replicants are having trouble recognising *us* as persons every bit as much as we have trouble with them. There is also one gut-wrenching effect that Scott leaves in; when Deckard shoots

Pris, she does not collapse and die like a human. Instead she thrashes around like a malfunctioning machine, an effect that shakes our previous acceptance of her as something just like us. Scott could have left all three of these touches out of the film; by including them, he balances the scales a little, and we can never totally forget that these things are machines as well as possible persons. (But note how the scales would have been tilted if Scott had *shown* the space-ship massacre, or if he had included the scene from Dick's novel where Pris coldly pulls off the legs of a spider one by one just to see what happens.)

Dick's book never allows us to forget the replicants' machine origins. But in the book we are told about things rather than seeing them; imaginative prose works upon our minds in an entirely different way from sounds and images. Much of the book has been lost for the film. We lose Mercerism, the strange and media-driven Gnostic-like religion, with all that it implies about the importance and manipulation of empathy. We lose Deckard's home life and the social importance of his pathetic ambition to own a 'real' animal, and so on. But this enables the film to focus more tightly, dramatically and emotionally, upon Deckard and his change. (Though it is another ambiguity of the film that we are never really sure if Deckard *is* the hero – Harrison Ford plays him with a remarkable lack of warmth – or if it is Roy who becomes the more admirable character. Deckard endures through to the end, but it is Roy's Nietzschean triumph over life and death in his dying moments that stays with us.[27]) Ultimately the film should act as a kind of philosophical mirror, making us look to see how we see ourselves.

This mirroring of the self, but within a different philosophical context, is a theme of my other exemplar film, *L'Année Dernière à Marienbad*, a film that has achieved a remarkable reputation ever since its release. Some people regard it as one of the most fascinating and innovative uses of film ever to appear anywhere near the mainstream cinema. Others regard it as a deliberately obscure and pretentious work whose possible aesthetic value is far outweighed by its difficulty. But I have come to regard it as a key instance of film *as* philosophy.

Since the film is about, among other things, the problems of narrative, it is impossible to summarise clearly the narrative of the film. Not everyone agrees with me on this. John Ward, for instance, in his early book on Resnais[28] believes that there is a simple narrative of what actually happened, and that once we can get clear on this we can concentrate upon the narrative effects, and what they tell us about memory, testimony, etc. (I disagree!)

But here is an attempted summary. The action of the film is set in a baroque chateau used as some kind of hotel or spa for the wealthy, circa 1960. We are not told these things and must estimate the date of the proceedings purely from the dress and hairstyles of the particip-ants. The action of the film is isolated from what we might be tempted to refer to as the real world, the world outside. Among the inhabitants of the hotel there are three central characters. We never learn their names – the script refers to them only as X, A and M. – or anything about their lives. The woman A and the man M are a couple of some sort – lovers? Man and wife? The other man, X, is the central character of the film, because he is also the narrator. On one level the plot is simple: X meets A and tells her that they have met before, last year at Marienbad. Or Frederiksbad, or Karlstadt. (Time is important in this film, not space.) He claims that they fell in love and that she agreed to go away with him, but did not. And now X wishes to resuscitate their relationship, and once more persuade A to run off with him. A, however, denies all of this. She claims she does not remember their agreement, doesn't remember meeting X at all.

So the film, says Resnais, is really about a single action, a persuading. X tries to persuade A. He tries to persuade her to remember their past, and he tries to persuade her to join him in the future. The whole action of the film may, then, be summed up in one line from a famous Hollywood song: you *must* remember this.

So far, so simple. But unfortunately the film's narrative is nowhere near as simple as this. Because, in the course of the various encounters between X and A, we are offered a series of events which don't seem to fit this narrative, or which contradict each other. These sometimes adopt the form of a flashback, though, since the entire film sometimes appears to be a flashback, this may not be the right term to use. Alain Robbe-Grillet, who wrote the film and the ciné-novel on which it is based, started from the premise that the cinema audience was now so used to the conventions of the flashback that they could be used to subvert what he called 'the linear plots of the old-fashioned cinema which never spare us a link in the chain of all-too-expected events.'[29] Our minds, Robbe-Grillet claims, do not usually operate in this pedestrian narrative fashion. Instead

> our mind goes faster – or slower, on occasion. Its style is more varied, richer and less reassuring: it skips certain passages, it pre-serves an exact record of certain 'unimportant' details, it repeats and doubles back on itself. And this *mental time* with its peculiarities, its

gaps, its obsessions, its obscure areas, is the one that interests us since it is the tempo of our emotions, of our *life*.[30]

Hence the narrative structure of the film, for the whole story is told to us by X. It is, in a sense, *his* flashback. And Robbe-Grillet rejects the old Hollywood convention that a flashback must be seen as an objective and reliable narrative of events, for it is in the very subjectivity of narrative that he finds the greatest interest. This is only a partial explanation for the complexity of the narrative, for it remains possible that not only is the narration unreliable, so is the identity of the narrator.

Let us rehearse briefly some possible explanations for the events of the film, starting with John Ward's summary[31]: a year ago a man X met a woman A at Marienbad in a chateau where they were both guests. Under the nose of her husband M, he began an affair with her. After trying several times to persuade A to leave with him, X is warned off by M. Finally M kills A, and X is left alone to mourn. The narrative is a grief-stricken interior monologue by someone trying to reconstruct or revise the events that brought him so much unhappiness. Whatever happens in the film, then, is X's version of what was said and done, with all that that means for its possible reliability. But we are also offered other possibilities. There is a suggestion – a flashback within a flashback? – that X responded to A's resistance then with an act of rape, an act of which he is now so ashamed that he keeps trying to blot it out. Perhaps what X is really trying to re-write here is his own past and character, as well as those of A, to show that he was engaged in a relationship which A welcomed, and not one that repelled her.

Or perhaps it was actually X himself who died last year, in an accidental fall, a death that interrupted his relationship with A, and it is this event that he is trying to airbrush from of his past. The film, then, is a ghost story, the interior narrative of a disembodied Cartesian spirit seeking to make sense of the events that brought about his death. Or those of a heart-broken lover seeking to make sense of the death of his beloved that he somehow brought about. Or perhaps they are all dead: this is a vision of hell, an endless slow minuet of characters with no past and no future, partaking of events that seem to have no ultimate meaning. None of the events within the chateau go anywhere: plays, conversations, games, but none of them relating to anything outside of this enclosed world.

The film is something of a feminist nightmare. It has no female characters, only A, but she is not a woman, merely X's memory or fantasy of a woman, passive and ultimately persuadable. If Resnais sees the film as a persuading, we can also see it as a seduction, and of the worst kind. X is not primarily persuading a woman to *do* something, but to *remember* something she would not otherwise have remembered. (Or perhaps *quasi*-remember since it is not clear that the events of last year ever happened, at least not to her.) If, as Lockeans hold, personal identity is composed out of chains of experiential memory, then X is recreating A, literally, making her the person he wants her to be by re-ordering her personhood, substituting his version of the past for hers, giving her the 'memories' she needs to have in order for her to be the person he wants her to be. In that way A becomes the woman that X has always desired. How, then, we interpret the sublimely ambiguous ending of the film may depend upon what character we give to this persuading.

Others have seen the film as being about time. Rather than interpret the events, all we have to do is place them in the right order to make sense. Our problem here is that all of the events have the same time, i.e. they are all primarily events within the narrative of X, within the mind of X. Whether they have any objective time, whether they refer to some other, differently-ordered sequence of events in the 'real' world, is something that we are not in a position to know.[32] For all of the events of the film take place within the solipsistic universe of X's mind. To say of a memory that is truthful or not is to say that it accurately records or mirrors an event of which it is a memory, an event usually outside the mind. But we cannot get outside this mind: all we have access to are the various contents presented to us in the course of X's narrative, which we must try to make as consistent as possible. Ward's narrative is one way of doing this, and I offer others. But what makes one narrative better than another? That it includes more? Leaves behind fewer problems? Or smaller problems? Solipsism leaves us with an indefinite number of choices here.

Since everything we know, everything we see, is communicated to us via the mind of X, we have to make some judgement about the reliability of the narrator. But without access to the external world, we have no grounds for making any objective judgement here. All we know is what X lets us know. All we know of X is what he tells us. So we can only judge him on this basis. Yet X himself is no suave and self-assured narrator, since other narratives keep breaking in, brief bursts of other stories which X himself tries to suppress – the rape, the fall, the shooting. Are these mere delusions or are these fragments of some more central truth that X is trying to keep from us? They cannot all be true – they contradict one another – though they may all be false.

X may be insane. Perhaps this is all his delusion. There are certainly features of his narrative that chime with traditional accounts of mental illness. Notice, for instance, how all the passing and barely overheard remarks of the other hotel guests can be interpreted as having a bearing on the situation of X and A.[33] Everywhere there seems to be meaning, even in places where the rest of us would not look for it. It is one of the symptoms of schizophrenia that the patient seeks and finds meaning in what the rest of us would regard as random or contingent events and features. Part of their problem, perhaps, is that their meaning-detecting equipment is *too* aware, *too* sensitive.[34]

Interpretation, then, may be impossible. Consider the statue in the garden: it plays a central role in some of the dialogues between X and A. It is, if you will, a piece of time frozen, a stone snapshot of an action interrupted. But what action? Yanking a momentary slice out of time renders it impossible to interpret accurately: is he pushing her back protectively? Is she pushing him forward? Can we even tell who they are? The classical interpretation at one point is countered later by the claim that the statue too is baroque, partaking of the 18th century convention for decking out contemporary figures in classical apparel. If even their clothing cannot be guaranteed to help us, then we have no idea who these figures are. But that is just as true of X and A and M. (The statue here reminds us of the picture Wittgenstein describes of an old man either climbing up or sliding down a hill[35]: even this simple drawing is ambiguous in its meaning when seen out of context. Context is essential, but there is no context to this film outside of what we see and hear in front of us.)

And the chateau itself, the fourth real character in this film, is equally problematic, for what appears – because we may pay so little attention to it – to be at least an objective backdrop to this story, turns out to be no such thing. Resnais himself subverts this notion: on one occasion we pan through a doorway into a room, yet later the same movement takes us into an entirely different room. The gardens are subtly different at different times in the film. A's room was, of course, plain, or else ornately decorated, dark or else white, with a mirror over the mantelpiece. Or a snow painting. The chateau changes its clothing from memory to memory, just as poor A does. We cannot even rely upon the scenery here; in the famous long garden-shot, only the people are real, *for only the people cast shadows*: it is almost as though the chateau and its gardens are the real ghosts.

In our everyday lives we seek to construct narratives with as great a degree of objectivity as possible. But should we then do this within the world of art? Cinema has always been seen as the most linear of all art forms, reflecting its material linearity as a single long strip of film moving through a projector. And since we regard our lives in the same linear fashion, so too do we try to interpret our films. It is this quest for objectivity that is under attack here.[36]

But nothing happens, complain some viewers. And that may be precisely the point. For a key theme of the film is the idea of stasis. (This is in some ways an un-moving movie!) The film opens with movement and nothing else: the constant wandering of a viewpoint through an ornate setting while an unclear narration struggles to be heard across discordant music. This progress leads towards a conversation, and the sight of a man and a woman talking, but this turns out to be a play within the screenplay. The action freezes and unfreezes, as does the conversation of the play's audience afterwards. (As though time itself were freezing and unfreezing within this viewpoint.)

Note the number of times the word 'frozen' appears in the dialogue and narrative, and the gossiping hotel guests' miraculous tale concerning the unlikely occasion when the lakes in the chateau's gardens froze. It is as though whatever it was that happened in the past (last year?) has sucked all the life out of this place and its inhabitants, leaving them frozen in place. (And isn't memory itself a kind of freezing, fixing the live events of our past in such a way that – like the statue in the garden – they will never move again and will become increasingly difficult to understand and interpret? Yet our memories wriggle and change shape against our will.) This freezing, this congealing of the world and its actions, is a feature of the schizophrenic experience, another hint about X's mental condition.[37]

I offer here a number of possible interpretations of the events of this film, but perhaps asking what a film is *about* is on a par with asking what a symphony is *about*; such things just exist, with all of their aesthetic qualities. In defence of *this*, we have Robbe-Grillet's own view of the film:

> We have decided to trust the spectator, to allow him, from start to finish, to come to terms with pure subjectivities. Two attitudes are then possible: either the spectator will try to reconstitute some 'Cartesian' scheme – the most linear, the most rational he can devise – and this spectator will certainly find the film difficult, if not incomprehensible; or else the spectator will let himself be carried along by the extraordinary images in front of him, by the actors' voices, by the sound track, by the music, by the rhythm of the cutting, by the

passion of the characters.... and to this spectator, the film will seem the 'easiest' he has ever seen: a film addressed exclusively to his sensibility, to his faculties of sight, hearing, feeling. The story told will seem the most realistic, the truest, the one that best corresponds to his daily emotional life, as soon as he agrees to abandon ready-made ideas, psychological analysis, more or less clumsy systems of interpretation which machine-made fiction or films grind out for him ad nauseam, and which are the worst kinds of abstractions.[38]

So there you have it. A set of puzzles on the nature of time, memory and subjectivity, an analysis of solipsism. Or a work of art that defies analysis by defying all notion of linearity or rationality. Difficult, if not incomprehensible; or the easiest film you've ever seen.

But why are *Blade Runner* and *L'Année Dernière à Marienbad* film *as* philosophy? Stephen Mulhall (another of this book's contributors) writes of the *Alien* tetralogy of films:

The sophistication and self-awareness with which these films deploy and develop [the issue of the relation of human identity to embodiment] together with a number of related issues also familiar to philosophers, suggest to me that they should themselves be taken as making real contributions to these intellectual debates. In other words, I do not look to these films as handy or popular illustrations of views and arguments properly developed by philosophers; I see them rather as themselves reflecting on and evaluating such views and arguments, as thinking seriously and systematically about them in just the ways that philosophers do. Such films are not philosophy's raw material, not a source for its ornamentation; they are philosophical exercises, philosophy in action – film as philosophising.[39]

And that summarises nicely how I feel about the two films here: neither *Blade Runner* nor *L'Année Dernière à Marienbad* are just a compendium of useful exercises and illustrations about the nature of intelligence and humanity. But what *more* must a film possess if watching it is to be *doing* philosophy rather than merely thinking in a philosophical way about the issues the film throws up?

This question has been central to a recent discussion of Mulhall's book in the on-line journal *Film-Philosophy*.[40] Here Nathan Andersen clarifies Mulhall's claim as:

...part of what makes films like *The Matrix*... and the *Alien* series so entertaining is precisely that they engage the viewer in much the same way as a philosophy text might. They call upon the viewer to ask questions about basic issues, to search for evidence, and to reflect not only upon the world presented within the film but on its significance for making sense of the reality they face in the everyday world.... For Mulhall, to consider a film as philosophical is not to see if it conforms to a pre-existing philosophical theory, but to approach it in such a way as to consider the extent to which the film itself poses questions and develops answers of a philosophical nature.[41]

In a later contribution to the debate, Julian Baggini recognises that 'Mulhall is not thinking about film as philosophising in the sense that film can offer explicit arguments, a series of articulated syllogisms',[42] and this is clearly so. If we demanded this from film, then it would indeed be impossible for us to see film *as* philosophy.

The claim that Mulhall makes above is that the truly philosophical film thinks 'seriously and systematically' about philosophical arguments and issues. But this must, by the very different nature of the form, be something different from the written arguments and analyses we are used to in standard philosophical texts. Perhaps Mulhall wants us to think of films as *showing us* philosophy rather than telling us about philosophy, which is what the usual written text does.[43] If philosophy hopes ultimately to tell us something about the world in which we live, something real or true, how could a fictional film hope to do this? Baggini is clear on the problem:

...by their nature what they show is not reality but a fictional construct. This is especially true within the genre of science fiction, where the action is premised precisely on the fact that the world depicted is different from the real world we inhabit. So to show something within a film is not necessarily to show something which is true of the world. This might seem antithetical to the project of philosophy, which is surely about, in some sense at least, revealing the nature of reality, the structure of logic, the essence of being, and so forth. If this is true, then how can fictional representations hope to show the nature of reality in a philosophically rigorous way?[44]

Much here depends on this notion of being true of the world.[45] Bernard Williams defines truthfulness as a virtue that includes an 'eagerness to see through appearances to the real structure and motives that lie behind them',[46] and truthfulness in this sense is a property that a film could share with other sorts of texts, including the philosophical.

Baggini argues that seeing the matter in this way makes more sense of the claim that film can be philosophy, for

> Film, like philosophy, can represent reality to us truthfully in such a way as to make us understand it better or more accurately than before. Film can achieve this through fictions which can include non-literal modes of representation such as metaphor, whereas philosophy usually achieves the same goal through more literal modes of description. Philosophy thus *says* while film *shows*, its form of showing being distinct from more literal forms, such as demonstration.[47]

The showing (and the looking, the audience's engagement with the cinematic experience) must therefore be crucial to the achievement of philosophy here.

The point is made more clearly by examining a different sort of film entirely, Kurosawa's *Rashômon* (1950). This is not a science-fiction narrative, but a realistic re-telling of a single event from four different viewpoints. For Baggini it makes a clear philosophical point about the nature of objectivity and appearance. But it does so *as* a film, in a way that another form of text could not do.

> What we are really being shown then is how one event, which in certain respects objectively occurred, since its key details are not even contested by the inconsistent accounts, is nonetheless recalled differently because the participants did not merely experience the events as detached, objective observers, but as participants who saw, in their actions and the actions of others, motives, feelings, and moral commitments that were not simple, publicly observable facts. Hence we are shown how to make compatible a kind of non-relativistic view that there are objective facts with the truth that events are ineluctably perceived differently by each individual.
>
> Obviously this is just a sketch of the philosophically deep waters *Rashômon* gracefully swims through. The purpose of the sketch is merely to bring out two important points. The first is that this is an example of how film can take forward a philosophical debate in a specifically cinematic way. Although one can to a certain extent formalise the 'argument' of the film in standard philosophical discourse, the argument of *Rashômon* is stronger on screen precisely because it is more effective in this case to show than to tell. This is because – and this is the second key point – the showing provides

reasons for us to accept the philosophical position being shown. It demonstrates the possibility of what might, simply described, seem impossible, and in showing it in the context of a story that is all too believable – all-too human in its moral and emotional projection, fallibility, and self-serving bias – it provides evidence that this is actually the way the world is. In short, the argument presented is coherent, it explains things about truth and belief in novel ways and it fits our understanding of how the world actually is.[48]

And this encapsulates the claim I want to make about both *Blade Runner* and *L'Année Dernière à Marienbad*. In the first of these films we address the question of what it is to be a person. Being *told*, as Dick tells us in his novel, that the replicants possess all of the Dennettian qualities for personhood, that they are intelligent, rational, language-using entities, tells us something at an intellectual level. But it is essentially a dry and lifeless proposition. To *see* the replicants, indistinguishable from human beings in their appearance and behaviour, to empathise with their plight and their quest, to see them empathising with each other and – at the end – with Deckard, the man (or replicant) come to kill them, is to engage in a form of life with them, to come to feel them as a part of our lives, as something we cannot avoid thinking of as being like us.[49] Film brings the bare functional proposition to life, makes it plausible, in a way that mere argument on paper cannot do. Film leads us into the lives of the replicants and the humans, and makes us realise that the former are closer to our real life than the latter, and thus it tells us something about ourselves and *our* world. (It approaches the problem cinematically via Wittgenstein's insistence on showing rather than telling.)

The same can be said of *L'Année Dernière à Marienbad*. It does not just *illustrate* philosophical themes, though it certainly does this too: it forces the audience to engage with them. By taking up and subverting all of the traditional dramatic and technical features of the cinema – the scenery, the narration, the flashbacks, etc. – Resnais and Robbe-Grillet challenge the audience to take on the film in a different way. We seem to have – as Robbe-Grillet pointed out in the quote above – a natural rationalist or Cartesian tendency to impose order, to look for clear narratives. *Marienbad* challenges this throughout.

What philosophical work does this film do? It is in some sense a challenge to this rationality, and specifically to the story of Descartes' *Meditations*. In the philosophical book we are invited, via Descartes' first-person narration, to understand and accept the possibility – perhaps ontological, certainly epistemological – of solipsism. Only when this is understood and accepted can we proceed to the *cogito* and beyond. But in the philosophical film, we are not invited to judge solipsism, we *are* solipsists. We inhabit solipsism.[50] Each member of the audience finds themselves located in the inexplicable space of the narrator X. Once we understand *this*, everything else falls into place. But it doesn't fall into the place of neat narrative, for – despite Ward's rather Procrustean efforts – this cannot be done. To construct a narrative means deciding which of the events we see and/or hear are real, which imagined, fantasised, desired or remembered, and deciding which events came before which others. But none of these things are possible for the solipsist, for whom there can be no external standard of reality against which to test mental contents. The mind at best mirrors itself here: it cannot be, as Rorty said in a different context, a mirror of nature.[51] And the solipsistic consciousness has no access to any independent temporal ordering: before and after make sense only within the consciousness. Thus Resnais' many flashbacks may equally well be flashes 'forward' or 'sideways': the mental/cinematic event itself contains no information referring outside of itself that could enable us to know which.

There is, then, no possibility of constructing a narrative. But what we are watching and listening to is someone precisely engaged in this project.[52] Through the film we see (and especially *hear*, on the narrative voice-over) X trying to produce order. At times, he is trying to produce order in his own thoughts, to get things clear to himself. But at other times X tries to order the world, to get the events outside of himself to match his mental picture of them. In the most notorious instance of this, what appears cinematically to be leading towards a depiction of X's rape of A is headed off by a burst of ecstatic music and images while X's voiceover denies almost hysterically what is being implied. ('Non, non, non! C'est faux!... Ce n'était pas de force.... Souvenez-vous....' No, no, no. It wasn't by force.... Remember...) That last 'remember' is not a question but an order, a command that reality get into line with how X wants it to be/to have been.

But this is madness.[53] For the solipsist has no reality outside of their mental contents. There is no logic, there is no order, there just is the present mental state. Hume's claim in the *Treatise* that we could tell our immediate perceptions and ideas from imaginings and rememberings by their vivacity is plainly false. But here we *see* this falsity in action. If we are confused, it is because the solipsist must inevitably be confused. If all that we as an audience can do is sit back and let the film proceed, let ourselves 'be carried along by the extraordinary images in front of him, by the actors' voices, by the sound track, by the music, by the rhythm of the cutting, by the passion of the characters',[54] then all the solipsist can do is sit back passively and let experience happen.

Thus the film becomes a refutation of the Cartesian project.[55] It refutes it not by *telling* us, not by demonstrating the falsity of a proposition involved or the invalidity of a logical move, but by *showing* us, by showing us solipsism in action. If we cannot make sense of the film, then solipsism doesn't make sense. And we can't. And it doesn't.

If we are right then film genuinely can be philosophy. Not always deliberately philosophy – I make no claims that Scott or Resnais were *consciously* engaging in this kind of philosophical work – but philosophy for all that. And therefore *watching* film, engaging both perceptually and intellectually with the cinematic events in front of you, can be another way of doing philosophy. That, at least, is the claim of this book, of the various authors who have come together here, that we can see film *as* philosophy, as Stanley Cavell claims that we can see 'even' many classic Hollywood movies as philosophising, as *thinking*. And if we are right then maybe Wittgenstein really wasn't wasting his time in those Cambridge cinemas.[56]

Notes

1. In Cavell, 1999, p. 25.
2. Though some dedicated Wittgensteinians insist that LW *never* laid down the burden of being a philosopher, and so like to picture him applying his intellect to even this unpromising material.
3. As they are in Walker Percy's fascinating novel *The Moviegoer.*
4. Someone interested in *this* approach to cinema could do no better than start with Noel Carroll's 'Towards An Ontology of the Moving Image', in Freeland & Wartenburg (1995).
5. As Mel Brooks' *Blazing Saddles* (1974) is when the action at the end spills out from the film's original setting and runs riot through the studio where it is being made, through the sets of other movies, and out into the 'real' world. A similar 'post-modern' self-referential attitude towards the film itself can be found in other light-hearted Hollywood works of the 1940s: see Olsen & Johnson's *Hellzapoppin* (1941) or a number of the Warner Brothers cartoons featuring Bugs Bunny, Daffy Duck, etc. of this period.
6. Released in 1993, it consists of 77 minutes of luminous blue 35mm screen accompanied by a personal narrative soundtrack. A moving (in one sense of the word but clearly not in another) metaphor for Jarman's own encroaching blindness, *Blue* is a probably unique challenge to the visual nature of cinema. A lesser challenge comes from von Trier's *Dancer in the Dark* (2000), also a film about blindness, wherein the screen is entirely black for three minutes.
7. And there have been some very useful recent books exploiting this approach. See, for instance, Falzon (2002) or Rowlands (2003). We, however, aim to go considerably beyond such an approach.

8. These are only the most obvious examples. One can use *The Matrix* to shed light on other philosophical traditions, on questions of religion, and so on. For more details, see Irwin (2002) or the excellent essays by Colin McGinn, Hubert Dreyfus and others at the website *Philosophy and the Matrix*.

9. As the Wachowskis found out when they inserted rather ponderous and self-conscious philosophising into *The Matrix Reloaded*.

10. Though the film itself is not in this sense analytical. I do not count here the admirable project being undertaken, especially in the US, to produce video interviews and biographies of great philosophers while they are still alive. See, for instance, the set of films made with and about Quine. (Details in bibliography.) As academic tools and historical documents these films are enormously valuable. Their aesthetic quality, on the other hand, tends to be minimal, production values being utilitarian rather than artistically driven.

11. In Vitale (1978), (accessed on-line 10/9/04).

12. As my co-editor pointed out to me, this is a stunning encapsulation of Schreberian themes, for Quayle's last fantasy has a superb paranoid grandiosity to it.

13. We can see these aspects of the film as being a metaphor for film itself, for the escapism, the desire to undergo 'experiences' that aren't our own that takes us into the darkness of the cinema when we are not being philosophers.

14. On the *Film and Literature As Philosophy* unit that Read and I teach at UEA. From teaching this unit emerged our desire to make this book.

15. One could, I suppose, argue that Jesus – the protagonist of a number of films from Hollywood and elsewhere – was a philosopher. But his *thought* is not usually a central feature of these films. (It is certainly rather hard to detect it in Mel Gibson's recent *The Passion of the Christ*, for instance, though even this film may raise philosophical issues for discussion in the manner of the films of our first category.) Scorsese's 1988 *The Last Temptation of Christ* may be an honourable exception here.

16. McKenna (2002), (accessed on-line 28/7/04).

17. Hence perhaps the novelty of Descartes' first-person narrative of the *Meditations* or Hume's occasional importation of himself into his *Treatise* ('when I enter most intimately into what I call my *self...*'). There is a counter-tradition of philosophy starting to work in just this way. It is sympathetically presented in the recent work of Alexander Nehamas.

18. Anyone with doubts should watch the Derrida movie mentioned above for ample evidence of the charisma and popularity. (And perhaps the lack of rigour!)

19. Or, to be accurate, to have sex with Maud: for our hero does indeed sleep with her, swathed in blankets on top of the cover of her bed, but nothing more.

20. And of course, in the cinema *no* character really has free will, since all are preordained to carry out the instructions of the director. Even when they seem to be revolting *against* the will of the director, as in the fight scene at the end of *Blazing Saddles*, this too is ultimately ordained – here, by Mel Brooks, the *real* director.

21. One might, then, see *MNCM* as a working out of a version of the argument from design, an exploration of its possible compatibility with notions of free

will. In this sense, *MNCM* may be seen as moving towards film *as* philosophy, and the more I think about the film, the more sympathetic I am to this view.

22. And note that these four are laden with mythological significance, representing wisdom, evil, purity and the spirit respectively, though the artificiality of the owl and the snake crucially alter the significance of wisdom and evil here. 'Wisdom' is not – or is more than? – wisdom. The same may be true of evil.

23. A term that doesn't exist in the original Dick novel, but was borrowed by Scott from the title of a story by Alan E. Nourse. Scott presumably liked the idea of a name that captures the idea of living on the edge.

24. And in considering this property, we should note the relevance of Cavell on acknowledgement here.

25. See Dennett (1981).

26. This is a continuing thread throughout *Philosophical Investigations*. See, for instance, I, 283 through 309.

27. And note the sublime ambiguity of Roy's last speech (improvised by Rutger Hauer) that starts '*I've* seen things you people wouldn't believe...' 'You people' as opposed to 'we non-people'? That makes sense, but our natural reading on first hearing it is the reading we would give it in our own usage, the more inclusive 'you people' as opposed to 'we people'.

28. Ward (1968).

29. In the introduction to his ciné-novel, *Last Year At Marienbad* (1961) p. 7.

30. *Ibid.*

31. See Ward *op. cit.* p. 39.

32. Or so I argue. Followers of Bergson, McTaggart, etc. are welcome to discuss this issue in the foyer.

33. The first lines of real dialogue we hear in the film are 'Don't you know the story? It was all everyone talked about last year?' This could refer to anything, but X takes it to mean *his* story, the affair with A that he claims took place last year.

34. The hyper-sensitivity of the schizophrenic is explored in an artistic context (with references to *LDAM*) by Louis Sass in his (1998).

35. In (1953), I, 139.

36. As it is in more recent films like *Memento* with its ornate and reversed narrative structure.

37. These experiences are explored in Sass (1994).

38. Robbe-Grillet, *op. cit.* p. 13.

39. Mulhall (2002), p. 2.

40. *Film-Philosophy* (ISSN 1466–4615) (See bibliography for address.)

41. Andersen (2003).

42. Baggini (2003).

43. The *unusual* text, like much of Wittgenstein's writing, may be excluded from this claim, at least if we take Wittgenstein often to be showing us rather than telling us.

44. Baggini, *op. cit.*

45. One might also consider that some films show us reality by a process of *exclusion*: they 'show' us the absurd by running outside the limits of thought and language. One thinks here of some of Peter Greenaway's films, *LDÀM*, *Memento*, *Natural Born Killers*, etc.

46. Williams (2002), p. 2, quoted in Baggini, *op. cit.*
47. Baggini, *op. cit.*
48. Baggini, *op. cit.*
49. As being, in context, more like us than *we* are, for it is one of the ironies of the film – deliberately inserted by Scott & co. since it is not found in Dick's novel – that the replicants are capable of greater emotional response than the humans. It is not the least of the film's ironies that the opening scene where a (presumably) human investigator gives the Voight-Kampf test, a futuristic equivalent of the Turing test designed to identify the *lack* of correct responses in replicants, throughout the scene it is the *replicant* that shows emotions while the human is cold and machine-like, a reversal of traits that we find throughout the film.
50. And thereby we inhabit its absurdities. Witness how the rational ordered house and garden become finally a labyrinth from which escape is impossible. And thus we have the final lines of the film, making clear the profound aloneness of a would-be solipsist: 'It seemed at first glance impossible to get lost here... at first glance... down straight paths, between the statues with frozen gestures and the granite slabs, where you were now already getting lost, forever, in the calm night, alone with me.'
51. Much more could be said about this, and the many rôles that the mirror, reflections and mirror-imaging play in *Marienbad*.
52. And we have something similar in Leonard Shelby's attempts at narrative-construction in *Memento*.
53. And perhaps literally so. Reading Sass (1998) throws up many indications of the sorts of madness that might be at work in *Marienbad*. See, for instance, his discussion of 'The Invention of Morel'.
54. Robbe-Grillet, *op. cit.* p. 13.
55. Though I do not wish to argue that this is *all* that can be found philosophically interesting in *LDÀM*.
56. I am grateful to the many UEA students with whom I have discussed film and philosophy, and to Rupert Read for his detailed and helpful criticisms.

Introduction II : What Theory of Film Do Wittgenstein and Cavell Have?

Rupert Read

In this second Introduction to the volume, I attempt first to unanswer this question, and then to sketch through 'abstracts' what the individual essays in the volume consist in, especially in relation to the concepts of 'theory of film' and of 'film *as* philosophy'.

This collection consists largely of efforts to 'read' an extremely diverse set of quality films *as* philosophy, and to critically assess such efforts. The authors in this collection see (some!) film(s) as actually doing philosophical work, rather than merely illustrating philosophical theses. If this book succeeds, then, it will succeed among other things in showing that diverse films can be/do philosophy.

But why should it be thought that such a task uniquely has to do with Wittgenstein and Cavell? Is it because these two philosophers have a powerful film theory which can reach films – or aspects of those films – beyond the grasp of 'Psychoanalytical theory' or 'Cognitive theory'?

No, it is not.[1] It is a striking feature of the essays in this collection, especially evident perhaps in the essay by Critchley, that they do not attempt to apply any film theory, not even an allegedly 'Wittgensteinian' one, to the films they discuss. In most of the essays in this collection, there is then an implicit challenge to the very idea of 'Film Theory'.

But nor is it simply a coincidence that the authors in this collection, all of them powerfully influenced by Wittgenstein or Cavell or both, have developed the particular kind of interest in film that suited them[2] to being gathered under the auspices of the title 'Film *as* philosophy: Essays on cinema after Wittgenstein and Cavell'. There are a number of (inter-related) features of Wittgenstein's and Cavell's (inter-related) thought which crystallised that title and this gathering of authors.

Some of those features have already been brought out by my co-editor in 'Introduction I', above. Some are implicit in subtle or vivid ways in the essays that follow, and I will not labour them here. Three are however worth mentioning immediately.

First is the belief, shared by all or virtually all of the contributors to this collection, that Wittgenstein's thought helps *to clear the way* for an appreciation of how films can philosophise. Wittgenstein's questioning of the utility of theory in philosophy generally, his non-theoretical approach to aesthetics (see Glendinning's essay, especially), and his emphasis on the importance of not thinking but looking, all conduce to approaching films not in the spirit of master approaching pupil, but in the spirit of an admiring co-conversationalist.

Second, and not unrelated, is the belief that films quite often succeed in philosophising, where they succeed, in ways that mirror aspects of the activity of Wittgenstein's own philosophising. That is to say that films can engage the audience in a *therapeutic* process of 'dialogue' (see 'A philosopher goes to the cinema', above, and Hutchinson and Read's essay, and Rudrum's), that films can investigate the absurd, can probe and 'show' journeyings beyond the limits of thought, can deliberately collapse under their own weight just as many of Wittgenstein's thought-experiments do (examples of such films perhaps include much of Peter Greenaway's oeuvre up until about *Prospero's Books*, *Memento*, and *Last Year at Marienbad*),[3] and yet that films can also show the life of human beings and their others in ways that, as Wittgenstein himself suggested, argumentative prose could not (see for instance Mulhall's essay).

Third is the belief that Stanley Cavell has – in a manner quite unencumbered by any tedious larding with quotations from or invocations of Wittgenstein, but yet implicitly informed by the first and second beliefs just mentioned – shown and exemplified more clearly than anyone else the way in which one can practice an understanding of the intellectual thinking of films. Cavell has done so with regard principally to great Hollywood fare,[4] not with regard to the 'art' films which might more naturally have been thought easy meat for his 'method'. Cavell has provided an existence proof for a 'method' of approaching (some) films which, while philosophically-sophisticated (embodying for instance the acknowledgement of 'acknowledgement' that is write so large in much of Cavell's (and of Mulhall's) oeuvre), makes in practice a good case for being a 'method' that sees serious conceptual thought in these films without either being *governed* itself or seeing *them* as governed by any set of thoughts systematic and pre-formatted enough to be worth calling a theory.[5]

So a number of the essays in this volume can be read with profit as attempting to understand film(s) not, as is usual in philosophy and film theory, by means of simply subjecting film to philosophical ana- lysis using pre-arranged criteria, criteria alien to films themselves, but rather, beginning from suggestions in Wittgenstein and Cavell, by means of seeking to understand (in part, from examples of films them- selves) how we have learnt to find cinema both a *natural* thing and an inherent source of philosophy and of *paradox*.

It is worth noting that a number of films discussed in this collection (for instance, *Fight Club*, *Memento*, and most of the films discussed by my co-editor, above) harbour, as did Wittgenstein, and as do Cavell and after him a number of significant Wittgensteinian thinkers such as Louis Sass, James Guetti, James Conant and Ray Monk (besides some of the authors in this collection), an abiding fascination with 'mental illness', and indeed more specifically with the paradoxes of delusion, with madness. Again, this is hardly a coincidence. With filmmakers such as Harmony Korine and the *Dogme 95* directors such an integral part of today's cinematic scene, it is perhaps increasingly obvious that films think, that films are no longer merely to be viewed as illustrative material for pre-existing philosophies (as films are typically presented as being in philosophy teaching of film) nor as illustrative material for pre-existing ideologies or theories (as films are typically presented as being in Film Studies). And much of this thinking, for reasons that are worth further exploration,[6] is done, is (I would submit) *naturally* done, on film.

Broader acknowledgement of all this within *Philosophy* may depend largely on whether Wittgenstein and Cavell come to have the influence on the philosophical reception of film that the papers in this collection believe – and argue – they should. An influence not usefully expressible in terms of a statable set of propositions, but rather in terms of a distinctive conception of philosophy: as a non-doctrinal activity. As a set of methods of questioning whatever can be successfully questioned and being careful not seriously or literally to question anything else. As an unfolding of reason which is reliably self-conscious about both the perennial danger of an overweeningness of reason *and* the perennial danger of committing oneself to absurdities about 'the limit of thought'. As a way of clearing the way for films to show us the thinking that they accomplish, and for us to think with and through them, not as a way of substituting for either of those processes.

This collection aims to advance philosophy – understood after Wittgenstein as a subject which does not advance in any respect resembling the advance of science – by fostering an understanding of how the new medium of film can be seen as engaging in the same: as reasoning and as exploring the 'limits' of reason. As, after Cavell, helping us to understand what a movie is,[7] and what *we* are not, and are.

Cogito Ergo Film: Plato, Descartes, and *Fight Club*   Nancy Bauer

This paper provides a reading of the film *Fight Club* as a commentary on two revolutionary moments in the history of philosophy, Plato's allegory of the cave and Descartes' *cogito*, both of which construe philosophy as exposing the epistemic unreliability of everyday experience. *Fight Club* explicitly figures its characters as prisoners in Plato's cave who, adopting what Stanley Cavell has identified as the stance of the modern philosopher, both yearn for and continually attempt to deny their yearning for a world in which they can conscience investing themselves. *Fight Club* suggests that discovering this world is a matter of finding a place from which to judge the status of the one we find ourselves in, a place that turns out to coincide with a seat in a movie theatre.

In Space No-one Can Hear You Scream: Acknowledging the Human Voice in the Alien Universe   Stephen Mulhall

This paper summarises and extends some of the argumentative themes of Mulhall's treatment of the 'Alien' series in his *On Film* (2002). It brings into the foreground the degree to which Ripley's situation in the Alien universe is represented cinematically in terms of the status (specifically the repression and reclamation) of her voice; and Mulhall uses this image to explore the relation of the individual directors of the films in this series to one another, to their central character and to the medium of their work. This process adapts various ideas of Stanley Cavell's, and concludes with a consideration of the role of philosophy in the ongoing conversation surrounding these films, and hence film as such.

Memento: A Philosophical Investigation   Rupert Read and Phil Hutchinson

Read and Hutchinson explore the anti-Cartesian philosophy of the protagonist (Leonard Shelby) of the recent philosophical film *noir*, *Memento*.

They argue that the film achieves its teaching, which is not by any means identical with Shelby's, through *showing* the viewer the alleged world of a seriously psychologically (though not necessarily neurologically) damaged person, and then forcing the viewer to understand how that 'world' collapses under its own weight, somewhat like the *Tractatus* or Wittgenstein's 'builders' thought-experiment. One way of summing up the central question of this paper is as follows: How does Leonard know to look for the photographs of people he has met in his pockets? Isn't that knowing, that repeated action of his, itself part of his 'filing system', his mind in action, in much the same way as Wittgenstein (in laying out the philosophical inadequacy of Empiricism, of 'imagism', etc.) describes in *PI*?

The Everydayness of Don Giovanni **Simon Glendinning**

Glendinning looks at Joseph Losey's film version of the opera, using critical and aesthetical tools from Kierkegaard, Wittgenstein and Cavell, and seeks to explore a sense in which the opera (at least as filmed) itself develops and expounds a sense of the 'everyday', in something like Wittgenstein's sense of that word. Glendinning argues that the film has the capacity literally and figuratively to *refocus our vision*, a capacity to defamiliarise and *thus* to bring into focus the everyday. What is at issue in this case is not the defamiliarisation of 'everyday perception' but the defamiliarisation of our sense of *the everydayness of Don Giovanni himself*. Ultimately, it is a defamiliarisation which enables us to acknowledge that the Don is not just a clever seducer who desires beautiful (that is aesthetically worthy) women, but is an arbitrary, frighteningly predatory force, indeed, virtually a demon himself.

Silent Dialogue: Philosophising with Jan Švankmajer **David Rudrum**

What happens when communication breaks down? When the conversations through which we supposedly 'talk things over' and 'work things out' fail, to the point where a dialogical interaction can't really be said to take place at all? These are the themes that the Czech filmmaker Jan Švankmajer explores in his short film *Dimensions of Dialogue*. Divided into three sections ('Exhaustive Discussion', 'Passionate Discourse', and 'Factual Conversation'), each part symbolises a form of failure and collapse in a form of dialogical exchange.

This essay uses Švankmajer's masterpiece in order to shed light on three very (very!) different philosophical conceptions of dialogue.

'Exhaustive Discussion' explores the Lyotardian notion that since dialogue requires commensurability, it is reductive of difference and entails a form of discursive violence. 'Passionate Discourse' addresses Bakhtin's philosophical conception of dialogue as an essentially benign moment, a process of 'sympathetic co-authoring' that he claims is 'akin to love'. Finally, 'Factual Conversation' illuminates the kind of practical dialogue discussed by Wittgenstein: everyday communication that entails ways of acting, and facilitates the performing of tasks. This final section is developed at the greatest length.

By allowing the wordless, visual medium of film to critique philosophy of language, the essay demonstrates that philosophical understandings of dialogue all too often underestimate the possibilities of breakdown, failure, and stand-off, whilst their enactment on screen realises these possibilities as a disconcerting and troubling fact.

Calm: On Terence Malick's *The Thin Red Line*   Simon Critchley

Critchley reads Malick's recent film as yielding an existential 'message' concerning calm in the face of death, but a message not accessible through reading the film simply through any pre-existing philosophical text (e.g. Heidegger's), nor through the philosophical influences on Malick (e.g. Stanley Cavell, his Harvard teacher). Rather, one must allow the film itself to work on one, and one must be willing to hear and see *its* philosophising. A philosophising expressed through character/voice pairings, *mise-en-scène* and developments of atmosphere and of moral point of view that Critchley lays out for the reader.

Habitual Remarriage: The Ends of Happiness in *The Palm Beach Story*   Stuart Klawans

Pursuits of Happiness, Stanley Cavell's study of 'the Hollywood comedy of remarriage,' is marked by what seems to be a significant omission: a near-total silence about Preston Sturges' *The Palm Beach Story*. By means of a Cavell-inspired reading of this film, and through an un-Cavellian fleshing out of the description of the central performance, 'Habitual Remarriage' tests the terms and the limits of *Pursuits of Happiness*.

'What Becomes of Thinking on Film?' **Stanley Cavell** *in conversation with* **Andrew Klevan** *on film as philosophy*

This interview elucidates Cavell's up-to-the-minute views on the topic(s) of the volume. Andrew Klevan, a distinguished young Film Studies scholar, engages in dialogue with Cavell, bringing in interdisciplinary perspectives and the point of view of practical film criticism. The title of the conversation, 'What Becomes of Thinking on Film?', is intended to evoke two of Stanley Cavell's essays on film: 'What Photography Calls Thinking' (in *Raritan*, Spring 1985) and 'What Becomes of Things on Film?' (in Cavell (1984)). In sum, how do philosophy and film meet each other in Stanley Cavell's thinking and writing, and how might their association profit the criticism, theory and teaching of film?

Notes

1. To quote a robust statement of a similar '(non-)position' elsewhere in 'human science': 'Despite our disclaimers...we will no doubt be read as...having sought to advance, perhaps surreptitiously, an alternative 'theory of mind and behaviour'. If we have offered anything that may remotely be construed as a theory, it would be a 'theory of language', but only if the word 'theory' is used in the most attenuated sense... . To state our position as starkly as possible: we refuse to become embroiled in the spurious antinomies which permeate so much of philosophy, psychology and sociology, which polarise realism/constructivism, idealism/materialism, dualism/monism, realism/instrumentalism, behaviourism/mentalism. We favour *none* of the above.' (These are the concluding remarks to the Conclusion of G. Button *et al* (1995)) In short: you can call what is advanced in this book a 'theory of film' and/or a 'theory of language' if you wish – provided you recognise that the word 'theory' is being used then in the vaguest, most bloated and attenuated sense imaginable.
2. And there are many others who could, I think, quite comfortably have been gathered under the same title, had they the time and had we the space. See for instance many of those who have written in and edited the collections mentioned in note 4, below. And also the work of the next generations, graduate students of Cavell, Conant, myself, and so on.
3. Harold Garfinkel famously remarked that social and cognitive scientists '...often suppose that taking away the walls is the best way of revealing what keeps the roof up.' (p. 223, Button *et al*, *ibid*.) And indeed it is not; but sometimes, *providing one recognises fully the nonsensicality of one's enterprise,* one can learn much (about oneself, about us, about the temptations of (un-)reason that we are subject to) by doing just that in imagination. By imagining, or showing, what one imagines it would be (like) to step outside 'the bounds of sense'.
4. Of great utility in understanding Cavell's work on Hollywood film are two recent collections: *Stanley Cavell: Cinema et philosophie* (eds S. Laugier and

M. Cerisuelo; Paris: Presse de la Sorbonne, 2001), and A. Crary's and S. Shieh's forthcoming collection from a major conference on Cavell's work.

5. We have included Stuart Klawans's essay as the voice of a distinguished film critic who, while not convinced by some of Cavell's readings, does at least – unlike some critics, film theorists and philosophers, very clearly appreciate what Cavell is trying to do. Klawans is thus a kind of dissenting voice in the collection, but the best kind of dissenting voice – a *comprehending* voice. See also n. 1, above.

6. For such exploration, see for instance the forthcoming work of a student of mine, Emma Bell. Arguably, the *naturalness* of the limits of reason and the 'limits' of thought being much explored in great (filmic etc.) art is itself thematised in such recent works as *The king is alive, Fight Club* and *Donnie Darko.*

7. See p. 3 of Mulhall's *On film* (2002) for further explication.

Part I
Essays

Cogito Ergo Film: Plato, Descartes and *Fight Club*

Nancy Bauer

A central concern of Stanley Cavell's in his writings on the movies is to dramatise the extent to which film, by virtue of its nature as a medium and as a matter of historical fact, tends to be preoccupied with philosophy's preoccupations.[1] Everywhere and always, Cavell puts pressure on the view that, at best, a given film might do a good job of *illustrating* a philosophical problem or position – a view that, alas, most of his colleagues in the world of professional philosophy would probably accept (that is, were they to find themselves thinking about the relationship between philosophy and film). This mainstream view concedes that sometimes it is useful to show a film in a philosophy class, since films can rouse the passions of students and thereby get them more invested in the issues. Of course Cavell would never disagree. But a pressing issue for him is not *whether* films rouse passions but exactly why and how they succeed in doing so. An intimately related question for Cavell, one that drives all of his work, is the relationship passions have to reason. Professional philosophy these days is apt to follow Kant's increasingly influential lead and identify reason as whatever is left of the human mind once the passions are excluded. But films by their nature relentlessly – you might even say absolutely – resist this picture. How and why they do so, Cavell finds, is not something one can discover apart from careful criticism of individual movies – what he calls 'reading' films. In the spirit of this discovery, I want here at least to begin a reading of David Fincher's *Fight Club*, released in 1999. What's of particular interest to me about this film is the way that it develops a vision of the intimate relationship between reason and passion in terms that appear to have been lifted from the work of two philosophers whose work turns on denying this relationship – one of them, Descartes, the quintessential modern philosopher, and the other, Plato, its avatar in the ancient world.

Film's resistance to Plato's and Descartes' conception of reason and its relation to passion, a resistance I find to be epitomised in *Fight Club*, is bound to make philosophers of a certain stripe nervous. If passion is exactly what reason is not – if, that is to say, passion is on the side of irrationality – then to the extent that they play on our affective capacities, films must be seen to lie essentially outside of the philosopher's purview. Engaging students' interest by rousing their passions is dangerous business; once a film shown in class does its job, the task of the philosopher is to bring students safely back over the border, to the side of reason. Famously, Plato in the tenth book of the *Republic* warns that philosopher-kings must banish poetry from their realms; for art, in all its beauty, seduces the hoi polloi away from what philosophy shows us rationality reveals and demands, and substitutes at best a distorted copy of reality and a suspect vision of what being human requires of us. Contemporary philosophers of course want film to have a place in the culture – only not one in the culture's seat of rationality, which of course is to be found, if it is to be found anywhere, in the philosophy classroom. Of course, there are some philosophers who take film to be an object worthy of serious philosophical interest. But these philosophers tend to be centrally focused on making the case that films appeal not 'merely,' as it were, to human affect but also to rationality – where, of course, the implicit assumption, the one that forestalls most philosophers from taking film seriously as a philosophical medium – is that we've got two distinctly different capacities on our hands here.[2]

Even those philosophers who are willing to concede that whatever line there might be between reason and passion is at best fuzzy are likely to resist Cavell's idea that film is, by its nature, a philosophical medium. For professional philosophy these days is governed by the idea that the business of the discipline, a business that is not at all compatible with the business of art, is to propose theses and construct theories and then employ certain established methods of argumentation to support them. This broadly scientistic understanding of what philosophy is good for represents a decisive rejection of the picture of philosophy that we find, as Cavell has noted, at the inception of the discipline in Plato's early dialogues, in which the work of philosophy takes place literally in the marketplace, where the philosopher, epitomised by the figure of Socrates, undertakes the task not of arguing for or against various positions but of attracting his friends to converse about the assumptions that undergird and guide their lives.[3] Plato's picture turns on an understanding of philosophy not as an argument-producing machine but as a mode of education, one that depends essentially on the having and trusting of friends. This is a vision of philosophy that, unlike the conventional conception, is at least in principle congenial to the suggestion that *film* is a medium of philosophy. For the power of both film and, on this vision, of philosophy, can be seen to depend upon our willingness and ability to talk with our acquaintances about what they care about.

But of course competing visions of what philosophy is and does find their parallel in equally competing visions of what film is and does. Professional philosophy's repression of the early Plato is mirrored in the tendency of film scholars to imagine that their job is to construct a priori theories about how movies work on their audiences and then point to this or that film as evidence of the power of the theories. On this conception of how to think about films, one's movie-watching experience – the ways one finds oneself responding to particular films – is fundamentally not to be trusted and indeed inevitably stands in need of criticism via the lens of a theory, the job of which will sometimes be not just to explain the experience but to explain it away. On Laura Mulvey's extremely influential theory, for example, the pleasure we derive from narrative films – *all* narrative films, she says – hopelessly and insidiously turns on their inevitable objectification of women and therefore must be disavowed.[4] In questioning the priority that Mulvey assigns to theory in characterising how we experience (all) movies, one need not insist that viewers are always in control of the way that the movies they watch affect them, or that the effects in question are unadulterated by the movie-watcher's sometimes morally worrisome investments. But we also need not reject the idea that films have the power, on their own, to engage these investments – and, as often as not, to challenge rather than confirm them. What film theory seems to require is the conviction that films are not, as it were, on top of their own powers – that they lack something like a self-consciousness of what they are all about.

In its certainty that film as a medium stands in need of systematic explication – that one's experience of a film cannot, on its own, ground any serious intellectual work – film theory finds what is perhaps an unlikely bedfellow in academic philosophy. The practice of professional philosophy in fact is premised on the idea that experience isn't the source of explanations; to the contrary, it's what stands in need of explaining. We are to dope out How Things Fundamentally Are With the World 'a priori,' quite apart from whatever particular experiences we may have had. If we make an appeal to experience, it is because we need an example of what stands in need of explanation or because we wish to show how our favourite theory happens to get confirmed by experiential evidence. In fact, a film might end up coming in handy in this enterprise; it can dramatise how chaotic raw experience is and how desperately it stands in need of being ordered via a philosophical theory. Take Tim Robbins's film *Dead Man Walking* (1995), for example. This movie is loosely based on the real-life experiences of Helen Prejean (played in the film by Susan Sarandon), a nun who was forced to learn about both sides of the death-penalty debates when she agreed to serve as the spiritual counsellor to a death-row murderer and rapist, played by Sean Penn. A philosophy teacher might screen this movie with the purpose of impressing on students the viability of his decided view that the death penalty is morally execrable – or, perhaps, tolerable or even laudable. The assumption guiding this use of the film is that, because it is 'just' a film, it has precisely no independent philosophical import.[5]

This assumption constitutes a denial of my experience of *Dead Man Walking*, which is that the film aspires to change the terms of the death-penalty debates. It does this, I find, in two principle ways. First, the director, Tim Robbins, via certain cutting and framing techniques, dramatises the lengths to which the state goes to protect individuals who carry out death-row executions – and, for that matter, ordinary citizens – from the fact of their own participation in these killings. In numerous point of view shots, for example, various prison employees are shown to attend only to very small moments of the condemned man's execution – the strapping down of his arm or the pushing of a button – actions that together add up to the state's taking of a human life. These shots and others, I submit, press on us the question of what a state is and what it is for a state to act in the name of citizens it strives to keep completely anonymous as they carry out its business. Second, Robbins uses inter-cutting to bring to light the difficulty, papered over by the tit-for-tat structure of our punishment system, of comparing the passionlessness and sterility of a state-sanctioned murder with the chaos and savagery of those murders that land people on death row. In my experience, the philosophical interest of *Dead Man Walking*, a respectable if not brilliant Hollywood movie, lies not in any support or condemnation it might lend the idea of a death penalty, though philosophers who comment on it are inclined to reduce it to these terms. Instead, the film draws our attention to features of state-sanctioned killing that have been scarcely articulable in the current death penalty debates. The potential power of even *Dead Man Walking* to change the terms of our conversation points to at least one reason not to regard films as in principle inferior to written philosophical works.

There is another important reason that I am resistant to the project of relegating films in an a priori way to a lower philosophical status than the books and essays that constitute the philosophical canon, but I cannot articulate it without first considering the question of *why* philosophers are inclined to deny the integrity of films as philosophical texts. This task, it turns out, will require a detour into the history of philosophy, starting with the founding of the modern version of the enterprise in the mid-17th century and working backwards to the roots of the profession in Plato.

The text that gets modern philosophy off the ground is Descartes' *Meditations*, which, according to legend were conceived by Descartes after he spent a restless night in an overheated room – a fact I mention only because insomnia will eventually become a central theme of what I wish to say in this paper. In the *Meditations*, famously, Descartes tries to get his knowledge in order – as it were, to separate the epistemological wheat from the chaff. But this project is mortally threatened almost immediately: it turns out that its first result is Descartes' finding himself forced to worry that the world as he knows it is a figment of his imagination. He notices, to take things a little more slowly here, that all of his experience can be explained just as well by the hypothesis that he is dreaming or that he is being systematically manipulated by an all-powerful demon as by the ordinary idea that there's a world out there with which he interacts. By the end of the first meditation, Descartes is in a panic: does anything at all actually exist? What begins to reassure him of the genuine materiality of the world is the fact of his own thought: no matter how screwed up his understanding of things is, it's still <u>his</u> understanding, so at the very least he must, as a mind, exist. Cogito ergo sum: I think; therefore, I am.

After this climactic moment in the *Meditations*, Descartes tries to bring himself back to his senses by convincing himself that his most basic beliefs are underwritten by a perfectly beneficent God, one who would not trap us in our own heads, as it were. Notoriously, however, this proof is considerably less than decisive, so that the most salient legacy of the *Meditations* is an image of a disembodied man who lacks the resources to judge the status of his own experience of the world. Descartes' own term for this state of extreme skepticism about the epistemic reliability of our ordinary experience is 'madness.' And it could be said that in the 350 years since the publication of the *Meditations*, we philosophers have been trying to regain our sanity. *The* task of modern philosophy has been to identify and secure the foundations of our ordinary experience – as though by failing to sublime this experience philosophically we are systematically and relentlessly imperiling ourselves.

Before Descartes, during the ancient and medieval periods, philosophers conceived of themselves as in the business not of securing the foundations of our knowledge but of describing the world in terms of what they *already* knew to be true – what Homer or the Scriptures, for example, had said. The guiding purpose of philosophical inquiry was not to theorise one's way back from the brink of madness but to propose a grand vision of how to live, and this inquiry took the form of a revaluation of everyday experience. The methodology of philosophy was to bring us to a new vision of our everyday lives, and this point is epitomised in what is perhaps the most famous image in the history of the enterprise: Plato's cave. Since this image is important to what I will go on to say, I want to rehearse in some detail the way Plato constructs and uses it.

Plato asks us to imagine an underground cave at the bottom of which is a group of prisoners, shackled so that they cannot move their heads

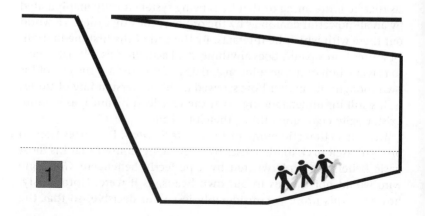

and are consigned to face the cave's back wall. Behind these prisoners, Plato says, we are to imagine a ledge on which other people are manipulating various everyday objects and making corresponding sound effects.

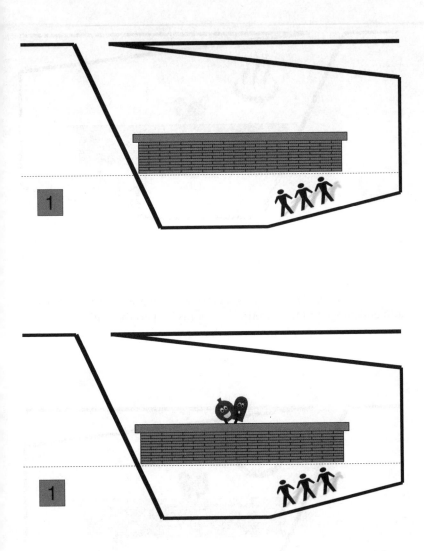

And behind the ledge there is a huge fire, the light from which casts shadows on the prisoners' wall. For the prisoners, Plato observes, 'reality' will consist exclusively in what's on the wall in front of them.

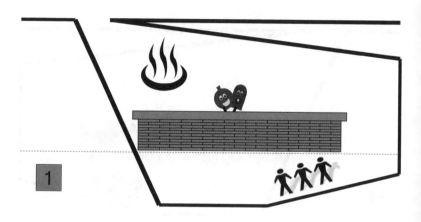

Now suppose, Plato suggests, that one of the prisoners is unshackled and encouraged to turn around, to set his back to the wall.

At first, Plato speculates, the strong light from the fire would blind him, and he would attempt to turn back to what is familiar. But if he were courageous and curious enough, he would not turn back, and gradually his eyes would adjust to the light. Let us imagine, then, that he walks away from his fellow prisoners – the '2' in the graphic below is to indicate that this is something like a second perspective on the world, as Plato sees it. When he reaches this place the newly freed prisoner will recognise that what he previously took to be real was actually a mere representation of what now appears to be the ultimate reality: the ledge, the objects being manipulated on it, and the fire.

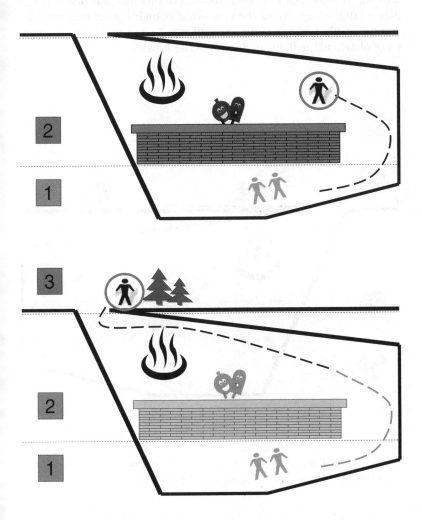

Plato now imagines the freed prisoner's being encouraged to walk past the ledge, the objects, and the fire, toward the mouth of the cave. Once again, the prisoner will be loathe to leave behind what he takes to be real. And since the light outside the cave will be much brighter even than the light of the fire, he will once again be blinded and will have to overcome the strong urge to turn back. But, if he is blessed with the right temperament, he will bring himself to leave the comfort of the cave.

(Again, the '3' indicates that we're at what Plato takes to be a third perspective on how things are.) When his eyes adjust, the former prisoner will discover that what he previously took to be real – the people's moving the objects on the ledge in front of the fire – was just so much play-acting: a copying of the real world (which means that what he was originally looking at on the wall was a copy of a copy – a mere piece of art, by the lights of Book X of the *Republic*).

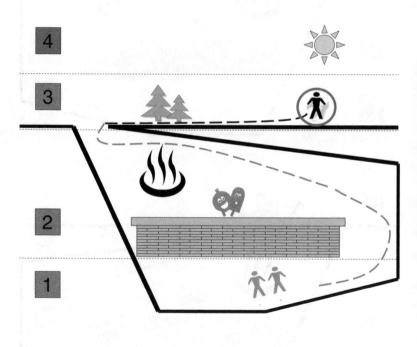

Eventually, Plato suggests, the prisoner may discover in himself the desire and fortitude to look upward and behold the sun.

Now, Plato believed that the things of this world – the things one finds at what I'm identifying as level 3, the things of our everyday lives – are themselves copies of ideal forms, emblematised by the sun and accessible (at level 4) only to people well trained in thinking, that is, to philosophers. This means that from the point of view of the philosopher what the prisoners at level 1 are viewing is merely a copy of a copy of a copy.

Notice that what Plato conveys via the figure of the cave is *not* the Cartesian idea that our ordinary experience is unreliable, nor, à la a later version of modern skepticism that we find in Kant, that the truth of how things are with the world – whether or to what extent the world is merely the product of our powers of imagination and speculation – is in principle beyond our grasp. Rather, what Plato's image suggests is that we, that is to say, the prisoners in the cave, are fixated on the light and shadows the world casts and that what we need to do to think and live truly is to muster up the courage to turn around and walk away. Let me put this point in a more provocatively, the way Cavell has taught me to do: Plato is exhorting us to walk out on the feature presentation. His prisoners, hypnotised by the shadows that play on the wall, composing a world out of these effects of artifice, are … watching movies.[6]

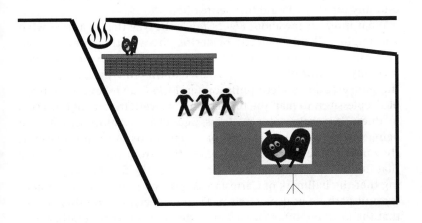

If we remind ourselves that Plato wished to ban all art from his republic on the grounds that it entices people away from the hard work of philosophy and drugs them into contentment with mere shadows of reality, we can appreciate Cavell's suggestion that at its founding moment Western philosophy in effect defines itself over and against film, as though delimiting itself by pointing to what it is emphatically not.

The difference between this founding moment and the modern one that Descartes inaugurates is that the moral of the Cartesian story appears to be the *impossibility* of the turning around Plato recommends to us. We are enslaved in our own consciousnesses, consigned either to go on watching the wall of shadows or to shut our eyes. I said earlier that philosophy today continues to be controlled by Cartesian skepticism. I can now put the claim this way: the conditions that define modern philosophy are strikingly similar to the conditions of watching a film. In both cases, the existence of the – or, in the case of film I should probably say 'a' – world is at stake. You might think that a major difference here is that the philosopher is desperately trying to *confirm* the existence of the world of his or her ordinary experience, while the filmgoer, as the cliché would have it, willingly suspends disbelief in the world that any decent narrative film conjures up. But Cavell's view is premised on the sense that something like the opposite is true here: our culture's craving for films is a sign of our desperate desire to believe in a vision of the world, and a place for the human in it, while the philosopher's madness results from his developing our uncanny capacity to ward this desire off.

What interests me about *Fight Club* is the way that it studies what you might call this dialectic of desire, the way that it evokes our yearning for a coherent world in which we can invest ourselves, precisely by scrutinising the resistance to this craving epitomised in the stance of the modern philosopher. *Fight Club* relies on the trope of sleeplessness to map the topography of a certain state of Cartesian madness. It identifies this madness, figured as insomnia, as a state of being unable to feel or express one's emotions. And this apathy is shown to produce a profound separation from other people, one that in effect denies their existence, so that the film ends up implying that the hallmark of Cartesian skepticism is an extreme, violent form of pathological narcissism. *Fight Club* claims, in other words, that the most important legacy of Cartesianism is ethical rather than epistemological.

Fight Club is the story of an anonymous corporate drone, played by Edward Norton, who begins to suffer from terrible insomnia. His sleeplessness is alleviated only by his sobbing his heart out at all sorts of support groups for diseases he doesn't have – testicular cancer, brain parasites, degenerative bone disease, tuberculosis, organic brain dementia, sickle cell anemia, and on and on. When the protagonist cannot cry, he cannot feel anything; and when he cannot feel anything, he cannot sleep. But when he invades Remaining Men Together, he sleeps, as he puts it, better than a baby. The plot of *Fight Club* is set in motion by the protagonist's meeting a woman named Marla Singer, played by Helena Bonham Carter, who, just like the protagonist, is a support-group junkie. Marla both deeply attracts and deeply repulses the protagonist, for she recognises <u>him</u> under all the fakery and thereby disrupts it. Marla makes it impossible for the protagonist to cry – hence feel, hence sleep. In the deep state of insomnia that ensues, the protagonist meets the seductive Tyler Durden, played by the seductive Brad Pitt, who draws him further and further into violent resistance against the culture that has spawned his meaningless life. At the core of this resistance is a nationwide network of 'fight clubs,' ever-growing groups of alienated men who get together late at night, when other people are sleeping, in warehouses and industrial basements – so many underground caves – and do what can only be described as beating the shit out of each other. Tyler Durden interprets these men's desperate need to feel something – their collective insomnia, as the film figures it – as a form of socially mandated emasculation. So it's no wonder that his recipe for relief, his way of Remaining Men Together, takes the hyper-masculine form of, at first, giving and receiving punches and, later, all-out acts of terror against corporate America.

Toward the end of *Fight Club*, we come to learn (and I'm afraid I'm about to spoil things if you haven't seen the film) that Tyler Durden does not exist – or, rather, that his reality is a function of the protagonist's insomnia. When the protagonist drifts off at night and at other moments of extreme exhaustion into a hellish state that's neither wakefulness nor dreaming, Tyler, it turns out, takes over his body. Tyler is Cartesian skepticism distilled to its essence: a personality whose existence is perfectly coextensive with his thinking. And yet, unlike the protagonist, through whose body and voice, we are given to understand, he commands legions of men, Tyler makes himself known to other people – though not to the protagonist, whose recognition of Tyler's true nature lags even behind ours. The protagonist's unwillingness to let others know him is signified in his abiding namelessness, which is underscored by the different pseudonyms – Cornelius, Rupert, Travis – he uses on each of his 'Hello, my name is...' support-group badges. The other members of Fight Club call the protagonist 'Tyler.'

So does Marla, the woman from the support groups, with whom the Tyler persona, much to the disgust of the oblivious protagonist, has been having an affair. Marla and the rest are not exactly mistaken in calling the protagonist 'Tyler,' of course – just as it would be wrong to say that *we* are mistaken when we refer to Brad Pitt in this film as 'Tyler.' Indeed, I wish to claim, an achievement of this film is the way it invites us to ask what it is that a human being's name names, which is to say, what a human being is.

This question takes its highest form, perhaps, in the film's response to the requirement – demanded by the transformation of Chuck Palahniuk's story into the medium of film – that the roles of the protagonist and Tyler Durden be played by two different actors. The coherence of the film depends on our accepting at one and the same time on the one hand that Tyler Durden is a figment of the protagonist's imagination and, on the other, the presence of Brad Pitt on the screen. The most unnerving moments of the film may well be those in which the contradiction is shoved in our faces, as Pitt, via security cameras within the mise-en-scène, flashbacks, and so forth, seems suddenly to evanesce, and we see Edward Norton punching *himself*. At the heart of this film, then, is the paradox that Brad Pitt's body is an essential part of the film *Fight Club* and yet it does not, cannot exist. And this paradox doesn't govern just what goes on within the film; it's an essential condition of the possibility of the film itself: there is no Brad Pitt, no human being, literally, in front of us – just lights and shadows cast on a screen in a dark place sealed off from the real world.

But for that matter, the Cartesian in us has to wonder: is there *ever*, even when we imagine we're dealing with the real thing, 'literally' a human being in front of us? I've never met the flesh-and-blood Brad Pitt. Is he computer-generated? Is he who he is on screen? Who is Brad Pitt? What does the person who gets paid for Brad Pitt's roles have in common with the figure I have come to know on film as 'Brad Pitt'? And suppose my ship were to come in and the 'real' Brad Pitt showed up one day on my doorstep. How could I know with absolute certainty that I hadn't just dreamed him up? These questions are on the same page as the ones over which philosophers have obsessed for the last several centuries. What *Fight Club* suggests is that this sort of obsession is a cover for a deeper, more human, more passionate question about what it means to recognise another person's existence – and, specifically, in the film's world, the existence of Marla. The achievement of this recognition, or what Cavell would call 'acknowledgment,' is further shown to require a willingness to allow another person to recognise you, to use your name. The protagonist's willingness for mutual recognition is what eventually kills off Tyler Durden, what brings the protagonist back from the limbo between being asleep and being awake. What fosters this willingness?

Let us return, for an answer, to an early moment in the film, at which the protagonist identifies insomnia with the condition of the prisoners in Plato's cave, which is to say, as I've suggested, with the watching of a film: 'With insomnia,' he says, 'nothing's real. Everything's far away. Everything's a copy of a copy of copy.' This would imply that the cure for insomnia involves bringing the real thing closer, as Plato's freed prisoner does when he journeys toward the sun. But the opening credit sequence suggests otherwise. The credits roll over a cinematic trip from deep within the Edward Norton character's brain outward to his nasal passages and then onto his skin and back away from his face, at which point we discover that we have just traveled up what turns out to be a gun in his mouth.[7] Though that excursion through the brain was of course computer-generated, the sweaty skin, those hair follicles, those pores the camera exposes – they consist of hundreds of extreme close-ups of Edward Norton's face. I take it that this opening sequence warns us that coming to understand the character Norton plays (which, in turn, will help us understand who Norton is on film) is not in fact a matter of looking very closely at him, but rather establishing the right distance from him, not too close, not too far. What exactly is this distance?

Like any really good movie, *Fight Club* proposes directions for thinking about the deep questions it poses. I will discuss two of its responses to the question of distance. First, there is the sequence in which the protagonist reminds us how a movie is put together. This sequence, which is aimed directly at us, occurs about a half hour into the film, right after Tyler proposes for the first time that the protagonist hit him and thus gives birth to the idea of 'fight club.' At this juncture, the protagonist as it were causes the frame to freeze and he explains to us how Tyler splices frames of pornography into the films he handles in his job as a projectionist.[8] Even a hummingbird may not be able to flap its wings as fast as a projector pixilates the frames of a film. But the hummingbird can't catch Tyler at work, as the protagonist notes, not because even it isn't fast enough but because it is incapable of understanding what Tyler is doing and why. *We*, however, are in a position to worry about these matters, and this sequence is explicitly exhorting us to, as it were, take off our chains and look around more carefully. The exhortation comes in quite direct form: both the protagonist and Tyler are explicitly figured as film directors. The protagonist has stopped Fincher's film in order to speak directly to us, as he does, via voiceovers, throughout the film; the 'cigarette burn' comes in exactly on Brad Pitt's cue; and Tyler of course helps himself to the director's task of deciding which available frames of film belong in what will be screened. So what do they want from us? *How* are we being asked to look more closely? Perhaps we should look for single, out-of-context frames spliced into *this* film. In fact, this search will be rewarded. Brad Pitt flits in and out of the frame in a split second several times, once, notably, when the protagonist, numbly working at a Xerox machine, talks about how his insomnia renders his representations of the world, as he puts it, à la Plato, copies of copies of copies.[9]

We are also treated, at the very end of the film, right before the credits role, to six or seven pornographic frames depicting a man's genitalia. What's important is that the penis we see for a quarter of a second or so is clearly something that is *not* important, not meant to work on us subconsciously: like the split-second appearances of Brad Pitt earlier in the film, it's a joke that, at least after more than one viewing of the film, we are at least in principle in on. It's as though Fincher is suggesting that what ought to be disturbing when it comes to watching this film is not its pornographic dimension – its sex or violence – but rather what is right in front of our faces, what we look at but may not see.

I said that I would discuss a second way that *Fight Club* provides us with directions for establishing the right distance from which to fathom Edward Norton's character. Let me suggest that *Fight Club* proposes that, in our current condition, at least, we as a culture cannot consider the question of the distance from which to understand others' existences in ungendered terms. For the protagonist's descent into madness, into perpetual insomnia, is triggered by the depth of his feeling for Marla Singer, the woman whose palpable desperation at the support groups matches his own and threatens to expose him to, not least, himself. We can scarcely avoid reading the protagonist's conjuring up of Tyler as a massive flight from his panic in the face of his feeling for Marla, which, since it's his feeling, constitutes a flight from himself. Shortly after the protagonist stops going to support groups and casts his lot with Tyler, Marla takes an overdose of Xanax and phones the protagonist for help. But it is Tyler who comes to her rescue, Tyler who keeps her from falling fatally asleep by what can be described in literal terms as making violent love to her, and Tyler who, in his hyperbolic investment in a hyperbolic conception of masculinity, confirms her sense of her own worthlessness. The protagonist begins to see Tyler for who is, begins to judge what's real, only when he is able to acknowledge his own, albeit unconscious part in Marla's degradation. His killing off of Tyler requires his acknowledging the Tyler in himself – his recognising the extent to which he both is and is not Tyler.

At the end of the film, as Tyler's last and grandest plot comes to fruition and one corporate building after the next comes tumbling down, Edward Norton's character discovers where he has to stand in order to see the world clearly, which in his case means to acknowledge both his own and Marla's flesh-and-blood existence. The protagonist has just killed off Tyler, mythically by shooting *himself*, but, in reality, as it were, by gazing through a widescreen window at Marla as she is getting dragged off the bus by Tyler's thugs, and finding himself able to believe in his desire for her. Marla, who is absolutely furious, is hauled to the protagonist's side and then stopped dead in her tracks when she sees the massive wound in his face.[10] As the protagonist reassures Marla that he is in fact all right, the buildings outside the window begin to implode; and the two reach for each other's hand as they stare at the window. The right distance from which to bear witness to what's real, to judge the status of the world, this film seems to claim, is not the one that would have you staring into the sun. Rather, it proposes – apropos of both Plato and Descartes, I claim – that the right distance is the one at which you are inclined to watch a movie with someone you love.

Notes

1. Cavell's writings on film include *The World Viewed: Reflections on the Ontology of Film* (1971/1979); *Pursuits of Happiness: The Hollywood Comedy of Remarriage* (1981); *Contesting Tears: The Melodrama of the Unknown Woman* (1996); 'On Makavejev on Bergman,' 'North by Northwest,' 'The Thought of Movies,' 'What Becomes of Things on Film?' and 'Appendix: Film in the University,' all from *Themes out of School: Effects and Causes* (1984) 'A Capra Moment,' *Humanities* (August 1985); *Cities of Words: Pedagogical Letters on a Register of the Moral Life* (2004) 'Psychoanalysis and Cinema' in Smith & Kerrigan (eds) (1987); 'Two Cheers for Romance,' in Gaylin and Person (eds) (1987); and 'Who Disappoints Whom? *Critical Inquiry* (Spring 1989).
2. The school of thinking I have in mind calls itself 'cognitivist film theory.' See, for example, Cynthia Freeland's argument in *The Naked and the Undead: Evil and the Appeal to Horror* (1999). Freeland's view is that horror movies can be taken seriously by philosophers because they appeal to both our

emotional and cognitive capacities (where of course these capacities are conceptualised by Freeland as essentially distinct). She writes, e.g., 'Horror films are designed to prompt *emotions* of fear, sympathy, revulsion, dread, anxiety, or disgust. And in doing so, they also stimulate *thoughts* about evil in its many varieties and degrees.... We may experience standard or predictable emotions (fear, revulsion, dread, relief), but then we also reflect on why and whether it is right to do so' (3; Freeland's emphasis). Other writings on cognitivist film theory include many of the essays in *Film Theory and Philosophy*, (ed. Allen & Smith), (1999) and *Passionate Views: Film, Cognition, and Emotion*, (ed. C. Plantinga & G.M. Smith) (1999). See also G.M. Smith, *Film Structure and the Emotion System* (2003). Other prominent cognitivist film theorists include Noël Carroll and Gregory Currie.

3. Plato seems to succumb in his later dialogues – including the tenth book of the *Republic* – to the temptation of turning Socrates into a mouthpiece and the marketplace into a bully pulpit. But in the early dialogues Plato seems committed to the picture of philosophy I have sketched here. For speculation about why Plato became preachier in his later years, see the late work of Gregory Vlastos, especially chapters 2 and 3 of *Socrates, Ironist and Moral Philosopher* (1991). For Cavell's most sustained discussion of the early Plato's vision of philosophy, see the introduction and chapter 1 of *Conditions Handsome and Unhandsome: The Constitution of Emersonian Perfectionism* (1991) and chapter 17 of *Cities of Words*, cited in note 1 above.

4. Laura Mulvey, 'Visual Pleasure and Narrative Cinema', in her *Visual and Other Pleasures* (1989), 14–26. The essay was written in 1973 and originally published in 1975. It has been anthologised countless times and is arguably the most well-known essay in the history of academic film studies.

5. Of course, most professional philosophers are not completely thick, and so they would not deny that a film might be, in and of itself, an object of aesthetic interest. It's perfectly respectable within professional philosophy to worry about whether a film is really a work of art – about, that is, what a work of art is and whether some films, at least, meet the criteria. You can engage in the cottage industry of talking about whether films work by appealing to our emotions or our cognition or both. (See note 2 above.) You can do what philosophers in general do and develop a top-down theory that *explains* what it is to be a film. What you can't do is suggest that films in and of themselves aspire to full participation in, and not just provocation of, philosophical conversation. You can't put any film, no matter how good it is, on an equal footing with the likes of an Aristotle or a Kant or a Heidegger.

6. Again, see Cavell's *Cities of Words*, chapter 17.

7. See *Fight Club*, 00:00:33 to 00:02:07.

8. See *Fight Club*, 00:32:10 to 00:33:33.

9. For this moment, see *Fight Club*, 00:03:57 to 00:04:10. For other moments in which Brad Pitt flashes into the frame for a split second, see *Fight Club*, 00:06:07 and 00:07:25.

10. See *Fight Club*, 02:15:13 to 02:16:10.

In Space, No-one Can Hear You Scream: Acknowledging the Human Voice in the Alien Universe

Stephen Mulhall

In my recent book, *On Film*, I offered (amongst other things) a reading of the four *Alien* movies which originates in response to the specific mode of monstrousness that the alien species embodies. My suggestion was that, beyond the threat of their violence (to which terror is the proper response), we are horrified by their drive to involve human beings in their essentially parasitic mode of reproduction. For that process – whereby the alien inserts a long, flexible member into the body of its host through one of that body's orifices, and deposits thereby a version of itself which develops within the host's torso to the point at which it must force itself out again – is a nightmare vision of human heterosexual intercourse, pregnancy and birth. The alien species is, in other words, an incarnation of masculinity, understood as penetrative sexual violence; but as such, it threatens the human race as a whole with the apparently monstrous fate of feminisation, forcing our species to occupy the sexual role (that of being violated, playing host to a parasite, and of facing death in giving birth) that women are imagined to occupy in relation to men.

This interpretation of the monstrosity of the alien helps to explain Ripley's emergence as the heroic protagonist in the first *Alien* film. Whereas the men of the *Nostromo* find their forced occupation of a female subject position – their unprecedented vulnerability to rape, impregnation and parturition – profoundly traumatising, it is far less alien to the women; and it is utterly unsurprising to the female crew member who shows herself most instinctively sensitive to the need to protect the integrity of her vessel against alien penetration (as when she tries to prevent the stricken Kane's return to the ship). In short, Ridley Scott's most effective subversion of the hybrid genre in which he is working (his association of femininity with heroism rather than

57

victimhood) is in fact dictated by the logic of his monster's monstrousness, and by its replication of his hero's understanding of her femaleness.

What I want to do here is to focus on a further aspect of the aliens' monstrousness that I noted in my book, but left relatively undeveloped, or at least inexplicit, in that context – the insistent orality of their uncanny parasitism, and the implications of that fact for our understanding of Ripley's intimate loathing for them, and of her often unmanageable relations with the other human beings in her world.

Ripley's voice

Beyond the fact of the alien species' insistently oral self-presentation – its incarnation of devouring insatiability at every stage of its life-cycle, from the metallic incisors of the chest-burster to the teeth-within-teeth of the warrior – its facehugger variant impregnates its victims through the mouth. On the assumption that its mode of reproduction is a monstrous image of the human mode, this implies that to occupy the role of women in relation to men is to have one's mouth stopped or gagged, to be rendered mute – an implication reinforced by the alien species' insistent avoidance of any form of negotiation or other mode of communication with its victims, its absolute refusal of conversation or (non-reproductive) intercourse with its intended hosts. Thus, heterosexual masculinity appears as aiming to silence the woman's voice, to deny her the most fundamental expression of her individuality. Accordingly, for the human race to be feminised is for human individuality as such to be threatened, as if the alien's monstrosity declares that something about the acknowledgement of individuality (in particular, the relation of individuality to sexual difference) sticks in our throats, makes us gag.

The first *Alien* film connects this aspect of the aliens' orality with Ripley's experience of the human world she inhabits, by underlining the degree to which her voice fails to register in that world. Her questions and orders for the repair of the *Nostromo* are avoided and ignored by Brett and Parker (they render her literally inaudible by allowing steam to vent throughout their conversation with her, making her utterances mere wasted breath); and when she forbids Ash from opening the hatch to allow Kane to be brought back on board, he acts as if she had not spoken. As the crew member who most intimately identifies himself with the aliens, his inclination to behave as if her words had no weight – as if she didn't exist – is entirely in character;

and when he attempts to prevent her from sabotaging his secret mission to return an alien specimen to the Company, he does so by forcing a tightly-rolled pornographic magazine down her throat – perhaps the film's most explicit equation of male violence with the desire to annihilate the female voice, and of individual human existence with the ability to speak for oneself, to have a voice in one's own history. (The same theme is reiterated in the film's climactic sequence, when Ripley proves unable to countermand her earlier self-destruct order to the ship's computer, Mother; Mother's utter lack of response to her daughter, her deafness to her hysterical screams for attention, threatens to be literally lethal.)

But of course, Ripley avoids the fate that her masculine, technological world attempts to force upon her. First, she drives herself through the terrifying business of preparing to eject the alien from the airlock by reciting a song to herself, as if needing to hear the sound of her own voice to retain a grip on her own existence (as if finding herself by finding a way of interweaving words with melody and rhythm – singing herself out of death into life). And after the success of her plan, as she puts her cat and herself into hypersleep for the journey back to Earth, the film's soundtrack is given over to Ripley's enunciation of a message sent to those whom she hopes will rescue her. In other words, her triumph is marked by her recitation of the circumstances that brought her to her present pass in the form of a mayday broadcast – an appeal to the universe that is also her voicing of her own history. It proclaims her existence, staking a claim to life that asks for a hearing; but it remains unclear whether anyone is attending to Ripley's words.

Certainly, she confronts the same avoidance or denial of her voice in the world of *Aliens*. Her testimony at the board meeting, its extended recapitulation of the narrative of her life, is entirely discounted by her interlocutors; and even when the Company acknowledges its need for her experience by offering her a place on the Marine rescue mission, the commanding officer tells his men that they can learn what they need from Ripley by absorbing a computer record of her story. It is as if the value of her witness to the events of the first film is reducible to the information content of her testimony – so that the fact of her having experienced those events, the reality and value of her status as a participant in the story she narrates, and so her individuality, need find no acknowledgement from her comrades-in-arms.

In this second film, Ripley's reiterated recovery of her life as hers to own is prepared for by the opening events of her relationship with Newt. The marines conclude that the young girl has been rendered mute by her experience of the alien attack; but Ripley's ability to elicit a verbal response from her shows rather that her muteness is an effect of the soldiers' coerciveness. Their mode of attending to Newt is as unresponsive to her human individuality as is their dismissal of Ripley; but Ripley, by contrast, allows Newt to find words for her experience by presenting herself as a conversation partner – as someone capable of listening. After the Marine's disastrous initial foray into the alien nest, Ripley attains a commanding voice in the future proceedings of the expedition when Corporal Hicks finds himself able not only to listen to her words, but to endorse them – to find them genuinely responsive to the reality of their circumstances and properly expressive of his own perspective upon it, hence not neurotically private or empty, but public or social. It is not that Hicks' repetition of Ripley's lapidary phrase 'we'll nuke the planet from orbit – it's the only way' grants authority to these words; it is rather that his voice attains its proper authority insofar as it acknowledges the authority inherent in hers. The remainder of the film is devoted to attesting to the mutuality of that acknowledgement, and hence to the possibility of modes of masculinity that seek not to stifle but rather to accommodate the female voice, and modes of femininity that can acknowledge and incorporate something more or other to masculinity than our worst nightmares of it.

In *Alien³*, Ripley's initial powerlessness in the human community she is attempting to defend is once again epitomised by her voicelessness: her testimony is as firmly discounted by the prison governor Andrews as it was by the Company board meeting, and the extremity of her exclusion from this all-male world is matched by a physical inability to articulate (the sore throat which marks her rape and impregnation on the *Sulaco*). Only three men are willing to converse with Ripley, and hence to raise the question of whether masculinity must deny the female voice. Clemens' openness to intercourse extends to the sexual, but is annihilated by the film's incarnate nightmare vision of that realm. Bishop exchanges compliments with her, but he also gives voice to the history of her rape and impregnation, as well as a despairing refusal of his own dilapidated state, and he is not, in the end, human. Dillon at least finds fitting words for the cremation of her spouse and child; but his refusal of her pleading request to assist in her suicide is balanced on a knife-edge between denial of her suffering and encouragement towards its overcoming.

It is therefore fitting that the film's climactic scene begins with what might be its most meaningful conversation – between Ripley and an apparently human being who claims to be the creator (and is certainly an exact image) of Bishop and his generation of androids. This man's voice is full-throatedly seductive, responsive to every lineament of Ripley's desire for a solution to her predicament – for children, for a life of her own, for the death of her foes. But it is false: its true meaning emerges as the unsuccessful attack on its possessor (by stripping Bishop II's ear away from something other than bone) uncovers the possibility that this 'man' is not Bishop's creator but simply another instance of that android type (as if, given his true reason for conversing with Ripley, precisely nothing hangs on whether he is human or not – as if masculinity endlessly clones itself as violent suffocation of the female). For either way, this interlocutor is simply the Company's mouthpiece, and Ripley's final achievement is to refuse any further intercourse with him – to say 'No', and to elicit the help of one of the convicts to annihilate her enemy by annihilating herself.

That this amounts to her reclaiming of her own life through the refusal of its continuance at any price is indicated by the film's marking of its own closure by repeating the concluding mayday message of the first: '...This is Ripley, last survivor of the *Nostromo*, signing off.' Her self-immolation is her way of affixing her signature to her life, her way of inscribing herself into and out of existence, of giving voice to her individuality in despite of the world's desire to stop her mouth. For it amounts to an enactment of the only words left to all the aliens' human hosts in these films – their despairing plea to 'Kill me' (with its implicit acknowledgement that alien impregnation amounts to individual annihilation, that in the gap between conception and birth the 'mother' is already, or would be better off, dead); but it makes those words mean otherwise. For Ripley's end is also the aliens' end. Her suicidal self-sacrifice thus incarnates the terms of her world in a way which deprives it of the means to perfect and totalise its silencing of the woman's voice; hence she opens up the possibility of its overcoming its fixation on that goal. In her wordless action, and in the face of absolute despair, Ripley in the end means to say 'yes' to human life.

In *Alien Resurrection*, Ripley's clone is introduced to the accompaniment of Sigourney Weaver's voice reciting lines first uttered by Newt in *Aliens*: 'My mummy always said that there were no monsters, no real ones – but there are'. This identifies Ripley's clone with the perspective of a child, and implies that her world will be the realisation of a child's nightmare – hence that the vision of human fertility and sexuality embodied by the alien species is best understood as giving expression to the fears and fantasies of a child, and thereby to a refusal or unwillingness to grow up. This resistance is not seen by Jeunet as groundless

– our brief glimpses of the clone's accelerated education, in which she acquires language through stun-gun reinforcement, suggest that nothing much in the male drive to subordinate the woman's voice has diminished over the centuries since Ripley's death. Neither, however, is such resistance seen as a viable stance; Ripley's clone's development to maturity may be artificially accelerated, but it is a journey no-one can avoid taking altogether.

Nevertheless, the main register of the clone's voice throughout the movie is that of child-cum-adolescent; its exemplary instances of conversational closure are akin to the nihilistic wit of US high-school mallrats. This is not in itself an indication of the clone's lack of individuality; it rather underlines that, as with any adolescent, she finds herself having to confront the adult world on offer to her as a whole. Any participant in the human social world must establish how far she will take responsibility for its particular arrangements from a perspective within them; but the adolescent looks upon that social world as if from without, considering whether it elicits her desire to participate at all. The costs of refusal are high for both parties. If the adolescent is to have the possibility of attaining genuine individuality, she must accept some form of communal existence; the refusal of the social world as such is the route not to privacy but to muteness. But if any particular inflection of the social world is to maintain and reproduce itself, it must find willing participants from amongst those born within it; their alienation would amount to its annihilation.

However, what Ripley's clone seeks to assess as a whole is not merely one amongst many possible forms of human life, but rather the human as opposed to another possible form of life – participation in the hive-life of the alien species. Hence, *Alien Resurrection* presents Ripley's clone as torn between the attractions of the external babel of aggressive, caring, altruistic and egoistic voices of her individual human (and android) comrades, and the internal, identity-dissolving babel of the alien hive that speaks to her through her bloodstream and cells. This conflict is ultimately resolved in favour of the human world; but the price for humanity is the denial of the alien hive's claims upon her qua mother – her willingness to witness her alien daughter's death, and to bring about the death of her alien granddaughter. Whatever comfort we might take from the thought that the clone is seduced by our humanity as such – her seeing more to humanity than there is to our present social (de)formations of it – is counterbalanced by the thought that the clone's refusal of alien life (and hence of its monstrous representation of human life) amounts to a refusal of maternity, of the fecundity of flesh-and-blood. Is such a route towards the achievement of a human voice a genuine acknowledgement of the claims and stakes of maturity, or a childish denial of them?

The director's voice

What might be gained, in understanding the nature of these four films, and of film as an artistic medium, in thinking of the director's contribution as a matter of voice as opposed to, say, vision? Is not talk of ways of seeing the obvious way of characterising central elements of work produced in a medium whose technological basis is the photographic reproduction of reality, and hence whose primary mode of appeal to its audience is through the eye? Why choose instead to articulate matters in terms of the mouth, and its complementary organ the ear?

It is worth pointing out, first, that my invocation of the human voice is not in fact opposed to talk of vision, any more than it stands in opposition to writing; the human voice can find expression (or fail to) in the field of writing (as well as that of speech) and in the field of vision (as well as that of language). The issues I aim to foreground – the affirmation and denial of one's existence, one's individuality, one's stake in one's own life – can also be brought out in (at least some versions of) these alternative vocabularies. Nevertheless, three distinctive aspects of the grammar of the concept of voice motivate its employment here.

First, there is the link, etymologically underwritten in German and systematically exploited by Heidegger, between '*Stimme*' (voice) and '*Stimmung*' (mood, or mode of attunement); this suggests that having a voice is in part a matter of being able to voice or to give voice to something – to be sufficiently receptive to a tone or register of a situation or world so as to be able to body it forth or give it expression. This relation between possessing a voice and being possessed by a voice or voices is repeatedly returned to in the *Alien* films – as when Bishop I's head ventriloquises the log of the *Sulaco* in order to clarify the reasons for Ripley's evacuation, or when Call reluctantly cedes her voice to that of the *Auriga*'s main computer. It seems a useful figure for the way in which any director of a sequel must attune herself to the underlying logic and mood of the world she is inheriting if she is not only to remain true to its significance but also to find a way of making her own contribution to its unfolding. Such submission to or submersion in a pre-existing reality is not an obstacle to the expression of directorial individuality, but its essential precondition; the cinematic *auteur* can flourish in the realm of sequeldom, but only by acknowledging rather than denying her belatedness – only by treating what appear to be constraints as conditions, by seeing that limits can empower.

A second thought captured by talk of the director's voice is that, in the context of a series of films, the various contributions to that series take on the aspect of moments in a conversation or dialogue. What gives that conversation its unity is its shared topic – say, the conceptual, dramatic and cinematic resources of the Alien universe – and a common desire amongst the participants to make the best of those resources, to essay the underlying truth of their nature and their human resonance. What gives the conversation its interest is the unpredictability of its overall trajectory, the distinctive way in which each film takes up its common inheritance, alters our perception of its essence, and opens up possibilities from which the next participant in the conversation must choose. And it is in those choices that the individuality of each participant finds expression; their collective subordination to the goal of saying what they see as the heart of the Alien universe is what brings out most clearly the distinctiveness of their perspective upon it.

With respect to the *Alien* films, this image of a conversation is particularly apt, since it positively invites the thought that each director's contribution to the unfolding directorial dialogue about the Alien universe is, in effect, their way of responding to Ripley's need and desire for an interlocutor, a worthy conversation partner, another who is willing and able to attend to what she is saying and to acknowledge her voice in the way they respond to it. It is this thought, the third thought encouraged by the idea of the voice, which I want briefly to pursue here.

In the terms provided by this image of a conversation between character and director, Ridley Scott appears not so much as one interlocutor for Ripley, but rather as the one who makes it possible for Ripley to encounter and assess future candidates for interlocution; for it is in the first film that the centrality of Ripley's character to the nature of the Alien universe – her claim to be a uniquely worthy opponent of the alien species – is first adumbrated. In the course of that film, she gradually emerges from an undifferentiated ensemble by refusing to accept her voicelessness, and hence her status as just one more potential victim, one more mute and traumatised body to be fed to a devouring masculinity. By its end, she can sign off as the sole survivor – she speaks in need of a hearer, more specifically in need of a rescuer, but she nevertheless speaks, and she speaks in her own individual voice, one which distinguishes her from the uniformity in death of her fellow crew-members even as it attempts to memorialise their individuality by recalling their names.

James Cameron thinks that he knows what Ripley wants, and needs. He presents her first moments as the undergoing of a nightmare, one which she relives every night until offered the chance to participate in the Marine rescue mission and (as Burke puts it) get back on the horse. His therapeutic message is clear; Ripley must relive her living nightmare if she is to overcome its traumatic effects on her life. Hence, Cameron's multilevel reiterations of the structure, themes, situations and images of the first film are in the service of psychoanalytic transformation. And he declares his belief that he has cured the ills of his analysand by offering Ripley the fulfilment she craves: a family, with Hicks as the husband and Newt as the child.

But the kind of family he gifts her, or more precisely the way in which he allows her to acquire it, shows that Cameron's conception of what it would be for Ripley to be healed is in fact a continuation of, hence is essentially complicit with, the very attitude to sexuality that locks her into her nightmare. For Ripley's family has a non-biological origin: her union with Hicks is not physically consummated, and she becomes a mother to Newt without conceiving, being pregnant or giving birth to her. In short, whilst Ripley's achievement of this director's conception of female fulfilment demands that she lay her body on the line for Hicks and Newt, it allows her to avoid any acknowledgement of her body's fertility. But what is thereby repressed is not annihilated; it is rather transposed onto the alien species, when Cameron introduces the alien queen into the picture, and presents her fertility – the emergence of new alien eggs from her quivering, semi-translucent, sagging egg-sac – as a new extremity of monstrousness. In other words, Ripley's directorial interlocutor is telling her everything she wants to hear; her would-be therapist is a mirror for her fantasies, perfectly attuned to their perverse valuations of human embodiment – a victim of transference. It is no accident that the jointly uttered words (and hence the acknowledgement of Ripley's voice) upon which Hicks and Ripley found their marriage – 'we'll nuke the planet from orbit: it's the only way' – give expression to a fundamentally genocidal impulse.

David Fincher is not prepared to make his conversation with Ripley into a reinforcing reiteration of fantasy. He declares his utter disagreement with Cameron's contribution to the directorial conversation by immediately depriving Ripley of her husband and child, and by forcing her to order and superintend an autopsy on her daughter. But the true subject of this dispassionate dissection is Cameron; Fincher extirpates his pivotal contribution to the series as if it were not only dead but potentially infectious, as if *Aliens* had taken the series away from itself, condemning it to inauthenticity and lifelessness. Fincher finds no more trace of genuinely alien life in *Aliens* than Clemens finds in Newt.

In Fincher's articulation of the Alien universe, things are both better and worse than Cameron can imagine. Worse, because the alien has, before the film has properly begun, already raped and impregnated an unconscious Ripley, thus fulfilling her worst nightmare; better, because Ripley's every waking moment thereafter – in other words, the whole narrative of her existence as this film presents it – is a concrete proof of her ability to survive that fulfilment, to exist beyond her fixation on its horror. Indeed, she even voices the desire for sex with Clemens, making space for a fully physical union with a man – as if her rape by the alien has demystified human heterosexual intercourse, allowing her a brief but intense moment of self-overcoming. In the end, however, Fincher is clear that the Alien universe is not constructed so as to accommodate anything other than moments of that kind; if Ripley is to mean what she says in this universe, she has to say 'No' to the hypermasculine, technocratic world that confines her – to find a way of saying 'Kill me' that affirms her individual existence. So (partly educated by Dillon's refusal of her first, failed attempts to do this) she signs off from that world through a wordless act which deprives it of its ability utterly to stifle the woman's voice, and hence declares a belief in the possibility of a world constructed so as to go beyond its fixation on denying that voice.

Jean-Pierre Jeunet implicitly accepts the totality of Fincher's critique of Cameron, and hence the substance of his intercourse with Ripley, by making the protagonist of his film not Ripley herself but rather her clone. She is not the same person, she is not even of the same species; hence her voice does not give expression to the same individual existence. But she has a voice, and it is female; hence it is striking that Jeunet's articulation of that voice brings out a certain register of childhood and adolescence. Its childlike inflection implies that the very resoluteness of Ripley's resistance to the aliens indicates a view of sexual incarnation that amounts to a refusal to grow up; but its adolescent intonation suggests further that to deny the legitimacy of the female voice (or the female register of the human voice) is to deprive ourselves of a perspective on our society as a whole, and even on our humanity as such, without which the community of human voices might descend into the bickering babel of the *Betty*'s crew.

We might also take Jeunet's attentiveness to adolescence as his way of saying that Fincher's total closure of the Alien universe did not so much exclude further conversation about it as relocate the perspective from which such conversation could continue. For Fincher forced Jeunet to find a way of restarting that conversation from scratch, yet without losing touch with its original topic; he forced Jeunet to take a view on the Alien universe as a whole, hence as if from outside, asking himself whether the conversation it had generated was sufficiently attractive to be continued. The fact of his film amounts to an affirm-ative answer to that question; and its ending, with Call and Ripley's clone poised to set foot on an Earth to which they are both strangers, further implies that Jeunet's affirmation has brought the series back to its origin, but with a sense that it is utterly unknown to us – that it has returned us to a genuinely alien Alien universe. What better way to renew the familiar conversation?

Philosophy's voice

Under this heading I want briefly to re-articulate and develop some themes in the introduction to my book on the *Alien* films – themes concerning the sense in which one might hear the voice of philosophy in the films under discussion, and hear my discussion of the films as having a distinctively philosophical register.

In my introduction I specified three ways in which one might think of the films themselves as attuned to specifically philosophical con-cerns. The first I called 'film as philosophising': this refers to the ways in which the films not only incite us to think about a variety of inter-related issues concerning human identity (the relation of human integrity to the body, sexual difference and nature) that have been familiar preoccupations of modern philosophy since Descartes, but are themselves thinking about those issues. They are reflecting on and evaluating various stances with respect to those issues, seriously and systematically engaging with them in just the ways that philosophers do; they are not philosophy's raw material or optional ornamentation, but rather exercises in philosophising.

The second mode of these films' philosophical attunement is that most commonly found in books described as 'philosophy of film' – a reflective, analytical interest in the nature of the medium of cinema, of the projected moving image, its powers and its limitations. In the

Alien films, their general preoccupation with human embodiment inexorably raises this question, since cinematic projections of moving images of ourselves are one of the necessary possibilities to which our embodiment subjects us, and we cannot fully understand that subjection without understanding the nature of photographic transcription as such. The more specific form in which the *Alien* films pursue this understanding is by focussing on the capacity of cinematic projections to translate certain individual physiognomies into movie stardom, as this capacity is exemplified in the camera's treatment of Sigourney Weaver. Her emergence as a star is (in fact and in myth) indistinguishable from her emergence as the heroic protagonist in *Alien*; and her identity as a star, the various ways in which it appears that she can and cannot incarnate certain character types and roles in other films, is inextricably linked with the development of her incarnation as Ripley throughout the series.

This incarnation in fact continues beyond Ripley's own death by virtue of her cloning; it is as if Weaver the star cannot shake off the integument of Ripley the character, as if to test the thought that photographic transcriptions of human beings are a kind of cloning, and that the transformation of actors into stars (their access to a strange new world of possibilities and powers) amounts to the establishment of a hybrid of human and alien (so that Jeunet's re-founding conception of Ripley's clone is an apotheosis of these films' increasing concern with the family resemblances between Weaver's physiognomy and that of Ripley's foes).

Furthermore, if Ripley's emergence as an authentic individual is figured by her acquisition of a voice in her own history, we might think of this film's study of Weaver's correlative emergence as a star as implying that the projection of her distinctive physiognomy into stardom is importantly dependent upon the equally distinctive physiognomy of her voice. In short, the *Alien* series' focus on Ripley's voice is also a study of the cinema soundtrack. It is a way of reflecting upon the capacity of talking pictures to present us with speaking as well as moving human beings, and hence to contemplate the human voice's dependence upon and independence of the human body.

For on the one hand, talking pictures emphasise the degree to which our sense of being presented with the individual human being placed before the camera is incalculably reinforced by an ability to allow her to speak; and they thereby underline the fact that human voices are necessarily embodied, and indispensable in articulating the individuality of their embodied possessors. But on the other hand, insofar as the cinematic acknowledgement of the marriage between voice and body is effected by techniques for synchronising what is in fact separately recorded, they imply the uncanny ability of the voice to divorce itself from any specific embodiment. When the *Alien* films repeatedly present us with Ripley's words in others' mouths, or in pure voice-over, or with Ripley giving voice to others' words, or with her responding to disembodied, re-embodied and otherwise dislocated voices, we are thereby invited to recall the ways in which prophets and oracles, gramophones and telephones, mediums and ventriloquists have variously effected ways in which the human voice might be encountered at a distance from its origin, to place cinema in this broader context, and to ask ourselves why such phenomena induce such a sense of the uncanny.[1]

The third mode of these films' philosophical attunement is manifest in their more general preoccupation with the conditions of their own possibility. I have already emphasised the degree to which the course of the series' development can be understood as the product of a dialogue between the different directors of each film in the series, which amounts to a serial dialogue between each director and the central protagonist of the films, which in turn amounts to a systematic reflective engagement with the relation between inheritance and originality that is the matrix of any serious artistic achievement in the making of sequels. In other words, the *Alien* series makes its own condition of possibility as a series one of its central preoccupations. But to make progress by reflecting on its own conditions of possibility is one way of characterising any truly rigorous philosophy, which can hardly refrain from demanding of itself just what it makes a business of demanding of every other discipline with which it presumes to engage. This is what I called 'film as philosophy'.

Hence, I hear the voice of philosophy in the *Alien* films in their exemplification of film as philosophising, philosophy of film and film as (in the condition of) philosophy. In what ways, however, might I claim that my articulation of these claims (and indeed all my other claims) about these films amounts to giving voice to a distinctively philosophical concern with cinema? I might, of course, simply argue that a philosophical ear is necessarily best attuned to the voice of philosophy in any and every place in our culture in which it is to be uncovered. And of course, when the specific films under consideration so persistently frame their human protagonists against the infinity of the cosmos, as if unmediated by the complex inter-weavings of culture and society, they positively insist upon being heard in metaphysical or elemental terms – as addressing the human condition as such.

But I want to go further, or at least further specify the mode of attentiveness that I take to be distinctive of a philosophical ear. For it is not just that philosophers are characteristically inclined to think systematically and insistently about issues concerning which no-one whose form of life is complex enough to be burdened with language can avoid thinking, if only briefly and infrequently. I would further claim that philosophy asks of us a certain kind of attentiveness to others – a willingness to remain awake to certain implications and unclarities and emptinesses of meaningful human speech and action with which other disciplines need have no concern (say, a certain kind of chafing or screaming at our human limits, a will to misrepresent those limits as limitations, to take the human condition as a constraint and to attempt to transcend it – perhaps by denying our fatedness to embodiment).

But if it is to overcome this will towards the unconditioned, the void, philosophy must first of all devote itself to articulating as accurately as possible the formations and deformations of our life with language that give it expression. Philosophy must, in short, allow its interlocutors to have their say; the philosopher must find the right words for, give fully responsive voice to, whatever her present conversation partner has it at heart to say or think. Philosophy's voice must thus give itself over to speaking (not for, or over, but) in the voice of its conversational other, thereby acknowledging her autonomy and individuality. Further, in encouraging its other to overcome her will to emptiness, it must draw upon no resources other than those available in principle to any and every competent language-using creature, hence restrict itself only to resources to which its other also has equal access (so that the philosophical voice is not one of expertise, as if authorised by some restricted species of knowledge).

These claims (unauthorised as they stand, but echoing remarks of Wittgenstein) together suggest that philosophy's voice must be sufficiently receptive to be capable of being possessed by any voice it might encounter in human dialogue, and assertive only in terms or tones which every human voice possesses. Its attunement thus appears as the very inverse of that with which the human beings of the Alien universe, and the aliens themselves, respond to Ripley's voice; it exemplifies an overcoming of this world's inveterate desire to suppress or suffocate that particular voice, and that particular register of the human voice. If this (this attunement, and this register) is not exactly Ripley's voice (since it must not simply reiterate childish fantasies), it is not exactly not that voice either (since it must remain attuned to the insider/outsider perspective of adolescence). At the very least, in being receptive not only to Ripley's but to the *Alien* films' desire for a voice in their own history, philosophy's voice acknowledges the otherness of those films, and hence the otherness of film and philosophy.

Note

1. This material is given an interesting articulation in Steven Connor's *Dumbstruck: A Cultural History of Ventriloquism* (2001).

Memento: A Philosophical Investigation

Phil Hutchinson and Rupert Read

This paper offers a reading of *Memento* as a therapeutic dialogue, one purpose of which is to loosen the grip of both dualism (the 'Cartesian'[1] picture of mind) and behaviourism. We do this by illuminating aspects of the film with a reading of the opening of Wittgenstein's *Philosophical Investigations* (hereafter, *PI*).[2]

The investigations

PI opens with the following (we quote at length and in full):

> 'When they (my elders) named some object and accordingly moved towards something, I saw this and grasped that the thing was called by the sound they uttered when they meant to point it out. Their intention was shewn by their bodily movements, as it were the natural language of all peoples: the expression of the face, the play of the eyes, the movement of other parts of the body, and the tone of voice which expresses our state of mind in seeking, having, rejecting or avoiding something. Thus, as I heard words repeatedly used in their proper places in various sentences, I gradually learnt to understand what objects they signified; and after I had trained my mouth to form these signs, I used them to express my own desires.' (Augustine, *Confessions*, I. 8.)
>
> These words, it seems to me, give us a particular picture of the essence of human language. It is this: the individual words in language name objects – sentences are combinations of such names. – In this picture of language we find the roots of the following idea: Every word has a meaning. The meaning is correlated with the word. It is the object for which the word stands.

Augustine does not speak of there being any difference between kinds of word. If you describe the learning of language in this way you are, I believe, thinking primarily of nouns like 'table', 'chair', 'bread', and of people's names, and only secondarily of the names of certain actions and properties; and of the remaining kinds of word as something that will take care of itself.

Now think of the following use of language: I send someone shopping. I give him a slip marked 'five red apples'. He takes the slip to the shopkeeper, who opens the drawer marked 'apples'; then he looks up the word 'red' in a table and finds a colour sample opposite it; then he says a series of cardinal numbers – I assume that he knows them by heart – up to the word 'five' and for each number he takes an apple of the same colour as the sample out of the drawer. – It is in this and similar ways that one operates with words. – 'But how does he know where and how he is to look up the word "red" and what he is to do with the word "five"?' – Well I assume that he *acts* as I have described. Explanations come to an end somewhere. – But what is the meaning of the word 'five'? – No such thing was in question here, only how the word 'five' is used. (*PI*: §1)

Now, the standard reading[3] of §1 of the *Investigations* reads it purely as an attack on the Augustinian picture of *language*. This is 'Augustine's pre-theoretical, pre-philosophical picture of the working of language which informs Augustine's own remarks on language as well as a multitude of sophisticated philosophical analyses of meaning' (*ACPI* I, p. 61). This picture of language, we are told, provides the paradigm within which Frege, Russell and Wittgenstein[4] were alleged to operate (see Baker and Hacker, 1980, pp. 45–59).[5] Baker and Hacker claim that what is of interest to Wittgenstein in *PI* §1 is not an 'inner' and 'outer' theory of mind, and other concerns that may be implicit in the passage from Augustine, but merely a number of related issues relating to word-meaning. They write:

[Wittgenstein] is concerned only with the points explicit in the quotation in (a).[6] (iv)Words signify or name objects. (v) Sentences are combinations of words. (vi) That a word signifies a given object consists in the intention with which the word is used. (vii) The intention with which a word is used (i.e. the intention to *mean* that object) can be seen in behaviour, bodily movement, facial expression, tone of voice, etc. (*ibid*: 61)

The trip to the grocer in paragraph (d) is taken, by Baker and Hacker, to illustrate different types of words (*ibid*: 63). They write, 'The example is designed to stress the fact that the contention that the three words are of different types rests on the differences in the operations carried out in each case, and on the ordering of the operations' (*ibid*).

We think this vastly underplays both the subtlety and the significance of *PI* §1:d. In what follows, we first outline a reading of (d) that we think captures the nuance – not to mention the philosophical import – of the example. We do this taking our inspiration from Stephen Mulhall's reading of the passage.[7] We then turn to a reading of *Memento* to show that this stands as a feature-length version of Wittgenstein's 'short', and in doing so *explores* the issues in play in a manner rich enough to provide one with further philosophical (therapeutic) insight of which Wittgenstein would have been proud.

There is something of a conundrum for all who pick up Wittgenstein's *PI*, and particularly for those who read the opening as Baker and Hacker do. Why did Wittgenstein choose a passage from Augustine's *Confessions* and not one from a recognised work in the philosophical canon? Indeed, after choosing to cite Augustine's *Confessions* he then chooses to cite in particular a passage from the autobiographical sections of the text rather than from Augustine's more overtly (and sometimes, indeed, explicitly) metaphysical writing. Furthermore, why did he choose to illustrate the limitations of the picture he identifies at play in the quote from Augustine with what is, on reflection, a decidedly eccentric depiction of a trip to the grocer? – the shopper appears to be dumb, the (rather mechanical) grocer keeps apples in drawers and counts them out individually after matching the colour with a colour chart.

Is it really a satisfying conclusion to write that the grocer example is an 'illustration of different types of words'? That it shows simply that

> 'Five', 'red', and 'apple' are words *each one of which belongs to a type the use* [our emphasis] of which is fundamentally different from the use of words of the other types. To say that 'apple' is the name of a fruit, 'red' the name of a colour, and 'five' the name of a number would mask deep differences beneath superficial similarities. Again, one might think 'apple' involves correlation with an object, 'red' with a colour, and 'five' with counting objects of a type, so all words involve correlation with *something*. The web of deception is readily woven. (*ACPI* I, p. 63)

Well, we do not find it so – or at least, the 'web' is not quite what Baker and Hacker say it is, and the difference is important. If there is a 'web of deception' here, it is a more subtle web. It is a web which Wittgenstein *wants* you to fall into and *wants* you then to struggle free from entanglement therein. A crucial part of the therapeutic work – that one does on *oneself* via the reading of the opening of *PI* – comes through the gradual realisation of just how *bizarre* the scenario(s) depicted by Wittgenstein is (are). It is one's temptation to (initially) see the shopkeeper scenario as a plausible enough scenario with philosophical morals following from it that is subject to a deconstruction that is illuminating – *a 'deconstruction' that one must perform for oneself.* What we consider the 'overture' to *PI*, the first 36 sections or so, is in effect Wittgenstein asking the reader over and over again, 'Will *this* satisfy you as being language? Perhaps not? Then will *this* be enough for you to regard what is happening here as language, with all the consequential results you think will accrue from such a designation? ...And are you not worried by your tendency to gloss over how peculiar the scenarios are that I have asked you to 'conceive' as language?'

By contrast, the Baker and Hacker reading is not satisfactory because:

a) It leaves so many questions and niggles hanging in the air, either unanswered or simply unasked, and
b) In saying that each word belongs to a different type of use, it implies there is a 'type of use' which can be definitively associated with each word in the language.

We think that responding efficaciously to both a) and b) is achievable, through a more subtle reading of the passage, expanding on the series of implicit questions that we just attributed to Wittgenstein as his intention in posing the ramifying set of 'examples' that the reader is confronted with, early in *PI*. We begin with b).

How does claiming that each word belongs to a type of use get us further than appealing to correlations with things, or words as names of things? All one has in fact done is exchange 'things' for a '*type* of use'. To come at this from one side, consider that both 'five' and 'red' can name things when embedded in certain sets of practices. When playing football I can readily name my mate Jim, the left back, 'Five', because that is his number in the team, the number written on his shirt; and, furthermore, it makes sense to do so because there are two players named Jim on our team. Similarly, Red Adair's friends were quite in order referring to him (calling him by name) as 'Red'. It was his name. The *suggestion* of an appeal to use that Wittgenstein makes in his later work is not to show that words have different types of use with which we can classify them accordingly; replacing our crude grammatical terms such as noun, verb, adjective, etc. But rather to show that words *might* play many different sorts of roles, and which one they do play depends ultimately on the usage in a context and on an occasion. Words do not '*belong* to types of use'.

The mistake here then is Baker and Hacker's thought that what is problematic for Wittgenstein – what he wants to critique in these opening remarks – is that words name things or correspond to objects, with the emphasis laid on the *nature* of what is on the other side of the word-Ω relationship. Rather, we contend that what is problematic in this picture is that words *must* be *relational* at all – whether as names to the named, words to objects, or 'words' belonging to a 'type of use.'[8] It is the necessarily *relational* character of 'the Augustinian picture' which is apt to lead one astray: Baker and Hacker, in missing this, ultimately replace it with a picture that retains the relational character, only recast.[9] There is no such thing as a word outside of some particular use; but that is a different claim from saying, with Baker and Hacker, that words belong to a type of use. For a word *to be* is for a word *to be used*. Language does not exist external to its use by us in the world. Language cannot, in John McDowell's phrase, be viewed from sideways on. This is a thought that animates Wittgenstein's thinking from the *Tractatus* onwards.[10]

The key to understanding *PI* §1, we think, is in reading the passage as a whole, but with particular attention to the remark, toward the end, of Wittgenstein's interlocutor, and to the way Wittgenstein then responds. Recall that in response to Wittgenstein's 'short story' the interlocutor says, and Wittgenstein responds, as follows:

> 'But how does he [the grocer] know where and how he is to look up the word "red" and what he is to do with the word "five"?' – Well I assume that he *acts* as I have described. Explanations come to an end somewhere. – But what is the meaning of the word 'five'? – No such thing was in question here, only how the word 'five' is used. (*PI* §1)

The question to ask, therefore, is why is Wittgenstein's interlocutor not satisfied with the scenario? What is it that she yearns for in asking her question? To take Baker and Hacker's line on this is to give no thought to the purpose of the interlocutor's remark but rather to interpret Wittgenstein's response to it as indicating that questions of the genesis of 'meaning' are not philosophical questions as they are contingent and thus of no philosophical import (cf. *ACPI* I: 64). But Wittgenstein is the author of the interlocutor's question (it is his question, he has this yearning or he at least sees it as a significant, appropriate, yearning); why author a question only to dismiss it as insignificant and inappropriate in the following sentence? A more satisfactory (to our eyes) interpretation of the purpose of the interlocutor's question is Stephen Mulhall's. Recent Mulhall argues that the question invokes the notion of 'meaning' coming from an inner mental process. The interlocutor is not satisfied with the explanation only being given with reference to outward criteria, or behaviour; the use of colour samples and the counting out of the apples one-by-one leaves her still wanting to know more about from where meaning might come. Mulhall writes, 'the cast of her [the interlocutor's] questions rather takes it for granted that nothing behavioural can settle the issue of understanding even in principle; only a transition to the entirely separate realm of the inner can give her the reassurance she craves' (Mulhall, 2001, 44).

It is our contention that the grocer example in *PI* §1 is analogous to (is a more profound precursor of) John Searle's famous Chinese Room example. However, rather than serving as an argument against strong AI, it serves more generally to bring to light the underlying prejudices that lead one to behaviourism and dualism and so forth. Searle's Chinese Room example is designed to prompt one to question whether the processing of symbols could ever be a sufficient condition for the attribution of 'understanding' to the processor. Wittgenstein sets up the grocer example in such a way that it leads one to crave something that will satisfy one to the extent that one would be happy to say of the grocer, 'He understands'.

Wittgenstein's example is designed to tempt us into positing inner mental processes of some sort. This, Wittgenstein's interlocutor does. However, this is only to begin to understand the reach of the example. For when we reflect upon what such a (inner) process might be we find that we want to describe something very similar to the ('external') behaviour that Wittgenstein's grocer does exhibit. Consider: A note is passed to him – *data is entered*. The words on the note are related to objects – *the input data is related to inner mental items (samples)*. More precisely: the word 'apple' is matched to the object 'apple' – *the apple-data is related to a mental image of an apple*; the word 'red' is matched to a colour sample – *the colour-data is related to a mental image of red*. Then, having ascertained what 'a red apple' 'means' – *having related the data with the correct mental image of what we call 'a red apple'* – we count five of them – *we mentally mark-off the lines in the five bar gate, or mentally slide the beads of the abacus across*.[11] The data is thus processed. The grocer retrieves five red apples and hands them to the note-bearer – *he 'understands' the request.*

Here is the point of the 'eccentricity' of the example. The example is structured to mirror the (alleged) form of inner mental processes. In tempting the interlocutor to ask for more so that she might be satisfied in predicating of the grocer understanding Wittgenstein tempts the interlocutor into undermining her own prejudices. Mulhall writes: '...if the public, externalised versions of such procedures were not in themselves enough to establish the presence of understanding to the interlocutor's satisfaction, why should their inner counter-parts?' (Mulhall, 2001, 45) Is it because they are inner? This is surely not enough.

However, the subtlety of Wittgenstein's example does not stop there. For, as Mulhall notes:

> If Wittgenstein's shopkeeper's way with words strikes us as surreal and oddly mechanical, to the point at which we want to question the nature and even the reality of his inner life, and yet his public behaviour amounts to an externalised replica of the way we imagine the inner life of all ordinary, comprehending language-users, then our picture of the inner *must be as surreal, as oddly mechanical, as Wittgenstein's depiction of the outer* [our emphasis]. (Mulhall, 2001, 46)

This brings us back to Baker and Hacker, because now we can gain a fuller understanding of what is misleading – and missing – in their account.[12] The purpose of *PI* §1 is not in the end that of *replacing* Augustine's picture with another – that of words 'belong[ing] to a type of use', but of facilitating one's realisation that Augustine's picture amounts to nothing one wishes to hold on to. It is the thought of words as *essentially relational* that is holding one captive here.[13] It leads one to yearn for inner mental processes when ultimately these can never be more satisfying than external processes. It leads one to con-tinue one's search for some*thing* to which one's words might *relate*.[14] Appealing to words belonging to 'type of use' does little to wean one off this because one can just as well appeal to the 'words' of (say) men-talese belonging to a 'type of use', while arguing (comforting ourselves) that (all) we are (doing is) taking the analysis to a more fundamental level. It is the relational view of words that leads to both dualism (in all its varieties) and behaviourism, or (most generally) to one or another variety of unnecessarily *theoretical* account of the mind.

Memento

Memento is the story of Leonard Shelby. On Leonard's own account he has an inability to form memories. This, he claims, is the result of neurological damage sustained during an attack on him and his wife, an attack in which his wife was raped and killed. In order that he can function and pursue his wife's killers he calls on a number of external resources (sometimes Byzantine in their strangeness or complexity) to 'replace' his memory. He has a file, similar to a police case-file, in which he accumulates evidence pertaining to 'John G' (his wife's 'murderer'); in addition he has a large wall-chart which he carries in the file, which is designed like a flow-chart or spider-gram employing notes and photographs. He has a Polaroid camera with which he takes photographs of people he meets, new belongings such as cars, and places such as the hotel in which he is staying; he then writes notes to himself on the back of these photographs. These notes might, initially, be just the person's name, but over time Leonard will add details such as 'Don't trust him' or 'She is your friend'. Leonard carries these annotated photographs about his person, constantly flicking through them as someone approaches who appears to know him. The final way in which Leonard compensates for his inability to make new memories is by having crucial information tattooed about his person. The tattoos are comprised of those that serve as reminders of his task – 'kill him' – and crucial pieces of evidence which will bring him closer to achieving his task – such as names or partial names of chief suspects: John G. This is Leonard's 'system'. He remarks repeatedly, 'You've gotta have a system.'

So far, we have presented this account straightforwardly. As anyone who has seen the film will know all too well, however, the film itself is not straightforward in its mode of presentation. The film opens with a scene in which one gradually comes to realise that, somewhat bizarrely, the film-spool is running backwards. After a couple of minutes, it suddenly reverses and runs forward for a few seconds. One's sense of relief at this, however, lasts a very short time. For one is thrown off one's guard again, as there is a cut to a completely different scene – this time in black and white – where the protagonist who one has just seen (who one comes to learn is called 'Leonard') begins to tell, from *media res,* of his confusion at the situation he is in. Soon the film switches to a colour scene, again unconnected, in which what one will come to see as the 'action' of the film begins. In the black and white scenes, which from then on are interspersed with the main action of the film, Leonard attempts to understand what is happening to him, and to explain to an unseen listener the nature of his condition, a condition that keeps him in a state of perpetual demi-confusion. Meanwhile, the 'main action' of the film proceeds in a sequence of scenes that run forward, normally – *but* one comes to realise that each scene is temporally prior to the action of the last, i.e. we are witnessing a story whose main action *goes back in time* as the film progresses.

One gradually comes to work all this out as one watches the film. The film is a puzzle that one has to work hard to try to unravel. Starting from a position of confusion, one tries to puzzle out one's 'condition', as the viewer of this film. Is the film's obscurity warranted? Or is it rather just a grand and clever trick, as some other recent 'cult' films such as *12 Monkeys* and *The Usual Suspects* arguably are?

The film sets out to induce in us an experience, an experience as of the very protagonist whose experience we are seeking to understand. One comes vicariously to inhabit Leonard's peculiar, confusing, tragic condition, by being placed in this position of oneself having to play the detective, as he perpetually does. One comes to understand, to know, for the first time, what it would be like to be like someone like him. There is no counterpart to this in most other 'trick' films. The reflexivity *Memento* requires of an attentive audience is something of intellectual substance.

So: we *inhabit* Leonard's position, vicariously. The film forces us to confront his deep difference from us. It enables us as viewers to progress in understanding what a mind might be that was unlike our mind, and what philosophical problems might be real to such a mind that are generally unreal to any of our minds.[15] *Memento* involves the attentive viewer in a prolonged, dialogical inquiry, in which the viewer must be active – and part of that activity consists sooner or later in trying to answer questions such as 'Just how similar to or different from Leonard are you? You want to identify with him; does he have what you are unreservedly prepared to call an ordinary human mind or personhood or a moral code when you see him doing *this*? Or apparently imagining *this*? And are you not increasingly worried by your tendency to gloss over some of the ways in which he is so strikingly different from you/us that perhaps you should have more reservations? (And reservations that extend to philosophical conclusions you may be inclined to draw concerning what must be in the head of someone, that is perhaps lacking inside his head?)'[16]

We suggested that Wittgenstein encourages us to *inhabit* the attractions of 'Augustinianism', far more than Baker and Hacker acknowledge. But will one have really gained anything, if one then simply lives in one of these apparent alternatives, as Baker and Hacker do, and dismisses all the rest? Philosophy for Wittgenstein is about liberation from the *compulsion* of any picture(s).[17] *Memento* involves a viewer who is actually watching it in philosophical work that involves a deeply similar struggle for liberation. The film's 'obscurity'[18] is warranted; and indeed, we suggest, intrinsic. It is the film's central brilliance.

Just what, then, are we to make of Leonard? Given the earlier discussion of Wittgenstein's grocer, we might make the following observations. One is tempted in watching the film to see Leonard's 'condition' as depriving him of the ability to form normal human relationships – he does not recognise the woman he slept with on waking the following morning; he only knows who are friends, who are trust-worthy, who are enemies etc. by having written as much on the back of a Polaroid of them. One is also made aware that his 'condition' makes him vulnerable to the manipulation of others – the Carrie-Ann Moss character (Natalie) provokes him into punching her, then leaves him alone in her house after removing all writing materials. She returns after a few minutes (when the thought has left him) and, bloodied and bruised, tells him that someone else had beaten her. Leonard is then sent off by her to get revenge on the person who she says (lying) 'beat' her, a person she wants run out of town or done in. Indeed the dénouement[19] of the whole film rests on Teddy (a corrupt police officer who has 'befriended' Leonard) confessing to using Leonard as a way of killing off drug-dealers and pocketing the cash – moving from town to town and feeding Leonard enough information so that he will identify the dealer as his wife's murderer. The two points are related: it is Leonard's inability to form 'normal' human relationships which allows for his vulnerability to the manipulation of others. In addition, we might say that in being so open to the manipulation of others Leonard could be said to be deprived of something further – his moral responsibility. Leonard, it would seem, cannot be held responsible for his actions because of his condition.[20]

Where does this lead? Well, one is – initially – tempted to the thought that it is his inability to form memories that precludes him from forming normal human relationships; this is also what makes him vulnerable to the manipulation of others and results in his lack of moral responsibility. But let us dwell on this thought. Were we to find a cure for Leonard, were we able to operate and repair those misfiring synapses, what then? Would we not, as did Wittgenstein's interlocutor, merely be implying that the internalising of those things that Leonard already does externally is enough to solve our problem? If the Polaroid photographs become *mental pictures* and the files and tattoos become *memories* what have we (and Leonard) gained? The very fact of interiority brings us nothing over what we (Leonard) already had.[21] And if you still incline toward thinking that interiority must be better, then try the following remark of Wittgenstein's:

> If I give someone the order, 'fetch me a red flower from that meadow', how is he to know what sort of flower to bring, as I have only given him a word?
>
> Now the answer one might suggest first is that he went to look for a red flower carrying a red image in his mind, and comparing it with the flowers to see which of them had the colour of the image. Now there is such a way of searching, and it is not at all essential that the image should be a mental one. In fact, the process may be this: I carry a chart co-ordinating names and coloured squares. When I hear the order 'fetch me [etc.]' I draw my finger across the chart from the word 'red' to a certain square, and I go and look for a flower which has the same colour as the square. But this is not the only way of searching and it isn't the usual way [!!]. We go, look about us, walk up to a flower and pick it, without comparing it to anything. *To see that the process of obeying the order can be of this kind, consider the order '**imagine** a red patch'. You are not tempted in this case to think that **before** obeying you must have imagined a red patch to serve you as a pattern for the red patch which you were ordered to imagine.* [Our emphasis][22]

Wittgenstein here establishes a possibility that frees us from the mental cramp of imagining that things *have to be* as Cognitivists *et al* imagine them to be. And let us now compare in more detail the second point Mulhall made regarding Wittgenstein's grocer. If Leonard's life with his 'aides memoirs' (and in Leonard's case they are just memories *period*) strikes us as surreal and mechanical, why does our interiorising such things make them less surreal and less mechanical? It does not – it only makes them *seem* less so, because of the psychological or cultural roots of philosophical delusion. A conception of mind as an inner realm populated by mental representations (whether pictorial or syntactically structured) which we access on the input of sensory data is precisely that which is being represented externally in *Memento*. The film then dissolves our appeal to an inner realm by showing – through Leonard's character – how such an appeal falls short of giving us what we want: *a person.*

What was it that we found in Leonard that made us think his 'condition' made him abnormal? We said he could not form normal relationships. We said he could be easily manipulated by those who chose to do so. We said this susceptibility to manipulation absolved him of the moral responsibility that we might accord a 'normal' person. But what is abnormal about the relationships Leonard forms? Well it is surely abnormal to wake up naked in someone's bed and then have to look through your selection of Polaroid photographs and match one with her, then turn it over to read her name and your comments on what you 'think' of her based on previous encounters. But *interiorise* that scene. Leonard wakes up naked in someone's bed, he sees a woman laying beside him, he looks through his selection of Polaroid photographs and matches one with her – *his senses send an image of her to his mind, the image is then matched with a mental representation of her*; Leonard turns the photograph over reads the name and comments he has written on the back which tell him what he 'thinks' of her based on previous encounters – *the mental image is associated with some memories of their previous meetings and this tells him what he 'thinks' of her.*

The first move in the viewer's diagnosis of Leonard then is not what one most likely thought it was. Leonard's inability to form 'normal' relationships is, we submit, not born of his condition preventing him from being able to form memories (new mental representations) but of others' awareness and exploitation of the fallibility of his system of forming memories. The awareness is informed by Leonard's own propensity to tell everyone he meets about his 'condition'[23] and outwardly manifest his 'condition'. However, we suspect that, more importantly, Leonard has submitted to a pathological pull toward being consumed by the desire to avenge the murder of his wife. Leonard's 'abnormality' – his seeming inability to form relationships and his heightened susceptibility to manipulation – do not result *in* his being devoid of moral responsibility but result *from* his abdication of moral responsibility. Leonard abdicates his moral responsibility, and his inability to form normal relationships and his susceptibility to manipulation by others results from that abdication.

This becomes more apparent at the 'end' of the film, when we see Leonard's understandable, yet repellently nihilistic decision to go after Teddy, the corrupt policeman who has been manipulating Leonard for his own ends. Leonard chooses to go after Teddy – to the point that he will finally kill him (at the 'start' of the film) – to give himself a reason to live. Leonard was our moral guide through the *noir* morass of 'humanity' around him in *Memento*. One inhabited (t)his world with him – only now, with this moral (and not merely cognitive) shock, does one realise what a revolting monster one has been party to.[24] This exercise in unreliable (and potentially therapeutic) narration and 'dialogue' parallels Wittgenstein's. *Memento* is merely more *clearly* moral in purpose than *PI*.

Memento: A philosophical investigation

To recap: *Memento* tempts one, as does Wittgenstein's grocer example, into the thought that the problems – of meaning, understanding or, in the case of Leonard, a fully human life where he *can* form friendships, be *able* to trust others and be responsible for his actions – can be solved by 'going inner'. That is to say, one is tempted to the thought that if one posits an inner realm then one will have provided sufficient conditions for the grocer understanding the note; and if one gives Leonard back his ability to form memories then one has sufficient conditions for Leonard to live a fully human life, forming friendships, trusting others and being responsible for his actions as a person. The way Wittgenstein's 'short' and Nolan's 'feature' are played out undercuts this move. All you do in making the move 'inner' is predicate of those same practices that they are inner; nothing is gained from the move, though much is lost. The move inner provides neither the necessary conditions for understanding nor the necessary conditions for living a fully human life.

Think again for a moment of the Chinese Room.[25] This is a technique of *'externalisation'*. It is Searle's rendition of this technique of Wittgenstein's. That technique is, we hope, now manifest in the opening of *PI* (and in *Memento*).[26] But the way it works contains more complexity – and (temporary) complicity – than Baker and Hacker assume. One needs to become aware of the subtle, even devious self-deconstruction[27] of many of Wittgenstein's 'thought-experiments', if one is not to miss his thought entirely. Take the 'builders', for instance, or take the 'wood sellers'.[28] Wittgenstein's 'webs of deception' precisely fool you into thinking that he is not giving you webs of deception. Baker and Hacker swallow the bait, but have failed to spot the hidden hook. (We return shortly to the question of just how fully *Memento* too self-deconstructs.)

Words do not *necessarily* play a relational role of any kind. One need not relate the word 'memory' with some inner process any more than one need relate the word 'red' to a mental representation of 'redness'. Our words having meaning does not require such a move. What does this mean for our thoughts on *Memento*? Well, it is not that Leonard cannot relate the woman next to him in bed to a mental representation of her, nor that he has no memories to relate to Teddy that will tell him whether he is trustworthy or not. It is not *this* inability to relate sensory experience to mental representations and memories that is the problem. It is rather, we wish to *posit*, that the narrative of Leonard's life has been radically disrupted, or even broken. The new narrative he is trying to construct leaves him vulnerable – recall when we as people normally set out on forming the narrative for our lives we are children and are cared for by guardians (parents, teachers, older siblings), indeed we are not generally considered responsible for our actions – the break and the resultant re-establishing of a narrative has for Leonard to be done without the benefit of childhood and the security that comes with it. Leonard is a child in an adult world (because not recognised as a child by others) but a child in *the most* adult of worlds because of his desire to avenge that which led him to his second childhood.[29]

As we have already hinted, Augustine is quoted, and a passage from childhood recalled in the autobiographical sections of his book, for good reason. We have noted that the shopping trip example is bizarre and somewhat eccentric. Why do we, as readers, accept it as a valid example at all? In other words, what makes Wittgenstein's example of the shopping trip appear, at least initially, plausible? Following Mulhall we take it that the example is in a sense mimicking children playing at shopping.[30] Think of an example of Cavell's. You visit the newsagent with a young child – let us say your 5 year old daughter. You take your newspaper and give sixty pence to the child saying 'Would you like to pay the man?' You hand sixty pence to the girl. She takes it in her hand, and then tentatively and somewhat shyly pushes her upturned fist forward, opening it to reveal the sixty pence in front of the shopkeeper. As the shopkeeper takes the money the child looks up at you and, somewhat proudly, smiles; the shopkeeper looks at the child, smiles and says in a self-consciously friendly manner 'Thank you very much'. Has the child entered the shop and *purchased* the newspaper? What condition do they have to fulfil to be said to have done so? Do they need to 'understand'?

We think they do need to understand. But an appeal to understanding here is not, as should now be clear, an appeal to an (a conception of 'understanding' as an) inner mental process. An appeal to understanding here is an appeal to the child's enculturation, their full participation in a form of life, their ability to *be*-meaningfully-in-the-world-with-others. What being able to understand means here, is, learning to *be*, being guided in one's attempts at *be*ing, and to *be*, with others, being trained to *be*, mimicking *be*ing. To understand, having understanding, is to be able to fully participate in the world with others. Of course there are a number of worldly as well as personal prerequisites for such a state. Leonard's moral pathology has returned him to a stage where he needs to re-establish those personal prerequisites. He needs to regain his understanding. Only it is much more difficult because his lack of understanding is not induced by his status as a child – he is not recognisably a child – though it is the guidance, training, learning that is accorded to children that Leonard requires. He actually gets the opposite from those adults that surround him in the film.

The narrative of Leonard's life has been subject to a radical break, and he is 'forced' into a second childhood, into the kind of position analogous to that gently and harshly characterised by Wittgenstein when he returns briefly to discussing Augustine in *PI* §32. But what, on our account, is the nature of the break? Has Leonard's wife been murdered? Or is he a moral nihilist, because of the shock caused to his system (sic) by his wife leaving him after the attack? Or is it all a result of guilt for the death of Sammy Jenkiss's wife, for which he was arguably directly responsible (in that he told her that Sammy was a faker of memory loss, when in fact he wasn't, and she killed herself at Sammy's hands as a result)? Is it even of any importance to decide?

It is interesting to note that the vertiginous expansion of possibilities as to what is really going on in *Memento* comes at the very moment, almost at the end of the film (i.e. at the start of the action), when one finally felt close to closure. One has come to understand the nature of Leonard's 'condition', one thinks. One has at last mastered what he has mastered intellectually, if not experientially. One's complacency is undermined by Teddy's 'dénouement' speech; and one begins trying to figure out all over again 'what the story' is.

So: which story *is* correct? We don't know. The film is puzzling, though less 'systemically' so than (say) *Marienbad*. But the counter-picture – to Leonard's own – that we think makes the best sense of the film draws on Teddy's speech, on what Leonard sees in his mind's eye during their dialogue, and expands on what we have already written concerning how Leonard's difference from us 'normals' may be less neuro-cognitive and more moral-psychopathological.

It doesn't matter if you find our story of the story less than fully convincing. Indeed, it is arguably even *better* that way! For it is enough that there is a real *possibility* that Leonard is not neurologically abnormal after all. Against those who want to 'go inner' to prove that Leonard is abnormal, it is enough to show that this 'move' actually takes us nowhere. The heart of the film's self-deconstruction is this, alluded to though not fully explicated by Teddy in his coruscating speech challenging Leonard: how has Leonard mastered his condition? *How can he know, as a matter of intellectual and historical fact, about his own condition, given that he actually does have such a condition?*[31]

Teddy suggests to Leonard that his wife survived the attack. That Sammy Jenkiss was a faker, not someone with an incurable neurological condition. That he, Leonard, was the one who had ended up in an asylum for a while. That Leonard killed John G. years ago, after Teddy helped him find him. And that Teddy has been using Leonard to kill people for his, Teddy's, corrupt ends, ever since. Teddy more or less insinuates then an identification or confusion on Leonard's part between himself and Sammy, and more or less insinuates that Leonard's condition may not be at all what he (Leonard) endlessly tells people it is.

Leonard is unsure what to think, now. Even his memories of his wife, seemingly so secure, start to disintegrate under the strain. (He learns the hard way that memory-scepticism cannot be confined.) The possibility that we think requires serious consideration at this point is that Leonard doesn't actually suffer from an incurable neurological problem at all. Rather, as his memory gradually returned or threatened to return after the trauma of the attack, he fought it off: because of the unbearable psychological pain that was caused him not so much by what had happened in the attack but by his wife being unwilling to bear him after the attack, and leaving him. He reconstructed his past such that his wife had indeed been not only raped but killed, and that he, the perfect caretaker and lover, was on an eternal quest to avenge her, a quest that in fantasy would then end with him sitting smiling in bed with her, with a tattoo saying 'I did it' (i.e. killed John G.) emblazoned on his chest.

His constant mental work – *his* distinctive innerness, his interminable deeply anxious doubts and his bombastic or dogmatic counter-assertions to those doubts – then stands in the way of facing the facts. He thinks; therefore he is not aware of something that he finds unbearably painful, something that must always be slightly outside of the frame of this film that we journey through with and through him. The deceptive aspect of the dénouement to the story we are now presenting, that comes at the end as we watch the film, but (as in *PI*) at the beginning of the 'narrative', is perhaps the story behind Teddy's story, a story that (re-)structures everything that 'follows' it. One is forced to rethink (through) the story/stories that Leonard has constructed (perhaps, temporally, in response to this story of Teddy's). (Compare *PI*: as the text proceeds, one is forced – at any rate, if one is attentive to the way the text is, so carefully, constructed, then one is forced – to reassess the thought-experiments and apparent-statements by Wittgenstein that one had hoped to rely on. This happens in the *Tractatus* in one gigantic explicit manoeuvre. In *PI*, it happens through continual piecemeal reflection: on the 'grocer's shop', on the 'builders', *and so on*.) Leonard's stories, built in reaction to what (at least according to Teddy) really happened to him, start to fall apart on him, and on one, all over again. The final beauty (and tragedy) of *Memento* is watching this happen – and then watching how Leonard stops the falling apart, and restarts himself on a freshly destructive and denying path.

Wittgenstein's pseudo-stories, and Wittgenstein's pseudo-theses, are not *meant* to hold up. Those who think that they do, those who like for example to extract 'grammatical truths' from Wittgenstein's work, have negated the spirit of his philosophy. 'Wittgenstein' is an unreliable narrator. You learn from him by bringing to consciousness what you are inclined to think about 'philosophical matters', by considering alternatives to those inclinations, by seeing those alternatives in turn collapse when you try to make them bear weight, and by as a result being compelled neither by the picture you started with *nor* by seemingly better, smaller etc. alternative pictures.

The dénouement to *Memento* gives one the surprising outlines, outlines we have now filled in a little, of an alternative possible plot-picture to that which one had been assured of by one's narrator. *His* philosophy, which is dogmatically 'anti-Cartesian',[32] much like Ryle and most 'Oxford' Wittgensteinians since, is thus thrown further into doubt. One is no longer *compelled* by (any of) Leonard's narration. With Teddy's midwifery,[33] one works through one's waning and waxing uneasiness with 'what one comes to understand' of Leonard's world, and *overcomes* it. Overcomes, that is, Leonard's self-understanding, his own philosophy, *and* the philosophies that would like to attack him (Cartesianism, Cognitivism) or that would incline to see him as in effect a fellow traveller (e.g. 'Logical behaviourism').

Whether the trauma that 'broke' him was his wife leaving him or his 'killing' Sammy's wife, the upshot is the same: our tentative diagnosis of Leonard is that he is a 'victim' of a *hysterical amnesia* resulting from the need to suppress the memory of a trauma and resulting in a continually-maintained bad faith. Thus a closing reason why *Memento* is film as philosophy is because it 'ends' by presenting one with an intellectual possibility not familiar from the Diagnostic and Statistical Manual nor from the likes of Karl Jaspers: namely, a form of bad faith undreamt of in Psychiatry's, Phenomenology's and Existentialism's philosophy. It presents a new possibility in (the philosophy of) psychopathology. Leonard has caught *himself* in a huge, awful and useful web of deception. His 'condition' leaves him terribly vulnerable to others' manipulations, and he experiences almost nothing but such manipulations in the course of the action of *Memento*. But in effect he takes this to be worth it. His tragic position is less bad than the alternative: facing up to what has happened to him, to what he has done, and to what he has made himself into.

Rather than maintain himself in such a constant state of anxious and delusional denial, Leonard could take a different route. The therapy offered by the film itself to its viewer, which is somewhat like the therapy offered by the entirety of Wittgenstein's text to his reader, is, we think, encapsulated in the beautiful motion of the camera as Leonard's car swings into and out of the yard of the abandoned building where the film starts and ends, and by its curve as he drives away 'into the future'. Living in the present, which requires acknowledging but not being possessed by the past (as those who obsessively remember it or obsessively 'forget' it are), would involve appreciating that beauty, which is visible to us as viewers, but which Leonard cannot see, locked as he is into an obsessive inwardness of thought and a bizarre externalisation of memory. As the car curves away down the road, we are given a point-of-view shot, for perhaps the first time in the film. We see the scene as Leonard sees it. It is beautiful; but he can see none of that. He has *trapped himself* in the present, which is the very contrary of *living* in the present.

Memento, more than the fabulous short story 'Memento Mori' from which it was adapted, and far more than Philip Kerr's interesting 'Wittgensteinian' detective-novel, *A philosophical investigation*, offers, we think, a philosophical investigation in the spirit of *Philosophical Investigations*. We have investigated *Memento* philosophically, and found that it not only shows but also *is* a philosophical investigation; one that depicts the soul of someone whose problem, perhaps, is actually that they cannot bear to remember, not that they cannot remember to forget.

Notes

1. We make no claim as to what type of dualism Descartes held. Much recent scholarship (see for instance the work of Gordon Baker and Katharine Morris) has done much to disabuse us of the ritualistic dismissal of Descartes as a crude substance dualist. When we use the term Cartesianism here we do so to indicate a pervasive conception of the mind, taken as distinct from the person, and animating that person (body). This therefore includes not only traditional self-proclaimed dualisms but also many 'materialist' conceptions of mind which deny their dualistic nature; we have in mind here for instance Jerry Fodor's psycho-semantics and Ruth Millikan's bio-semantics, as well as any theories which draw an analogy between the mind and computer software.

2. The sections of this paper that deal expressly with *PI* §1 and Baker & Hacker's reading of that section are expanded-upon versions of some sections of 'What is The Purpose of Elucidation?' by Phil Hutchinson.

3. We call this the 'standard reading' as this is the standard interpretation in Wittgenstein scholarship at present. We have in mind, primarily, that offered in *ACPI* i-iv. Similar readings of *PI* are offered by Hans-Johann Glock (1989, 2001b), P.M.S. Hacker (1996, 2001a, 2001b), Paul Johnston (1989), Anthony Kenny (1984, 1989), and Severin Schroeder (2001). Dan Hutto (2003) and Marie McGinn (1997) could fruitfully be seen to be on the fringes of the standard (elucidatory) camp. However, they both show considerably more sensitivity to the therapeutic nature of the work, though they both, crucially, hold onto the thought that there must be something more. As we've seen this is a move that has really quite drastic implications. It is important to note that Gordon Baker was co-author of the first two volumes of ACPI only. After this time he went through a radical change of mind. His later work, published between 1991 and his death in 2002, advances what he terms a 'radically therapeutic' reading of Wittgenstein's *PI* and, on his own account, has strong affinities with the readings advanced by Cavell, Conant, Diamond and Dreben. See Baker (2004) *Wittgenstein's Method: Neglected Aspects*. It may strike the reader as strange to therefore refer to 'Baker & Hacker' critically throughout. However, we follow Gordon Baker who in his later work referred to his own early work with Hacker in this way and used it as a stalking horse for his own new reading.

4. Gottlöb Frege, *Foundations of Arithmetic*; Bertrand Russell & Alfred North Whitehead, *Principles of Mathematics*; and Ludwig Wittgenstein, *Tractatus Logico-Philosophicus*.

5. It is of considerably more than mere passing note (given recent exegetical disputes) to observe that while Baker and Hacker argue the case for, and take themselves explicitly to have established the case for, Frege and Russell operating within this Augustinian paradigm, they – equally explicitly – stop short of making the same claims regarding Wittgenstein's *TL-P*. They write, 'it would be *absurd* even to try to give here a definitive proof that the *Tractatus* conforms to an Augustinian picture of language. Instead, we shall simply show that this is a plausible view of the book. [...] The exclusion of all matters of 'psychology' differentiates Wittgenstein's logical atomism from Russell's. It also makes it *pointless* to search in the *Tractatus* for many of the theses characteristic of the Augustinian picture' (*ACPI* I, pp. 58–59). Nevertheless, they *do* conclude by asserting that Wittgenstein was working within the Augustinian paradigm, following Frege and Russell.

6. Paragraph (a) of *PI* §1.
7. Mulhall's (2001) reading of *PI* 1 is what first brought to our attention the possibility of the topic of this paper. The critique of Baker and Hacker is ours as is the identification of the relational nature of language being, at root, what Wittgenstein identifies as holding us captive.
8. It is important to note the 'must' here. Of course words often refer to things in a trivial non-controversial sense; it is just that this is not a condition of their having meaning. Also, we take it as unproblematic that 'belonging' is a form of relationship. Belonging denotes a relationship holding between the possessor and possessed. Certain words are possessed by certain types of use. (For more on such relationality, and for our analysis of a mistaken version of it, mistaken in a way that closely parallels Baker and Hacker's mistakes, see our review of two books by Joseph Margolis, forthcoming in *Philosophical Quarterly*).
9. Thus our central criticism of Baker and Hacker could helpfully be phrased thus: they *reify* 'the Augustinian picture' as an ogre to be combated and avoided at all costs. Unfortunately in mis-diagnosing what is at fault in that picture, they themselves *recommend* what is *merely* a *variant* of it.
10. Note Wittgenstein's remark in the Preface to the *Tractatus*: 'This book will, therefore, draw a limit to thinking, or rather – not to thinking, but to the expression of thoughts; for, in order to draw a limit to thinking we should have to be able to think both sides of this limit (we should therefore have to be able to think what cannot be thought). The limit can, therefore, only be drawn in language and what lies on the other side of the limit will be simply nonsense.' Read and Crary's *The New Wittgenstein* (Hacker's rejoinder excepted, of course) could fruitfully be viewed as an elaboration of the 'thought' of McDowell's just cited alongside this prefatory remark that serves as a very fruitful guide to interpreting Wittgenstein's work as a whole.
11. Of course we do not wish to restrict ourselves to pictorial mental representations here. The syntactically structured 'mentalese' of Fodor's psycho-semantics and Millikan's bio-semantics will do just as well.
12. Here our account departs from Mulhall; as far as we are aware he does not make this observation and, by extension, critique of Baker & Hacker. The point regarding the relational view of language is our own.
13. It is this thought that informs many (would-be) Wittgensteinians' appeals to a somewhat reified conception of grammar and grammatical rules as a way of settling philosophical disagreement and dissolving philosophical problems. It is this easy brand of 'Wittgensteinianism' (*Rylensteinianism*) that has done much to marginalise Wittgenstein's work in contemporary philosophy.
14. When we talk of 'relating' and 'relational', we are talking of external relations, i.e., of (genuine) relations. Of course if we were to say 'all words relate either internally or externally' then there is no problem, at least in the sense that we state nothing. There's a sense in which to identify a relationship as internal (such as between a 'mental illness' and its central symptoms) is to say that there is no *relationship* at all, that they are (part of) the same thing. (For further explication, see Denis McManus's forthcoming book on the *Tractatus*, *The Enchantment of Words*).
15. For example, *Memento* does not play the relatively cheap philosophical trick of *The Matrix*, which simply tries to enforce Cartesian doubt (updated

roughly through Putnam's 'brain-in-a-vat' thought-experiment) on its audience. *The Matrix* first attempts to insist that you are just like Neo, the film's 'meditator', and then after a while, in an imperial gesture that attempts to negate its initial paranoid hypothesis, reveals the true reality behind appearances. *Memento* has no such imperial project. While one tries to identify with a film's narrator, *Memento* starts from the presumption that we are learning about someone's state of being who is very different from normal. (This presumption later gets questioned, such that the film gradually becomes a kind of dialogic experiment in the viewer's trying to figure out *where they stand* in relation to *Memento's* narrator. See also the next note.)

16. As we shall see, this set of questions too eventually gets trumped, as one starts to wonder whether Lennie isn't a lot more like you and I, cognitively or epistemically speaking, than he lets on or (alternatively) than he realises.

17. See Baker (2004) Chs. 1, 3, 8, 9. Also Hutchinson and Read (forthcoming) in Moyal-Sharrock (ed.).

18. It is worth recalling that Wittgenstein is frequently criticised, even by some of his 'admirers' such as 'Oxford' Wittgensteinians, as an obscure writer. Our thought concerning this is that there is an internal relation between the style and the 'substance' of Wittgenstein's philosophy. That true, deep philosophising is bound to appear 'obscure' to one unwilling to follow the train of thought (across superficially diverse 'subject-matters') that Wittgenstein takes, a train that passages close by and indeed through nonsense, endlessly. But that, as with *Last Year in Marienbad* (see Introduction I to this volume) and perhaps also films such as *The Man Who Wasn't There*, or *Memento*, if one is willing to follow that train of 'thought' open-mindedly, if one is willing to enter into therapy with the text, then this/these text(s) will seem the least forced and the least obscure of all.

19. Though in this case the end is just the beginning, as it were.

20. He is like a child. Here, we think that Cavell's (and Mulhall's) remarks on the crucialness of seeing that the person who 'shops' in *PI* 1, like many of the people in *PI*, is implicitly (like) a child are very salient. We expand on this point below.

21. Furthermore, isn't it true that, as Leonard says, memory is unreliable? Leonard can helpfully be *seen as* Empiricism, practiced, writ large. Everything is externalised, everything verified. 'Just the facts, sir' could be his motto. It seems absurd to suppose that this would be *better*, that it is *better* not to be '*encumbered*' by memory, as Leonard at times claims. Yes, it is absurd. But, as we saw Mulhall in effect remarking, above, *it is no more absurd than Cognitivism.*

22. Wittgenstein, 1958, p. 3.

23. We place 'condition' in scare quotes now as it is not really a condition but merely an external representation of the internalist picture of mind. As will become apparent, neither do we think it is a condition in the way in which Leonard says it is in the film. There are many clues in the film to point in the direction of another conclusion. [We discuss this in more detail later.] It is worth adding that there is one other thing Leonard tends to tell everyone

about: Sammy Jenkiss. We deal with the significance of this toward our conclusion.

24. As we elaborate later, Leonard, on our interpretation of *Memento*, is in the end normal, except for his pathological moral difference from us. As one is sequentially sympathetic to and then appalled by all the other characters in *Memento*, so one's identification with Leonard finally comes to an end somewhere; specifically, as one sees him deliberately turn himself into a killer. In other words, during the film one identifies morally but (unlike in for instance *The Matrix*) *not* cognitively-epistemologically with the film's main protagonist. But our suggestion that ultimately Leonard is to be distinguished from you or I *morally* but *not* cognitively or epistemologically brings with it something potentially uncomfortable: our long journey with him forces us to confront our own possible 'shadow' immorality or psychopathy.

25. The original version of which can be found in Searle (1980).

26. Another splendid instance/discussion of it can be found at Wittgenstein & Waismann, p. 26.

27. We do not wish to imply any particular identification with Derrida (or his followers) in our employment of this term. We employ it in accordance with ordinary usage.

28. Hutchinson (forthcoming) has shown how the builders example self-deconstructs (contra Rush Rhees's interpretation) by the end of *PI* §6. See Cerbone 'How to Do Things With Wood' in Cary & Read (eds) on the same regarding the wood sellers in *Remarks on the Foundations of Mathematics,* and Crary's paper *ibid.* Also see Cerbone's 1994.

29. In this regard, Lennie parallels the replicants of *Blade Runner*. See Mulhall (2002)'s exemplary reading for details.

30. This is also a prominent theme in Stanley Cavell's readings of Wittgenstein, something he returns to again and again.

31. It is worth bearing in mind that real individuals who have suffered complete long-term memory loss from after a certain point in their life and inability to 'make new memories' do *not* come to know about their condition. They are always at best confused, and tend to deal with this confusion *either* through a continual desperate effort to understand their condition that makes no progress *or* through a lack of interest in anything except the present and the distant past (including a lack of interest in their condition). See, e.g., 'Jimmy', the 'Lost Mariner' in Sacks, 1985.

32. Near the end of the movie, Leonard remarks, in a moment of self-doubt when he will not self-doubt, in a moment when the unpalatable reality of his existence threatens to break through all his resistances to it, that 'The world doesn't disappear when you close your eyes'. He then opens his eyes, confirms that the world is still there, and triumphantly drives on – toward murder.

33. Teddy's role here, somewhat like that of Hannibal Lecter in another fine philosophical film, *The Silence of the Lambs*, is that of an unreliable but nevertheless in important part true educator; a kind of morally-repellent Socrates.

The Everydayness of Don Giovanni

Simon Glendinning

'If ever any kind of history has suggested the interpretations which should be put on it, it is the history of philosophy'.[1] In a period of philosophical history which has managed to find itself largely indifferent to philosophy's historical character, Merleau-Ponty's sharp observation is a timely reminder that the resources for reading philosophical texts are not wholly independent of the texts of philosophy that have been read. Concerned in his own case that we may unwittingly fall back on traditional interpretive keys for reading a philosophical score that may be performing something new, Merleau-Ponty urges us not to conclude too quickly that we know what is emerging in the movement that is bringing phenomenology to being. It seems to me that a good deal of the controversy over the interpretation of Wittgenstein's later philosophy in general and the distinctive writing of the *Philosophical Investigations* in particular has been bound up with a similar problem. It is the problem of coming to terms with the novelty of its teaching, *a difficulty of reading* posed by the fact that the history of philosophy, its terms of criticism and self-understanding, may stand in the way of 'letting this book teach us anything'.[2]

If this point is granted, it quickly becomes clear that making a start in learning (to read philosophy) from reading Wittgenstein's writing demands special attention to the language he draws on to articulate his view of what opens philosophy, his view of distinctively *philosophical* difficulties. And, equally, one needs to attend to what one might call the strategies of responsiveness to those difficulties that one finds in his writing – or rather, as Cavell's attention to 'the way this work is written' helps us see, that *is* his writing.[3] On this view, understanding Wittgenstein's work is in a certain way a matter of becoming a new reader of philosophy.

The essay that follows is not a devoted reading of Wittgenstein's style of writing but a development of what, to kick off with, one might call its *aesthetic* orientation. With such a classically philosophical heading one is obviously walking headlong into what J.L. Austin calls the 'bogs and tracks' of traditional philosophy,[4] and so one risks just the kind of pre-determination of one's reading that I am seeking to resist. But I do not regard this launching indication as a last word in orienting a reading of Wittgenstein. Indeed, I am appealing to this word first in the knowledge that what today might be understood as a philosophical difficulty in aesthetics will not typically be different to the understanding of any other kind of philosophical difficulty. As I will try to explain, I want to start off with the classical heading of aesthetics because, in my view, what distinguishes Wittgenstein's thought from more traditional forms of philosophy is that while the latter presents itself as resolving or solving a problem of the intellect or the mind, Wittgenstein regards that understanding as itself a form of disorientation. And reorientation will require an understanding of the kind sought not in scientific or theoretical studies of phenomena but from the kind of understanding one looks for in the appreciation of a work of art.

What, then, should we say about philosophical difficulties as Wittgenstein conceives them? Among other words, Wittgenstein would often speak of them as 'puzzles'. Karl Popper hated that idea.[5] And one can certainly sympathise. Wittgenstein's way of coming to terms with, or at least on occasion finding an English expression for, his understanding of the nature of philosophical difficulties seems somehow to trivialise them, reducing them to difficulties of language, puzzle-games to be resolved, it seems, simply by looking at the 'ordinary use' of words.

That conception grates particularly with a traditional understanding of philosophical difficulties as the mark of a mind in a state of pre-theoretical ignorance. Unclarity here is, as it were, everyday life in the cave. Readers wedded to that idea are likely to find it hard to stomach Wittgenstein's finding satisfaction with the everyday. Indeed, from this point of view Wittgenstein seems to regard our pre-theoretical state as a kind of blissful peace, interrupted only by the confusions brought on by philosophising. And this seems true: Wittgenstein regards philosophical unclarity as a species of lived disorientation, so that one's condition is one of entanglement, bewilderment – empuzzlement – and without doubt he will want to contrast that condition with the way in which we normally take things in our stride.

There is, it seems, a massive gulf between the theoretical ambitions of traditional philosophy and the Wittgensteinian idea of leading our words back to their everyday use. Back to the rough ground, says Wittgenstein. That's back to the cave, says his opponent. When philosophical difficulties are just linguistic puzzles, philosophy becomes little more than a pastime for over-educated adults, not, as Cavell would have us have it, our second education, an 'education for grown-ups'.[6]

Perhaps some boys and girls who grew up with an only slightly modified fascination with puzzles and riddles might find the image of philosophical difficulties as puzzle-games congenial. However, while Wittgenstein might be more sympathetic than many to the idea that our adult ways are transformations of the ways of children, his appeal to the idea of a puzzle does not seem to me to be the belittling of a genuinely adult concern. I would rather follow Cora Diamond's recent suggestion that far from seeing philosophical difficulties as puzzle-games, as difficulties of language, Wittgenstein teaches us to regard them as opened up by experiences in which we are struck dumb by what she calls 'the difficulty of reality'.[7] This is a form of aliveness to the world which contrasts with occasions where one takes things in one's linguistic stride; indeed, to take Wittgenstein's example, it contrasts with the point of view of someone who, absorbed in the everyday, sees no special difficulty at all.[8]

Diamond invites us to conceive this troubled or astonished or awe-struck or otherwise defamiliarised condition as one marked by 'the mind's not being able to encompass something which it encounters', that there is a confrontation with something which it is 'impossible to get one's mind round'. She puts it like this, but then, in a footnote on a related turn of phrase, she pretty much takes it back. The word 'mind', since it 'may be taken to suggest a contrast with bodily life' is not, she suggests, really satisfactory. *As her responsiveness here hesitates Diamond's writing becomes an example of the condition she wishes to present to us.*

Holding off for the moment the inadequacy or perceived inadequacy of the word 'mind' here, what she expressly presents to us is a view of philosophical difficulties as akin to or perhaps even an instance of what is classically conceived as an experience of the sublime. Like the ancient idea that philosophy begins with wonder, that is, perhaps, a beginning. But as I have indicated, it is important to me that her own formulations on this point are not experienced as the end of the matter, that it is actually the experienced inadequacy of the response that is more relevant, more originary to the opening of philosophy, than is her actual presentation of the condition. Trying again, we might say that philosophy begins every time we find our words as failing to come to terms with the difficulty of reality. I find that the words at my disposal seem not up to expressing what I now find remarkable. With an eye to the Cavellian problematic of coming to terms with the novelty of Wittgenstein's writing we might want to call that a difficulty of reading too.

So let's not say an experience of the sublime. Indeed, 'subliming' our words is a form of responsiveness, perhaps *the* form of responsiveness to this experience, that Wittgenstein most closely connects with the 'misunderstandings' against which he struggles.[9] Not the sublime then, but a felt difficulty of coming to terms with or 'reading' what confronts us. Wittgenstein, deploying the most explicit of figures of disorientation, works to capture this with the suggestion that in my life with words I have become lost: 'I don't know my way about'.[10] When the way things are spoken of 'in the language-game' are found wanting we find ourselves without a path or passage (*poros*) available, and are left without knowing a way to go (*aporos*).

Wittgenstein's writing is, I think, best understood as an attempt to achieve a satisfying responsiveness to this kind of *aporia of inhabitation*. But it is also writing that is alive to how, in an effort to come to terms with that condition, we turn again and again to a disabling response of the mind. Diamond calls it the moment in which thinking suffers a kind of 'deflection', it is the moment where aporetic empuzzlement is transformed into something like a puzzle-game, an intellectual problem which demands demanding work by a clever adult mind – we seek 'results' and 'conclusions' which would solve the problems and so bring thinking on these matters to its end.[11]

How might one avoid having one's thinking suffer such 'deflection'? What kind of guidance does Wittgenstein offer here? Or again, when what is in question is an aporia of inhabitation what kind of guidance does he suggest we need? Wittgenstein famously compares his work in philosophy with the curative work of a psychoanalytic therapist. And with that in view it is interesting to note that it is not only the idea of a puzzle which many philosophers do not like about Wittgenstein's orientation in philosophy but that it is equally true, as Cavell notes, that 'many philosophers do not like Wittgenstein's comparing what he calls his "methods" to therapies'.[12]

Well, perhaps there is a lot that many philosophers do not like about Wittgenstein, but it seems to me important that the two points just mentioned go together with a third which, if anything, is even more likely to offend contemporary sensibilities. What I have in mind is not often recognised as a defining aspect of Wittgenstein's orientation in philosophy, but Cavell has marked it very clearly – and I will try to confirm it in what follows. In his presentation of Wittgenstein's 'methods' as comparable to 'the progress of psychoanalytic therapy', Cavell notes that the 'end' of such therapy is a situation in which 'you have reached conviction' but not because you have reached conviction about a proposition or a theory.[13] In an effort further to elucidate this suggestion, Cavell shifts from the purely psychoanalytic register (which could and often does, after all, understand itself as a *scientific* undertaking) to an explicitly *aesthetic* one. Out of the blue, more or less, and in a supplementary addition calling for a sentence leading off with a capitalised conjunction, Cavell adds: 'And this is the sense, the only sense, in which what a work of art means cannot be said. Believing it is seeing it'.[14]

The suggestion is that if Wittgenstein's work of reorientation achieves a 'result' or reaches a 'conclusion' this will not be because his readers will have acquired an understanding of the sort supplied by a scientific theory but because he or she will have achieved a point of view of the sort one arrives at when one comes to an understanding of a work of art. Wittgenstein himself captures the sense of understanding at issue here in the following remark:

> We speak of understanding a sentence in the sense in which it can be replaced by another which says the same; but also in the sense in which it cannot be replaced by any other. (Any more than one musical theme can be replaced by any other.)
>
> In the one case the thought in the sentence is something common to different sentences; in the other, something that is expressed only by these words in these positions. (Understanding a poem.)[15]

In the case where what we are trying to understand – the reality that poses a difficulty – is a poem, a creative work of words, we might want to speak of coming to understand the expression of thoughts, but the parenthetical comment at the end of the first paragraph invites us to project the use of understanding at issue here more widely, to the non-linguistic case of works of music for example. It is this suggestive comparison that I want to develop and exploit in this essay. In doing so I want to stay close to 'the difficulty of reading' introduced above, to allow that to be heard as a general expression for difficulties where what one aims at is an understanding where 'the first judgement is *not* the end of the matter'[16] and where the result of guidance is not a last judgement – but a readiness to return to the matter anew, to read and re-read (to see it over and over, to listen and listen again). Perhaps even to return to the matter without seeking further guidance.

Wittgenstein mentions musical themes as the sort of thing one can find irreplaceably fitting. But might one also want to speak similarly of specifically musical ideas or musical thoughts? In order to see how one might want to speak in this way – to find this way of speaking irreplaceably fitting – I want to consider some remarks on Mozart's opera *Don Giovanni* by Søren Kierkegaard.[17] With reference to Joseph Losey's film of the opera[18] I will eventually want to transpose Kierkegaard's invitation to listen to the opera back into what is an equally appropriate visual key: since 'believing it is seeing it', the imperative will be that we watch, watch, and watch again, Losey's *Don Giovanni*. To begin with, however, I want to introduce a first stab at the idea of musical thoughts – and of a filmed presentation of an opera – by considering Plato's view of art in terms of *mimesis*, and particularly the idea of *mimesis* in music.

Plato saw artistic creations as fundamentally a species of resembling representation, and he famously regarded such representations as lying 'a considerable distance apart' from the truth.[19] Now what does Plato say about musical arts? From Plato's point of view what matters in general is whether an artistic work represents its subject correctly or incorrectly: the issue is one of the adequation of the work to the represented reality, its resemblance to something real. How can this apply to music? When Plato has Socrates discussing song in Book Three of the *Republic* he begins by drawing a distinction between the words and the music. As far as the words are concerned, the principles of proper enculturation which applied to the selection of spiritually healthy poetry can be used again. But with respect to the music, on which Socrates admits to knowing very little, the principles are inapplicable, or at least cannot be applied directly: it is simply a matter of finding that style of music, *whatever it is*, which will best suit the appropriately selected words.

In fact, however, Plato does not altogether abandon the principle of mimetic representation even in the case of finding music that is merely expressively suitable to the characters being represented.[20] And, even if the idea of appropriateness and fittingness has a clear – and it seems not purely conventional – application in the case of 'finding music to suit the words', this retention of the idea that music *itself* represents some subject-matter in the sense that he supposes that pictures or poems do is far less compelling. Can music represent (in this sense of imitation) anything? One way of making music fit this model would be to say: If paintings can imitate all the sights of life, so music should be able to represent the sounds of life. Indeed, this is just the kind of representation which Plato seems to be thinking of in the passages where he discusses musical *mimesis*. The music will, for example, 'represent' appropriately 'the tones and variations of pitch' of a particular sort of person.[21] And, I suppose, Plato would accept that music might also imitate sounds in nature as well as characters and feelings expressed by the human voice and accent. (Consider the overture of *Don Giovanni*. Are the initial 'waves' of sound mimetic representations of the sound of waves? I think Losey invites us to allow this relationship to belong to what is heard. I will come back to this.)

But musical works which *do* purport to represent in this way are few and far between. It is perhaps for this reason that Plato assigns to music an essentially secondary role, that of an appropriate accompaniment, something expressively 'in keeping' to the kinds of words thought suitable for the education of the young.[22] In particular those which are appropriate to, because we can readily associate it with, a life of courage and discipline. So without finding it fitting to endorse a general mimetic model for music perhaps we should follow Plato and regard the music in opera as just such expressively appropriate accompaniment. Perhaps also we should regard a filmed opera as a mechanical recording of what could be got more originally by viewing a staged performance.[23] In what follows I want to use Kierkegaard's essay on *Don Giovanni* to reconfigure our thinking on these two suggestions. I want to turn the first back towards the thought that there are ideas whose most appropriate medium for expression is intrinsically (and not only indirectly) musical. And I want to turn the second towards the possibility – and interest – in an encounter with that expression which is mediated through a further medium, specifically the medium of film.

Kierkegaard's essay on *Don Giovanni* belongs to the part of *Either/Or* that is presented as written by a young man whose concerns are wholly wrapped up in an 'aesthetic' view of life. According to this young aesthete, Mozart was granted the extraordinarily good fortune of finding in the serial seducer Don Juan 'the only true musical subject'.[24] If this is to be believed then the opera *Don Giovanni* does not simply render in music a subject that might be equally well or even better expressed in some other form (as Verdi may be said to do in his *Otello*, for example); on the contrary, it renders in music a content that is somehow already intrinsically – irreplaceably – fit for music. Here then, if Mozart succeeds, expressive form and expressed content will be united in a remarkable internal harmony. And, there is no doubt that Kierkegaard's author thinks that Mozart is almost totally successful in this case. Indeed, he insists that 'anyone who wants to see Mozart in his true immortal greatness must turn his gaze upon *Don Giovanni*'.[25]

I want to try to go some way to explaining and defending this claim. In order to do so I must first explain why Kierkegaard's author thinks that getting our gaze properly turned upon the opera is itself a far from straightforward task.

If music is conceived as representing sounds, and pictures as representing sights, then we will not say that music is to any degree a rich medium for attaining truth, even at a second or third remove, and we will not think it worth giving special attention to a filmed opera either. Yet, surely, there is also the experience of listening to some music (or watching a film) and feeling 'This *says something*'. And one seeks satisfaction here wracking one's brains to find the right words for what it says. But then it may be that it doesn't 'say anything' that one might express in words: there may be no verbal paraphrase, no way of putting it differently. What should we say about such cases? First of all, it seems clear that on the occasions where one wants to say 'This music (film) really *says something*.' we almost never mean by that: 'This aurally (visually) resembles the sound (the sight) of something.' And that is so even if it does so resemble something. In fact, very often there may be no way of specifying 'what the music (the film) says' that takes us outside the music (the film) itself, no way of putting it differently which would get hold of this content in some other way. Here, then, we are dealing with what might be called the understanding of an intrinsically musical (filmic) idea. Here one may want to say: 'This music (film) expresses an idea alright, but it is an essentially musical (filmic) idea, not something one could adequately express in another medium.'

Expressing oneself in this way may be wholly appropriate, but it can easily seem unsatisfying, especially for listeners (viewers) who do not feel they understand the music (film) themselves. Saying it cannot be expressed properly in another way seems to leave such listeners (viewers) in the dark. If it cannot be expressed in another way, how might one begin to explain to others what one has grasped in such a case?

With this problem we are moving towards the kind of thing that concerns Kierkegaard's young aesthete. As he puts it himself:

> The difficulty is that what the music under discussion expresses is essentially music's proper object, so this music expresses it far more perfectly than does language, which makes a very poor showing in comparison... Consequently, what remains to be explained can only have meaning for a person who has listened and who continues constantly to listen.[26]

In order to hear what needs to be heard you need to listen to the music. But listening does not guarantee hearing (nor seeing believing), and any other form of explanation necessarily falls short of expressing what the music (the film) expresses. Quite a problem.

Perhaps we have to get in an appropriate mood for listening to Mozart's *Don Giovanni*.[27] For this purpose I would certainly recommend watching Joseph Losey's version of the 'ever-admired' overture to the opera. But perhaps we need an appropriate mood for watching that too. To make a start of sorts let us read what Kierkegaard's young author has to say about the overture, about what he calls this 'perfect masterpiece':

> This overture is no mere fabric of themes, it is not a labyrinthine hotchpotch of associations; it is concise, resolute, powerfully structured; and above all it is impregnated with the essence of the whole opera. It is as powerful as the thought of a god, stirring as the life of a world, trembling in its earnest, quivering in its passion, crushing in its terrible anger, inspiring in its zestful joy; it is sepulchral in its judgement, strident in its lust; it is unhurriedly solemn in its imposing dignity; it is stirring, shimmering, dancing in its joy. And it has not achieved this by sucking the blood of the opera; quite the contrary, it is prophetic in its relation to the latter. In the overture, the entire compass of the music unfolds; it is as though, with a few mighty wing-beats, it hovered over itself, hovered over the place where it is to alight. It is a contest, but a contest in the higher regions of the air. To someone hearing the overture after making closer acquaintance with the opera, it might perhaps seem as if he had found his way into the hidden workshop where the forces he has come to know in the opera display their primal energy, where they vie with one another with all their might.[28]

If it is possible, I invite you now to watch Losey's overture to Mozart's *Don Giovanni*. The glass-makers workshop, with its furnace and trumpeting blowers, provides a fitting site for the arrival by gondola not simply of the central individual, the Don himself, but everyone that he plays with, a matrix of forces circulating the fire that is destined to return at the end.

But explanations, preliminary stage-setting, overtures, efforts at attunement of all kinds, may get us nowhere. To see how Kierkegaard's lover of Mozart's opera hopes that he might nevertheless provide what he calls 'suggestions' that could 'move us to listen once more',[29] I want to look a little more closely at one of his basic suggestions here: namely, that a piece of music really might 'express a musical idea'. How, first of all, might someone's conviction that a piece of music 'expresses a musical idea' show itself? It will undoubtedly show itself in the fact that that person will not be satisfied if the music is played or sung just anyhow. If it is to properly express the musical idea then she will want it to be performed in a particular way: making a crescendo here, a diminuendo there, a caesura in this place... and so on. And this *may* be *all* she will want to *say* about it.

In other cases one might want to say more. That is, in some cases one can try to make more elaborate suggestions about how one wants to hear it performed. For example, someone might draw comparisons to other pieces of music, saying it is something like this piece and not at all like this one; or they might draw comparisons of a more figurative kind: as when one says 'At this point there is, as it were, a semicolon', or 'This is, as it were, the answer to what came before.' In some cases, one might try to offer a linguistic pointer, using descriptive language to direct someone towards the musically expressed content. One might say, for example: 'This music expresses sensual desire in its lived immediacy'. And then again perhaps one will want to make a film.

With respect to the problem that what needs explaining can only be grasped in the music itself, it is important to see that these 'suggestions' and 'pointers' might actually effect a transformation of someone's experience of the music. Through them we can be brought to notice features of the music we had not heard. And then, when we listen again, perhaps we hear it differently. Then we might say: 'Oh yes, yes. Now I get it'.

Wittgenstein is particularly interested in the kind of thinking which leads along the way to such an understanding of irreplaceable fittingness. In his 1938 lectures on aesthetics he describes it in terms which speak directly for the close kinship that, following Cavell, I am appealing to between the 'method' of reorientation in Wittgenstein's philosophical writings and the mode of achieving appreciative conviction sought for in aesthetic issues:

> The question is whether this [causal explanation] is the sort of explanation we should like to have when we are puzzled about aesthetic impressions, e.g. there is a puzzle – 'Why do these bars give me such a peculiar impression?' Obviously it isn't this, i.e. a calculation, an account of reactions, etc., we want – apart from the obvious impossibility of the thing.
>
> As far as one can see the puzzlement I am talking about can be cured only by peculiar kinds of comparisons, e.g. by an arrangement of certain musical figures, comparing their effect on us... Suppose a poem sounded old-fashioned, what would be the criterion that you had found out what was old-fashioned in it? One criterion would be that when something was pointed out you were satisfied.[30]

Bringing together as it does the concepts of puzzle, therapy and arriving at a certain kind of conviction, this passage clearly supports Cavell's supplementary comparison concerning the understanding of art and following Wittgenstein's writing in philosophy. This writing too develops its teaching through various 'examples'[31] of giving 'peculiar kinds of comparisons',[32] comparisons which reorient us when we are puzzled, and which also invite us to see that empuzzlement in a certain way. ('Obviously it isn't a matter of giving a causal explanation.') I'm learning to read philosophy again. I may see, for example, that while the aim has not changed – it is still what one will want to call *clarity* that we are after – I now understand that differently.

The 'sort of explanation we should like to have' and that one actually finds in both aesthetic criticism and Wittgenstein's writings in philosophy is closely connected to what Wittgenstein calls 'aspect perception'.[33] In the case of visual aspects, aspects in pictures and paintings for example, the formula is something like this: A visual aspect is something that one can fail to see without failing to see any of the visual surface. To take the over-used but still helpful case, one might look at the ambiguous picture of a duck-rabbit and only ever see a duck in it. Until, that is, someone makes what Kierkegaard's young aesthete calls 'suggestions' of certain kinds, points out features of the picture you are looking at, compares it to other pictures, perhaps does an imitation of a rabbit, and so on... So that, hopefully one then says: 'Oh yes, now I see it.' One sees that nothing has changed, and yet one sees it differently. As a result of the suggestive pointers, one has a new visual experience.

And so also with music (or film). Perhaps someone sees Losey's presentation of the overture to *Don Giovanni* for the first time – and then perhaps hears the waves of sound in the opening bars in connection to the cinematic cliché of breaking waves as symbols of sexual climax, and then further thinks of the waves as swooning waves of desire. Equally, however, one might develop the formal connections between the overture and the finale, and so with the entrance of the Commandatore that marks the beginning of the end for the Don. This is a connection that Losey marks by bringing together his costumed players around a glass-maker's furnace. On this reading it will be emphasised that the first 'voice' we hear in the opera is not simply that of Don Giovanni himself or Don Giovanni alone. This is the kernel of the young aesthete's description of the overture that I quoted to get in the mood. Here again, however, he is quick to insist on the radical inadequacy of any of his suggestions – concluding his description by noting that 'to express more of this is an impossible task; all one can do is listen to the music, for the contest is not one of words but a raging of the elements'.[34] In this case, then, the 'final word' cannot be either final or a word. Ultimately the opera must deliver its own elucidation, make its own suggestions. And then the important thing will be whether one is then 'moderately bored' or whether, on the contrary, one now wishes to hear it 'again and again'.[35] Hence, as the young aesthete puts it, all he can really do is push us to 'listen, listen, listen to Mozart's *Don Giovanni*'.[36] And then, perhaps, one will come to hear it differently. That is, while we hear that nothing has changed in the music, we will now have a new auditory experience.

What this elaboration on musical aspects suggests is that listening to music is never a purely aural or merely tonal phenomenon: what we first hear are not just conjoined sounds, or a series of tone data; rather, what we hear, and *what we get immediately*, are themes, melodies, tunes, rhythms, song. Again, what this brings into focus is that when we talk of someone 'understanding the music' this almost never means that they have 'come to see what it aurally resembles'. Rather, it means that they are able to listen and to hear its content, a content that is *in* the music, in the well-ordered arrangement of its internal structure.[37]

Moving us towards a transformation of one's immediate experience of the opera is, I think, exactly what Kierkegaard's young aesthete wants to achieve with his loving suggestions about *Don Giovanni*. Specifically, he aims to enable us to hear it in such a way that we will now be inclined to say that the opera is the expression of an essentially musical idea.

We can begin to appreciate what such an idea might be by holding fast to the thought that in music, unlike speech, the sonorous moment remains the constant matter of our interest – it is not, that is, just a starting point for a movement of reflection that may have scant further interest or regard for the sound.

Let me try to put this another way. With both music and speech, at the level of immediate perception something is heard (music in one case, words in the other). But in the case of the auditor of speech, this medium is something through which we achieve a consciousness of the conceptual content that is 'what is meant'. In the case of the auditor of music, however, there is no such movement, no break, from the level of immediate aural perception. Thus, if music 'says something', or can be said to 'communicate ideas', this cannot be conceived as something one grasps only by going beyond the starting point of what is immediately given. On the contrary one can and must hold fast to this starting point. Indeed, one does so even if the aural aspect changes and what is heard is transformed. We arrive here at the central claim of the essay on *Don Giovanni*: namely, that unlike a word-language, whatever music expresses can only be given in the immediate *in its immediacy*.

In distinguishing these two cases – expressive 'communication' in music and language – Kierkegaard's young aesthete draws on a crucial (and, he supposes, a fundamentally Christian) distinction between sensuality and spirit. And in these terms, his central claim develops into the thesis that *only* the well-ordered sounds of music (the inner structures of unity that we call tunes, melodies, harmonies, song and so on) can sustain an immediate relation to *sensual* experience. Music alone can express the immediately sensuous *in its immediacy* – without reflection and without conceptual determination, without reference then to spirit. This is, he proposes, 'what is given' when what is given is the immediate expression of the immediate.

On this view, when Don Juan is interpreted in music the listener is not presented with a general conceptual content – the distinctive character of a seducer for example – but *an immediate expression of seducing life as it is sensually lived.*

It is for this reason that Kierkegaard's young aesthete asserts that the opera *Don Giovanni* is unsurpassable as a musical work of art: for in it we find not music accompanying the thoughts or deeds of a certain kind of character or group of characters; but 'a world of sound' which is the immediate expression of the Don's sensuous desire as it is immediately

enjoyed. That is, the musical presentation of Don Juan is not the presentation of a distinctive persona but rather something akin to the
expression of a 'power of nature'.[38] A force which, as he puts it, 'as little
tires of seducing...as the wind tires of blowing, the sea of billowing, or a
waterfall of tumbling downward'.[39] According to this argument, the
expressive musical form is so uniquely united with its expressed content
in this case because the essence of Don Giovanni's existence resides on
the level of sensual immediacy – it is for this reason intrinsically fit for
musical expression.

As should be clear, this argument strongly suggests that an adequate
presentation of the opera has to be very careful to avoid unfolding the
'action' in terms of a sequence of dramatic situations; in terms, that is,
of the interplay between distinctive characters. What marks the existence of Don Giovanni is not his troubled and troubling relations to
others but the irrepressible inwardness of a passionate sensuality. And
so, for Kierkegaard's young aesthete, in the musical expression of that
existence his encounters with others are never just 'dramatic situations';[40] rather they are the immediate expression of the entwining of
passions that are set in motion by the movements of Don Giovanni's
radically sensual being.

On this view, the various figures in the opera are like expressive satel-
lites circulating in a kind of musical matrix around the stellar passion
of the Don. As the author puts it, it is Don Giovanni's passion and his
passion alone that resonates in and sustains 'the Commendatore's
earnest, Elvira's anger, Anna's hate, Ottavio's self-importance, Zerlina's
anxiety, Masetto's indignation and Leporello's confusion'.[41] Thus, even
when he is not visibly present in a scene, Don Giovanni's being remains
in full sway in the internal play of forces that are musically rendered
there. For this reason – that is, because 'he is not character but essentially
life'[42] – Don Giovanni is 'omnipresent in the opera'.[43]

As one begins to appreciate this intrinsically musical inner structure
of the opera, it is hard not to find the physical presence of a costumed
'cast of characters' a growing distraction from it: an annoying, if necessary, feature of live performance. One perhaps comes to feel rather like
the uneducated Rita who wants to resolve a staging problem by putting
the play on the radio. Indeed, Kierkegaard's aesthete arrives at a similar
resolution for himself:

> Well-attested experience tells us that it is not pleasant to strain two
> senses at once, and it is often distracting to have to make much use
> of the eyes when the ears are already occupied. We have a tendency,

therefore, to close our eyes when listening to music. This is true of all music to some extent, of *Don Giovanni* in a higher sense. As soon as the eyes are engaged the impression gets confused, for the dramatic unity afforded to the eye is entirely subordinate and defective compared with the musical unity which is heard simultaneously. My own experience has convinced me of this. I have sat close up, I have sat further and further away, I have resorted to an out-of-the-way corner of the theatre where I could hide myself totally in this music. The better I understood it or believed I understood it, the further I moved away from it, not from coolness but from love, for it wants to be understood at a distance. For my own life there has been something strangely puzzling about this. There have been times when I would have given anything for a ticket; now I needn't spend even a penny for one. I stand outside in the corridor; I lean up against the partition separating me from the auditorium and the impression is most powerful; it is a world by itself, apart from me, I can see nothing, but am near enough to hear and yet so infinitely far away.[44]

At this point one might well begin to wonder if Joseph Losey's filmed realisation of the opera is, for just that reason, simply debarred from bringing about anything like the shift in aspect that Kierkegaard's young aesthete seeks. Can Losey really offer anything more than what has been called 'canned theatre'? In the end, will we do better just to listen to the soundtrack on its own, freed from any baleful visual influences? I think not. Indeed, in my view, the excellence of the film lies precisely in its capacity to provide a visual mediation of an essentially aural phenomenon.

To understand this suggestion we need to distinguish Losey's production from filmed stage performances. Ultimately, my view is that the film is itself a work of art, and not simply the recording on tape of an art-work which is expressed in some other medium. But whatever one's judgement on the piece, even a muted sight of Losey's cast striding through the Italian countryside would indicate that he has produced something that is about as far away from the recording of a stage production as one can imagine.

So not a stage recording. Yet, of course the whole thing remains essentially staged. Film fiction, it seems, offers us the possibility of giving us the appearance of an opening onto what, following Bazin, but in Kierkegaard's words, we might call the 'world by itself' of Don Giovanni.[45] However, as I have indicated, I do not want this to suggest that Losey's film provides a realistic visual appearance of a fictional visual world. Indeed, in my view, if Losey's film succeeds then that is because his surreal staging offers us a new visual window on an essentially *aural* world. Or again, if Losey has achieved anything then what he has done in this film must in some way render 'visible', through a kind of visible figure or 'suggestion' for the eyes, the 'solar system' of passions that is Mozart's *Don Giovanni*.

For the sake of argument, let's credit him with some success here. However, even granted that, one might still wonder what one can get from Losey's film that one cannot get, at least in principle, from a live stage performance? Indeed, what in the last analysis *is* the difference between Losey's film and the recording of a live performance?

In my view the only chance of squeezing out a difference here is if the medium of film really can give rise to aesthetic effects or possess aesthetic virtues in its own right. Effects or virtues that Losey can in his own way appropriate to provide this 'visible' rendering of an essentially aural idea. And this can be achieved, I think, just in so far as the film has (and I think it has) the capacity literally and figuratively to *refocus our vision*, a capacity to defamiliarise the everyday. But now, and crucially in my view, what is at issue in this case is not the defamiliarisation of 'everyday perception' but the defamiliarisation of our sense of *the everydayness of Don Giovanni himself*. Ultimately, it is a defamiliarisation which enables us to acknowledge that the Don is not just a clever seducer who desires beautiful (that is aesthetically worthy) women, but is an arbitrary, frighteningly predatory force, a demonic force of immediate longing for femininity.

As Kierkegaard's young aesthete brilliantly puts it, we miss the identity of Don Giovanni entirely if we fail to see that for him 'every girl is an ordinary girl, every love affair an everyday story'.[46]

I would like to conclude by finally bringing Kierkegaard's Mozart and Losey's Mozart together. That Kierkegaard's aesthete might also have wound up recommending that one watch the Losey film – at the cinema or more readily on video or now on the digitally remastered widescreen version available from Columbia TriStar on DVD – can perhaps be indicated by looking at a brief review of a performance of *Don Giovanni* that Kierkegaard wrote two years after writing *Either/Or*, a review very much in tune with the earlier essay on the opera, criticising what he called 'a single point' in the performance he saw.[47]

The single point in question concerns a scene in which Don Giovanni attempts to add the peasant girl Zerlina to his list of conquests, terribly enough, on her wedding day. I'll present Kierkegaard's critical response to the production he saw, and then, if possible, one should watch Losey's version of the same sequence.

In his review Kierkegaard says that the aria was sung 'too reflectively' by the male lead. Instead of an unreflective, immediate and command-ing address *to* the girl, he sung it as if he were simply singing *for* her, aiming to arouse her passion by the beauty of his song. But, for Kierke-gaard, the expression in song is not a shift of mode (to the spiritual) for the seductive Don Giovanni. On the contrary it expresses the constant (sensuous) being of his existence. As we have seen, for Kierkegaard what is expressed in *Don Giovanni* is fundamentally already musical. Consequently, the aria that is 'the seduction of Zerlina' should not be read as the playing out of the strategy of a falsely amorous lover at the balcony, a reflective seducer intending to arouse erotic desire. As the immediate expression of his being it is without plan or intention whatsoever. It is, that is to say, simply the direct outpouring of Don Giovanni's desire: *this is what he does*. That it arouses the girl is not its reflective or intended object or effect but the upshot of primitive powers which can draw her in.

To acknowledge this properly, we would do well to recall the brutal words of Don Giovanni's servant Leporello who, flatly in the extreme, concludes his description of his masters conquests by noting: 'He doesn't care if she's rich or poor, ugly or beautiful ['*brutta*' or '*bella*']. So long as she wears a skirt…you know what he does.' And when we see Don Giovanni singing to Zerlina of her 'sweet, pretty face' a face which would, he suggests be wasted on a country bumpkin, we should be clear that she *is* a country bumpkin, and we should not be tempted to aestheticise her as a pure and simple, sweet and pretty peasant girl. The Don will tell her that she is 'not born to be a peasant' and will praise her 'roguish eyes', 'beautiful lips', 'hands white as cream, fragrant as roses'. But what really matters for the Don is that she is a woman, and she has eyes, a mouth and hands.

For Kierkegaard, no excellence of delivery can make amends for the total misconception of the opera which occurs if a single suggestion of reflective considerations is allowed to creep into the portrayal of the Don. This is not a drama of significant words and deeds, but an ex-pressive matrix of pure powers and energies focused on the sensual existence of Don Giovanni. Hence also the scene with Zerlina is not simply a 'dramatic situation' occurring between two characters in a story; it is the immediate expression of an essentially erotic enjoyment (the erotic as immediately enjoyed) in which the 'innocent' peasant becomes sensually entwined with the passion of Don Giovanni: she no longer wants simply to be strong enough to resist, and is finally delighted to be free of having to resist.

Kierkegaard was critical then of any presentation of *Don Giovanni* which allowed any moments of thinking or planning into the portrayal of the Don. For according to Kierkegaard he simply *is* desire in its inward sensuous immediacy. And so he seduces Zerlina not because she is a pretty or beautifully simple peasant woman, but rather, in common with every other woman who is the target of his desire, because she is a woman. If possible I want you to listen and watch Losey's rendering of this most astonishing of duets, watch again the unfolding of this most appalling (because most perfect) of love songs. Even the visual gag, teetering on foolishness – the comparison of the Don to the (filmed) Dracula or Nosferatu type – helps disclose the Don not as 'a lover' of women but as an insatiable natural force.

What Kierkegaard's young aesthete wants to stress in his essay on Mozart's *Don Giovanni* is that it is not a dramatic interaction of characters but a matrix of forces, a field of powers and energies in internal relations all devoted to expressing the passion of Don Giovanni as it is undergone in immediate experience. And it seems to me that in their wanderings around the Palladian villas of Vicenza, Losey's surreal cast of strange, almost alien creatures in big hats and big hair draws us closer to the everydayness that is 'the world of Don Giovanni' than does many a lavish production in the theatres and opera houses. Watch, watch, watch Joseph Losey's *Don Giovanni* – and, indeed, you may begin to hear the music anew.

Notes

1. M. Merleau-Ponty (1962) p. viii.
2. S. Cavell 1979, p. 3. (Word order amended.)
3. *Ibid.*
4. J.L. Austin 'A Plea for Excuses', in his 1961, p. 182.
5. See for example, K. Popper, 'The Nature of Philosophical Problems and their Roots in Science' in his 1963, *passim.*
6. S. Cavell 1979, p. 125.
7. C. Diamond, 'The Difficulty of Reality and the Difficulty of Philosophy', unpublished manuscript.
8. See L. Wittgenstein (1953), §93.
9. *Ibid.*, §38, §§93–4.
10. *Ibid.*, §123.
11. The relationship between this conception of philosophical difficulties and the distinctive style of writing of *Philosophical Investigations* is further explored in my 'Philosophy as Nomadism', in Carel and D. Gamez (2004) pp. 155–167.
12. S. Cavell, 'Aesthetic Problems of Modern Philosophy' in Cavell 1969, p. 85.

13. *Ibid.*
14. *Ibid.*, p. 86.
15. L. Wittgenstein (1953), §531.
16. *Ibid.*, p. 219.
17. Kierkegaard's essay on *Don Giovanni* is the first essay in the first major part of the book *Either/Or* (London: Penguin). However, while Kierkegaard wrote this book, there is an important sense in which the essay on *Don Giovanni* is not straightforwardly a presentation of his view. (His later review of the opera in his own name suggests that it is, however, pretty much his own view too. See below.) The book *Either/Or* is wrapped in several layers of pseudonymity. The two main parts (as it were 'Either' and 'Or') are assigned to two fictitious authors. Part of the first part is an extract of a diary by a third author, and part of the second includes a sermon by a fourth. On top of that the two main parts are introduced by a fictional editor in a preface. The essay on Mozart's opera is presented as coming from the hand of a young man whose concerns are wholly wrapped up in what the editor calls an 'aesthetic' view of life. Here the central exemplar is the Don Juan figure, the great seducer and lover of women, and, according to the youthful author of the first part, it finds its absolutely unrivalled presentation in Mozart's opera *Don Giovanni*. (I think he would have been delighted by Losey's film of the same.)
18. *Don Giovanni*, Director J. Losey, Conductor Lorin Maazel, Cast Ruggero Raimondi, José van Dam, Edda Moser, Kiri Te Kanawa, Kenneth Riegel, Teresa Berganza, Malcolm King, John Macurdy, Composer Wolfgang Amadeus Mozart, Librettist Lorenzo da Ponte. Columbia TriStar 2004 (DVD of 1979 movie).
19. Plato, *Republic*, p. 598b. Plato normally refers to artistic representations as lying at 'two removes' or 'two generations' away from reality (see p. 597e and p. 602c). However, since the artist aims at representing things not 'as they are' but only 'as they appear to be' (p. 598a), one can say that he regards artistic representation as three removes from the truth. The order at issue then is as follows:
Truth itself: The form
First remove: The particular as it is
Second remove: The appearance of the particular
Third remove: The representation of the appearance of the particular.
20. *Ibid.*, pp. 398c–399–400c.
21. *Ibid.*, p. 399a.
22. *Ibid.*, p. 398d.
23. One might see here a subterranean Platonism in the philosophy of Walter Benjamin's 'The Work of Art in the Age of Mechanical Reproduction'.
24. S. Kierkegaard (1843), p. 62.
25. *Ibid.*, p. 83.
26. *Ibid.*, p. 84.
27. I'm thinking here of Heidegger's discussion of the claim that one's 'openness to the world' or oriented 'going about' in the world in general – and hence also every (disoriented) encounter with the difficulty of reality – is always 'constituted existentially by the attunement of a state of mind' (Heidegger 1962, p. 176).

28. S. Kierkegaard, (1843), p. 128.
29. *Ibid.*, p. 84.
30. L. Wittgenstein (1966), p. 20.
31. L. Wittgenstein (1953), §133.
32. *Ibid.*, §130.
33. *Ibid.*, Part 2, Section xi, *passim.*
34. S. Kierkegaard (1843), p. 129.
35. L. Wittgenstein (1966), p. 4.
36. S. Kierkegaard (1843), p. 109.
37. See L. Wittgenstein (1953) §523: 'I should like to say "What the picture tells me is itself." That is, its telling me something consists in its own structure, in *its* own lines and colours. (What would it mean to say: "What this musical theme tells me is itself"?)' I take it that Kierkegaard's essay gives us one way of understanding what the suggestion in parentheses might mean (what it amounts to). Wittgenstein's wanting to compare understanding music and understanding a sentence is made explicit in *Philosophical Investigations*, §527.
38. S. Kierkegaard (1843), p. 99.
39. *Ibid.*
40. *Ibid.*, p. 135.
41. *Ibid.*, p. 121.
42. *Ibid.*
43. *Ibid.*, p. 133.
44. *Ibid.*, p. 122.
45. *Ibid.*
46. *Ibid.*, p. 103.
47. S. Kierkegaard, 'A Cursory Observation Concerning a Detail in *Don Giovanni*', published in *Fædrelandet* (*The Fatherland*) in 1845.

Silent Dialogue: Philosophising with Jan Švankmajer

David Rudrum

Jan Švankmajer does not appear to be a filmmaker to whom words come easily. Many of the short films for which he is best known (including all but one of the eleven shorts collected in the BFI's two-volume selection of his work)[1] are characterised by a wholesale rejection of the spoken word. Few contemporary directors are capable of making feature-length movies that contain not a single word of dialogue, but Švankmajer achieved this in his 1996 film *Conspirators of Pleasure*. Some of his experimental techniques might even be said to call into question the need for inventing Vitaphone.

The most commonly cited influences on Švankmajer's work are the distinctively Czech traditions of surrealism, animation, and puppetry, but to these should be added his accomplished background in visual arts, his early work with avant-garde theatre (including masked performance), and an interest in silent cinema. Notably, the media on this latter list are largely wordless, or, more accurately, do not rely primarily on spoken language. For to call Švankmajer's films 'silent' or 'wordless' is not strictly accurate. Many of them are structured around evocative music (for example, *J. S. Bach: Fantasy in G Minor*, 1965) and employ gruesome sound effects (as in *Dimensions of Dialogue*, 1982). Others, in the tradition of silent cinema, employ words on-screen, as text (for example, *The Death of Stalinism in Bohemia*, 1990), and elsewhere Švankmajer uses voice-over to skillful effect (as in *Jabberwocky*, 1971). To think of his films in terms of an absence or lack of language, then, is misleading. Rather, they practice a conscious rejection of conventional dialogue. Of the shorts that make up the bulk of Švankmajer's output, very few contain any verbal interaction at all: most fly in the face of it. Of his four feature-length films, only the most recent, *Little Otik* (2000), is scripted principally around dialogue. Previously, *Conspirators of Pleasure*

114

eschewed it entirely, *Faust* (1994) contained little, and *Alice* (1988) went out of its way to avoid dialogue by having a voice-over narrate the story and speak all the characters' parts. Unsurprisingly, the only scholastic study of Švankmajer's films claims in the blurb on its cover that they 'display a bleak outlook on the possibilities for dialogue'.[2]

Yet it is precisely the idea of dialogue that lies at the heart of some of the most interesting thought of twentieth century philosophers – from Ludwig Wittgenstein's philosophical investigations of words in every-day interactive use (i.e., in dialogue), to Emmanuel Levinas's view of a dialogical relationship, prior to language, as fundamental to being, to Mikhail Bakhtin's claim that both language and the self are constituted dialogically. These thinkers come from philosophical traditions about as different from each other as they could possibly be, yet their common emphasis on dialogue underlines the importance of this concept to the make-up of contemporary thought. On the face of it, such philosophical positions seem far removed from the concerns of Švankmajer's films. But I contend that Švankmajer formulates a scathing critique of our notions of dialogue that, in its scope and depth, deserves to be called philosophical.[3]

What happens when communication breaks down? When the conversations through which we supposedly 'talk things over' and 'work things out' fail, to the point where a dialogical interaction can't really be said to take place at all? These are the themes that Švankmajer explores in his short film *Dimensions of Dialogue*. Divided into three sections ('Exhaustive Discussion', 'Passionate Discourse', and 'Factual Conversation'), each part symbolises a form of failure and collapse in a form of dialogical exchange. I say 'symbolises' since, true to his roots in Czech surrealism, Švankmajer pursues his themes using striking visual metaphors, and, tellingly, not a word is actually spoken throughout the film. In what follows, I shall use Švankmajer's masterpiece to shed light on three very different philosophical conceptions of dialogue.

Part One: Exhaustive discussion

Two moving heads, animated from everyday objects in a pastiche of Arcimboldo's mannerist portraits, are seen approaching and confronting each other. The first 'head' (a collage made of fruit and vegetables) and the second (made of kitchen utensils and tools) stand face-to-face, as if interlocutors. But the 'dialogue' that ensues consists of the latter swallowing the former, its component utensils seen individually chewing and devouring the fruit and vegetables before the 'utensil-head' as a whole vomits forth their masticated remnants, which then reconstitute as the (now rather battered) vegetable-head. The two heads separate. The utensil-head is then confronted by a head made of items of stationery, which now performs a similar action, attacking and devouring the utensil-head and spewing it forth again in fragments which re-form a beaten-up utensil-head. The stationery head now meets the battered vegetable head, and is in turn devoured and regurgitated by it, thus completing the cycle. This pattern of dominance is replicated, and each time the devoured fragments vomited up become smaller, mushier, and less distinct. It becomes impossible to recognise the original objects from which this ever more homogenised matter was produced, until, eventually, what is spewed forth are lumps of clay, which congeal to form surprisingly realistic 'human' heads. When two such heads confront each other at last, an act of cannibalism ensues as one devours the other. Yet this time, the head that is vomited forth is an exact replica of both the devouring and the devoured heads, which itself promptly vomits forth an exact replica, which itself vomits forth an exact replica ... and so on.

The first 'chapter' of Švankmajer's film has been described as a metaphor for cannibalism. But despite its concern with the devouring of like by like, to suggest the episode is fundamentally about eating overlooks its avowed subject matter: this process forms a metaphor for the reduction of the different to the same perpetrated in dialogue. Švankmajer's stripping out of any actual dialogue deserves analysis. By replacing the cut and thrust of words with the metaphor of head confronting head, Švankmajer explores a relation that has been seen as underwriting the possibility of dialogue, which Emmanuel Levinas calls the 'face to face'.

For Levinas, the face to face is 'the irreducible and ultimate relation'.[4] It is a relation of immediacy and straightforwardness, yet it is also a profoundly ethical encounter (*Totality & Infinity*, hereafter *TI*, p. 202). It is the moment that makes interaction possible, although it takes place prior to language itself. Indeed, Levinas suggests that 'the face to face founds language' (*TI*, p. 207). Therefore, to be engaged in linguistic dialogue is to be engaged in the face to face: 'Meaning is the face of the Other, and all recourse to words takes place already within the primordial face to face of language' (*TI*, p. 206). In his own, distinctive way, Švankmajer is exploring this face to face relationship by muting its linguistic component and exposing its phenomenological structure through metaphor. Švankmajer and Levinas, then, share a concern with the immediacy of the encounter lying behind the moment of dialogue.[5] Above all, they share a concern with the ethical import of this moment. Their conclusions, however, are radically divergent. Fundamental to an understanding of both is the role of the face.

According to Levinas, the face is an experience of transcendence. It offers a 'gleam of exteriority' (*TI*, p. 24), an epiphany which reveals the Other and the infinity of his Otherness.[6] The face of the Other 'appeals to me' (*TI*, p. 194), it 'summons me to my obligations and judges me' (*TI*, p. 215), it 'opens the primordial discourse whose first word is obligation' (*TI*, p. 201). Yet this is a transcendent experience rather than a verbal one: the immediacy and the nakedness of the face need not be couched in words. The face communicates in its own right, and, claims Levinas, 'The principle "you shall not commit murder"' is 'the very signifyingness of the face' (*TI*, p. 262). Fundamentally, then, 'The epiphany of the face is ethical' (*TI*, p. 199), and 'to see a face is already to hear: "Thou shalt not kill".'[7]

To claim that this is also Švankmajer's standpoint would be misleading, yet nevertheless the similarity of his concerns is striking. 'Exhaustive Discussion' not just represents but enacts the moment of the 'face to face', in which each face is confronted by the infinite Otherness of the Other. Since Švankmajer's faces are made of completely different kinds of object, a sense of mutual radical alterity is conveyed, and the question of how to respond (and hence, how one *ought* to respond) to the manifestation of the infinitely Other is raised. Švankmajer's animation of this confrontation is rather less optimistic than Levinas's theorisation of it: both Levinas and Švankmajer concur that the experience of the face is 'a situation where totality breaks up' (*TI*, p. 24), but their different understandings of the nature of this 'breaking up' point in very different directions.

It seems that, for Švankmajer, being confronted with the absolutely Other does not entail the unqualified respect for its otherness that *Totality and Infinity* stipulates. *Pace* Levinas, Švankmajer's film shows that the otherness of the face is something that *can* be 'encompassed' and 'contained',[8] and quite brutally at that: it can be eaten, even cannibalised. 'Exhaustive Discussion' enacts such a temptation to violate the face, to reduce the Other to the same through violence, to devour the sacrosanct identity of one's interlocutor by assimilating it to one's own. For Levinas, 'The Other remains infinitely transcendent, infinitely foreign' (*TI*, p. 194), but Švankmajer shows that, on the contrary, the Other can not only be violated and appropriated, but utterly ingested and consumed. Nor does Švankmajer offer us some consolation in the possibility of somehow absorbing the ingested Other to nourish or enrich the same: instead, the battered remnants ('the Trace of the Other', perhaps) are bulimically expelled.

On the one hand, Levinas insists on the peaceable nature of the encounter with the face that underwrites the ethical heart of his philosophy:

> The relation with the face, with the other absolutely other which I can not contain, the other in this sense infinite, is ... maintained without violence, in peace with this absolute alterity. The 'resistance' of the other does not do violence to me, does not act negatively; it has a positive structure: ethical. (*TI*, p. 197)
>
> The face in which the other–the absolutely other–presents himself does not negate the same, does not do violence to it ... It remains commensurate with him who welcomes ... This presentation is preeminently nonviolence, for instead of offending my freedom it calls it to responsibility and founds it. As nonviolence it nonetheless maintains the plurality of the same and the other. It is peace. (*TI*, p. 203)

It is precisely this vision of the benign amity of the face, the ethical orientation of the face to face encounter, and the ensuing vision of respectful, benevolent, friendly dialogue that Švankmajer's film questions, even rejects. The face can never know that its welcome will be a peaceful one, can never be sure it will not be devoured. And since the structure of Švankmajer's film demonstrates that the devourer can instantly become the devoured, that the face that eats another face can itself be eaten by a third, the proliferation of violence permeates both sides of the face to face. Both my reception of the Other's otherness and my own being-towards-others are therefore haunted by the threat of aggression.

Accordingly, 'Exhaustive Discussion' takes issue with the very 'first word' of the dialogue spoken by Levinas's face:

> This infinity [of the Other's transcendence], stronger than murder, already resists us in his face, is his face, is the primordial *expression*, is the first word: 'you shall not commit murder.' The infinite paralyses power by its infinite resistance to murder, which, firm and insurmountable, gleams in the face of the Other, ...– the ethical resistance. The epiphany of the face brings forth the possibility of gauging the infinity of the temptation to murder, not only as a temptation to total destruction, but also as the purely ethical impossibility of this temptation and attempt. (*TI*, p. 199)

Whether Levinas is trying to argue here that murder is an *ethical* impossibility rather than a real impossibility is unclear. Jill Robbins suggests that 'The murderer who takes violent aim at the face of the other does not truly *face* the other. He thus loses not only the face of the other but also his own face'.[9] In other words, the 'total negation' (*TI*, p. 198) of murder is possible only outside the face to face relation.[10] Švankmajer, I contend, shows us this is not so. A true annihilation of the Other, a true negation of his otherness, his distinctiveness, and his identity can indeed be perpetrated in the destruction of the face–*by another face*. Only when one face meets the face that confronts it not with a welcome but with this cannibalistic violence is such a 'total negation' achieved: only a face, in the moment of the face to face, can truly annihilate another face. This 'de-facement' of otherness is what Švankmajer's film depicts. Furthermore, the structure of Švankmajer's 'Exhaustive Discussion' is such that my destruction *of* the Other and my destruction *by* the Other are figures for each other: the process creates a mutually destructive loop in which all three faces involved pulverise and are pulverised by each Other. Švankmajer has claimed that 'Abstract destruction does not exist in my films. ... Destruction in my films has ideological and philosophical roots'.[11] This cyclical downward spiral of violence is therefore significant.

In 'Exhaustive Discussion', the product of each Other's voracious appetite for the destruction of each Other is the creation (through destruction) of Infinity, symbolised by the constant replication of the same clay face at the end of this episode of the film. Yet this is not the Infinity of Otherness envisioned by Levinas, it is an infinity of the same, an eternal recurrence of identical faces. Švankmajer's vision of infinity, then, is achieved *not* through transcendence but through the cannibalistic assimilation process, by doing violence to the other and reducing it to the same. Levinas's position that 'The welcoming of the face is peaceable from the first, for it answers to the unquenchable Desire for Infinity' (*TI*, p. 65) may perhaps describe an encounter that takes place where there is a desire for an infinity of otherness, but Švankmajer shows us a very different situation where there is a desire for an infinity of the same.[12]

This is not to suggest, though, that Švankmajer's film is merely a convenient 'flip-side' to Levinas's philosophy, that 'Exhaustive Discussion' basically agrees with the structure of Levinas's phenomenology whilst reversing its values. If this were the case, 'Exhaustive Discussion' might be read as espousing the same message as Levinas's philosophy, only teaching it through negative example. Švankmajer's film actually poses more complex questions to Levinas's thought. For example, is not Levinas's creation of the very notion of 'the face' a moment of monolithic categorisation, itself supremely in-different to otherness?

What if there were different kinds of face? What if we responded differently to different kinds of face? Or if we all responded the same way to all faces? Or if our response to different kinds of face was always the same? These are precisely the kinds of question that 'Exhaustive Discussion' en-visages. Of course, they are not entirely new questions, nor are they uniquely Švankmajer's:

> In effect, the necessity of gaining access to the meaning of the other (in its irreducible alterity) on the basis of its 'face,' ... and the necessity of speaking of the other as other, or to the other as other, ... as the necessity from which no discourse can escape, from its earliest origin–these necessities are violence itself, or rather the transcendental origin of an irreducible violence.[13]

What Švankmajer adds to Derrida's critique of Levinas's in-different violence towards the face is a vivid dramatisation of the diversity and otherness that exists within the category of the face. (As an aside, it is interesting that it took an artist with a strong background in masked theatre, where the face is obscured, and *not* 'manifested', 'revealed', 'present', 'naked', or any such term from Levinas, to show us this diversity and otherness, and to do so using techniques of symbolism and allegory heavily indebted to the 'face-less' tradition of masked theatre).

By showing faces made from completely disparate kinds of object confronting each other in their difference, Švankmajer shows that the face to face relation can indeed be a meeting of others, but not in the way that Levinas intends. Švankmajer's vegetable-head, utensil-head, and stationery-head symbolise that there are indeed different kinds of face, and, hence, that our approach to the face of the Other cannot be a straightforward communion (an 'inter-face', perhaps) as Levinas envisions. The encounter with difference is something jarring, and Švankmajer conveys this sense with striking visual conceits: there is something deeply 'Other' about seeing a razor shave a cucumber, or a pair of pliers pulverising sugar-cubes in its teeth, or crockery being smashed by the chomping action of a book as it opens and closes. The oxymoronic oddness of these conceits conveys precisely the sense of otherness that is under investigation here. So the violence in Švankmajer's film is in no way critical or disparaging about difference and otherness: rather, if there is a Švankmajerian ethics, then it lies in conveying a sense of difference, otherness, and alterity that goes beyond the level envisaged by Levinas's account of the face.

In a sense, 'Exhaustive Discussion' ends where Levinas starts: with a single kind of face that, created in the image of 'man' (Levinas would say in God's image), allows for no more difference than the concept of 'man' has in western philosophy. Švankmajer shows this 'face of man' to be self-perpetuating, in an unsettling vision of infinity. True, there is peace (no more devouring now, only vomiting), but this peace has been made possible only by the reduction of three very different faces to the identity of this 'face of man'. Švankmajer invites us to suspect, then, that the peacefulness of Levinas's 'face to face' is the peace of like meeting like rather than Other meeting Other.

It is in Švankmajer, not in Levinas, that 'the primordial multiplicity is observed within the very face to face that constitutes it' (*TI*, p. 251). So radical is this difference that Švankmajer cannot but be pessimistic about our chances of appreciating it, of letting the Other be, and of letting him speak by himself, as himself, to us in dialogue. Of course, Levinas says repeatedly that we can never comprehend, grasp, or be adequate to the otherness of the Other, but Švankmajer takes this assertion more seriously by dramatising our inevitable failure and its disastrous consequences. To put it another way: Levinas, Michael Eskin has noted, was fond of Paul Celan's observation 'I am you when I am I'. This line encapsulates the substituting of one's self for the Other and taking responsibility for the Other that the face calls us to in Levinas's philosophy. Yet if I must first substitute myself for the Other, then my being-towards-others is essentially a being-towards-myself. This is the kind of situation that leads me not to peace with the Other, but to devouring his otherness. It is the kind of situation that Švankmajer, in 'Exhaustive Discussion', warns us about.

Part Two: Passionate discourse

Two lifelike clay figures, one male and one female, face each other across a wooden table. In a masterful claymation sequence, he smiles at her, their hands touch, and they kiss tenderly, stroking one another's bodies. As they cleave together, their forms merge until they are one mass of animated clay, undulating in waves of passion from which their gasping faces occasionally emerge. Eventually, their bodies separate from this mass and face each other again. But a small blob of animated clay remains behind on the table. This crawls over to the woman and tries, pathetically, to attract her attention. She brushes it away. It lands next to the man, who also knocks it aside. It returns to the woman, who tries to crush it, then to the man, who throws it at the woman. She throws it back in his face. In the anger that ensues, the two clay figures gouge out each other's faces and tear one another's bodies to pieces, until all that is left at the end is a seething mass of clay, now writhing in violence rather than passion.

According to František Dryje, this episode of *Dimensions of Dialogue* is 'a masterfully anecdotal and concise statement about the sad prospects for an elementary emotional life … [which] ultimately has the character of a parable'. Here as in many of Švankmajer's films, 'The erotic element is treated at a tragic, fateful level.'[14] Dryje reads the combination of tenderness and violence in the film as following the spirit of de Sade, one of Švankmajer's acknowledged influences. Yet a three minute fragment of a short that bears reading as anecdote, parable, and tragedy calls for a more interrogative, philosophical interpretation, in which the film's avowed status as a metaphor or allegory of dialogue is scrutinised.

Once again, Švankmajer's film challenges our overly optimistic notions of dialogue, questioning whether an intimate communion or coincidence between two minds, however close to one another they may be, is a positive end. Švankmajer is therefore at odds with the tendency, widespread in literary, cultural, and media studies throughout the last two decades, to valorise the notion of 'dialogism' as a dynamic, creative force in the makeup of culture, language, and subjectivity. This tendency is largely associated with the influential thought of Mikhail Bakhtin.[15]

Bakhtin's work sees dialogue as the lifeblood of language, as far more essential to it than notions of, say, reference or signification. Language, for Bakhtin, is always already intertextual, not in some deconstructive fashion, but rather because every utterance is uttered in an environment infused with other utterances:

> The dialogic orientation of discourse is a phenomenon that is … a property of *any* discourse. It is the natural orientation of any living discourse. On all its various routes toward the object, in all its directions, the word encounters an alien word and cannot help encountering it in a living, tension-filled interaction.[16]

According to Bakhtin, 'The word lives … on the boundary between its own context and another, alien context' (1981, p. 284), so that 'there is only the word as address, the word dialogically contacting another word, a word about a word addressed to a word.'[17]

At first blush, Bakhtin's conception of dialogue may seem unrelated to that dramatised by Švankmajer in 'Passionate Discourse'. Yet there is more to Bakhtin than the structure of words. Words, for Bakhtin, are always spoken *by* someone *to* someone, so that dialogue thrives on intersubjectivity as much as on intertextuality. As speaking subjects, our voices (and hence our selves) are essentially 'polyphonic', shaped by the person to whom – and for whom – we are speaking. Bakhtinian dialogism, then, is not confined to verbal interlocution. It enables subjects to interact, to intersect, even to merge. Hence the importance of 'the word as address': 'I am conscious of myself only while revealing myself for another, through another, and with the help of another' (1984, p. 287). Indeed, Bakhtin wonders whether a subject can exist and achieve self-consciousness outside of such acts of union with other subjects. He even moots a principle of 'Nonself-sufficiency, the impossibility of the existence of a single consciousness' (*Ibid.*, p. 287), and goes so far as to suggest that *'To be* means *to communicate'* (*Ibid.*), i.e. to share one's being with another.

So if we seem to have come a long way from Švankmajer's film, my contention would be that it is precisely the notion of dialogue as intersubjectivity, as a moment of sharing and, especially, *merging* of consciousness, that 'Passionate Discourse' enacts and works through to a brutal conclusion. Švankmajer shows us that the union of two selves in dialogue, overcoming the boundaries between them, is not as desirable a phenomenon as it might seem. Bakhtin's thought is particularly susceptible to the flaws diagnosed by Švankmajer's film because it is predicated on the importance of the role of love, about which Švankmajer is hardly encouraging. This emphasis on love is not often apparent in Bakhtin's work on language and literature, for which he is best known. But this work is preceded by an early phase of Bakhtin's career in which his interests are more strictly philosophical: he maps out a phenomenology of human interaction (a 'participative thinking'[18]) that, according to some commentators, lays down the coordinates of his later work on dialogue.[19] Through his philosophical works, one can begin to see that 'Passionate Discourse' enacts a scepticism towards the Bakhtinian understanding of dialogue.

The focus of Bakhtin's early philosophy is on the responsiveness and responsibility of people in relation to each other, on the architectonics of a participative 'answerability'.[20] Its emphasis on human interactivity underpins his later concept of dialogism. Bakhtin argues that the self is needed to consummate the other (and vice versa) through participatory processes such as 'co-authoring' and 'sympathetic co-experiencing'. On its own, the self remains incomplete, incoherent, and inchoate until consummated by the other. Bakhtin describes the processes of this consummation in very benign terms:

'Only sympathetic co-experiencing has the power to conjoin or unite harmoniously ... on one and the same plane' (1990, p. 81). 'Sympathetic co-experiencing' is 'akin to love' (*Ibid.*). Indeed, 'The notion of *sympathetic* co-experiencing developed to its ultimate conclusion ... would bring us to the idea of aesthetic *love*' (Ibid.), an idea that Bakhtin sees as essential to the process of consummation.

When Bakhtin later turned from philosophy towards language and literature, he translated his ideas about participation and self/other consummation into the concepts of dialogism and polyphony. Bakhtin's descriptions of dialogue thus take on the benevolent, loving aspects of his early philosophy. As Caryl Emerson has noted:

> Baxtin's potential other lives forever on friendly boundaries. ... This ... [is a] major troubling area in Baxtin's poetics, what we might call its presumption of 'benevolence' or 'benignness.' Just as in Baxtin's scheme of things an openness to others can never really be threatening, so Baxtin seems to assume that dialogue just naturally optimizes itself for its participants.[21]

She concludes that 'This benevolence of Baxtin's is the most appealing and perhaps the most troublesome aspect' of his work.[22] It is this understanding of dialogue as predicated on mutual loving interanimation that we see played out to tragic and destructive ends in Švankmajer's 'Passionate Discourse'.

At first glance, then, Švankmajer's film can be read as critiquing those of us who, like Bakhtin, are tempted to think of dialogue as a meeting of hearts as much as a meeting of minds, as a moment of unity or merger rather than mere exchange, perhaps even as a coming together of kindred spirits: in Bakhtin's terms, a consummation. 'Passionate Discourse' seems to ask questions like: what happens if a time comes when there is no longer any love lost between the participants in the dialogue? If the co-experiencing is no longer sympathetic? If it is no longer *co*-experiencing at all? What if the self or the other is not consummated during the interaction, or if their consummation is not the whole story? This episode of *Dimensions of Dialogue* enacts graphically some very negative answers to these questions, interrogating the optimism of a philosophy of dialogue founded on a moment of consummation grounded in love.

Yet such a reading is rather superficial, and does justice neither to Bakhtin nor to Švankmajer. In 'Passionate Discourse', the problematic moment is not that of the consummation, which is depicted in all its desire and passion. It is rather the aftermath of this moment that is troublesome. Relatedly, it is not the state of being consummated that Bakhtin valorises, but rather the *process* of consummation. As in Švankmajer's film, this is not problematic as long as it is ongoing. Interaction, for Bakhtin, is not a state but an activity. If it were a state, true 'inter-*action*' would have ceased. Thus Bakhtin asks, 'What would I have to gain if another were to *fuse* with me?'[23] Our selves would have become caught in stasis.

> 'If I am consummated and my life is consummated, I am no longer capable of living and acting' [1990, p. 13]. In order to live, one needs to be unconsummated–a person needs to be open for herself, one needs to be 'axiologically yet-to-be, someone who does not coincide with his already existing makeup' [*Ibid.*].[24]

Conversely, 'The consciousness of being fully consummated in time ... is a consciousness with which one can do nothing or with which it is impossible to live' (*Ibid.*, p. 121).

Is Švankmajer's film in agreement with Bakhtin, then? Both seem to envision a passionate moment of loving consummation in which two selves overcome their boundaries and merge. However, in Bakhtin's thought, the process restarts: each self goes on to interact with (and presumably be consummated once again by) other selves. In this benevolent vision, interaction fuels further interaction, dialogue fuels further dialogue, and so forth. The alternative, Bakhtin implies, is a form of death: 'To be means to communicate dialogically. When dialogue ends, everything ends. Thus dialogue, by its very essence, cannot and must not come to an end' (1984, p. 252).

Yet Švankmajer's 'Passionate Discourse' involves a pause for thought. Are there no consequences of these dialogues, interactions, consummations? Bakhtin affirms that selves are altered in these processes, but Švankmajer takes this possibility more seriously. Švankmajer shows that however ecstatic the moment of consummation, it must come to an end, and the two selves must resume their separate identities. Bakhtin overlooks the problematics attendant on this moment, because his thought does not dwell on the possibility of dialogue ending. How, then, do two people who have entered into a loving, consummating interaction sustain an interrelationship after this moment has ceased? What of our selves is left over, left behind, and how does this leaving affect our relation to our selves and to the other with whom we have interacted? Švankmajer's nondescript blob of animated clay, crawling between the separated lovers and pawing at both, is a poignant illustration that the self after a loving communion with another self can be *less* than itself. His is a very different version of the incomplete self from Bakhtin's: something of the self has been left behind in interaction, and this is not necessarily a positive thing (as the fact that the lovers refuse to enter into further dialogue, but prefer instead to tear each other apart, dramatises).

All in all, then, Švankmajer's 'Passionate Discourse' sees love and dialogue as an uneasy pair. The self in both is vulnerable and responds to this vulnerability with violence. It has been claimed that 'when the erotic motif is directly expressed in Švankmajer's work, it is always at the same time contaminated ... by its own negation'.[25] In this film, much the same might be said of the dialogue motif. And, since Bakhtin's thought is not troubled by such a contamination, 'Passionate Discourse' accordingly advises us to be cautious of its optimism.

Part Three: Factual conversation

Clay oozes from a drawer in a table. The mass separates and congeals to form two identical human heads, who face each other across the tabletop. Through the mouth of one emerges a toothbrush, which is proffered to the other. The other's mouth produces a tube of toothpaste, squeezing some onto the other's brush, whereupon the objects retract into the mouths. Similar interactions follow: a slice of bread is proffered by one mouth, and is buttered by a knife emerging from the other; an unlaced shoe appears from one and is threaded by a shoelace from the other; a blunt pencil appears, and a pencil sharpener, wielded by a grotesque tongue, sharpens it. Then there is a pause as the two heads change places. In the second 'phase', the same objects appear, but in more awkward pairings: the slice of bread is toothpasted, the toothbrush sharpened, the shoe is buttered, the pencil tied up by a lace, the bread sharpened, the shoe toothpasted, the pencil buttered and so forth. These pairings become ever less successful: the toothpaste and butter knife try to smother each other, for example. When these pairings are exhausted, the heads change places once again, now visibly exhibiting large cracks around the mouth. In the third 'phase', each object confronts an identical object and does animated battle with it: two shoelaces tie each other into a tangle; two butter knives fence with each other; two sharpeners try to sharpen one another, and so forth. After all eight battles result in the objects' mutual destruction, we see the two clay heads, cracked to the point of disintegration, their grotesque tongues panting from the effort.

Commentators on Švankmajer's films have again seen in this final episode of *Dimensions of Dialogue* a parable that is essentially philosophical:[26]

> The final 'movement' of *Dimensions of Dialogue* ... is a tour de force both of animated technique and of conceptual argument. Here Švankmajer achieves a genuine synthesis of sensation and idea, tossing out tactile and visual impressions in abundance while assaulting the viewer's mind with intellectual riddles. As a ... meditation on taxonomies and the organisation of knowledge, it is most stimulating and lucid. I find it a most telling example of an argument sustained by moving images.[27]

So what, then, is the philosophical content of this filmic parable? Here is one suggestion:

> its object permutations have a tactile matter-of-factness which derides rationality, whilst at the same time appealing to a certain logic. It is as if Švankmajer were pondering the limits of commonsense association and assertion, using everyday objects as a way to query our human habits, both of material usage and of thought. Each morning, we 'think nothing' of squeezing toothpaste onto a brush, or of spreading butter on bread. (Cardinal, 1995, pp. 90–1)

What is being overlooked in this reading, once again, is the film's manifest concern with the idea of dialogue: after all, these everyday objects, many of them tools, appear through the mouths of two interlocutors. And the notion of everyday language as a set of tools acting in (and on) ordinary usage and patterns of thought finds a clear analogue in the philosophy of Ludwig Wittgenstein:

> §11. Think of the tools in a tool-box: there is a hammer, pliers, a saw, a screw-driver, a rule, a glue-pot, glue, nails and screws. – The functions of words are as diverse as the functions of these objects. (And in both cases there are similarities.)
>
> Of course, what confuses us is the uniform appearance of words when we hear them spoken or meet them in script and print. For their *application* is not presented to us so clearly. Especially when we are doing philosophy![28]

There is a striking amount of common ground here. The first 'phase' of this episode of Švankmajer's film effectively dramatises the most familiar theme of Wittgenstein's thought: linguistic interaction as a remarkable set of implements that we use to get things done. It also conveys a tension similar to Wittgenstein's preoccupation with the everyday: the components of linguistic conventions are perfectly ordinary, everyday objects, yet we should never forget that even at its most ordinary, language is a truly *extra*ordinary thing. Švankmajer relays this sheer extraordinariness through his remarkable dramatisation of Wittgenstein's 'tool' metaphor: the mouths literally spout everyday objects and perform everyday jobs with them.

Yet Švankmajer is not simply concerned with a philosophy of ordinary language – and neither, of course, is Wittgenstein. 'Factual Conversation's second 'phase' soon turns into a meditation on linguistic extraordinariness. As Roger Cardinal has it:

> As an affront to commonsense, this perverse algebra of improper equations is most upsetting, for we are asked to digest not only the unsuitable pairings but also the filmmaker's jovial attempts to make them 'work'. For when the butter-knife meets the shoe, its response is to spread it with butter; the shoelace knots itself suavely round the pencil; the tube of toothpaste enters the pencil-sharpener and is sharpened until its contents ooze disgustingly forth. (Cardinal, 1995, p. 90)

The film seems to be asking us: how can we think language through when ordinary circumstances give out, when the tools and conventions of everyday language do *not* get the job done? Put simply, what happens when we talk at cross-purposes?

Whilst, visually at least, this 'phase' suggests a devastating philosophical challenge to the Wittgensteinian tool metaphor, it is not the thoroughgoing critique it seems. There are many moments in Wittgenstein's thought where he anticipates Švankmajer's scepticism about the straightforwardness of conventional everyday dialogue:

> What is it like for people not to have the same sense of humour? They do not react properly to each other. It's as though there were a custom amongst certain people for one person to throw another a ball which he is suppose to catch and throw back; but some people, instead of throwing it back, put it in their pocket.

In a conversation: One person throws a ball; the other does not know: whether he is supposed to throw it back, or throw it to a third person, or leave it on the ground, or pick it up and put it in his pocket, etc.[29]

These passages, similar to the second 'phase' of 'Factual Conversation', convey the sense of oddity, confusion, and shock that arises when the everyday conventions of ordinary language break down, when inter-locutors 'get their wires crossed', and in effect no longer play the same language game. Švankmajer and Wittgenstein recognise that the con-ventions that make our language work can frequently cause the kinds of problems they normally solve: theirs is a philosophical vision of lan-guage and dialogue that makes room for disagreement and misunder-standing. As Wittgenstein says, 'If agreement were universal, we should be quite unacquainted with the concept of it'.[30]

The third 'phase' of 'Factual Conversation', however, offers a more radical challenge to any philosophy of dialogue. In it, like confronts like (as in 'Exhaustive Discussion') with destructive consequences, in a typically Švankmajerian downward spiral of violence and destruction. By showing shoe confronting shoe, toothbrush confronting tooth-brush etc., the film invites us to contemplate a vision of linguistic chaos in which the tool-kit of everyday speech can achieve nothing, to imagine a language in which questions are simply met with more ques-tions, assertions with counter-assertions, orders countermanded with conflicting orders. Wittgenstein remarks that 'Orders are sometimes not obeyed. But what would it be like if no orders were *ever* obeyed? The concept 'order' would have lost its purpose'.[31] Yet this is precisely the kind of situation Švankmajer's film is asking us to contemplate.

Perhaps this is why *Dimensions of Dialogue* was originally received as a politically subversive film: Švankmajer remarks that on its release (and instant banning) in 1982, it 'was shown to the ideology commis-sion of the Central Committee of the Czechoslovak Communist Party as an example of what had to be avoided.'[32] The sequence is certainly a meditation on a theme of non-conformism. In Wittgenstein's terms, it shows not just the bending and breaking of rules and conventions: it challenges them outright. Roger Cardinal compares it to Surrealist poetry in its advocating apparently bizarre experimentation with everyday items as a positive moment of playful liberation.[33] However, the final vision of mutual destruction leads one to question whether Švankmajer implies such a challenge is a wholeheartedly positive thing. It results, after all, in the end of the dialogue and even the end of the speakers.

There is, no doubt, an ambivalence that runs through Švankmajer's film: dialogue is represented as both creative and destructive. A similar ambivalence permeates much of Wittgenstein's later thought, where language appears both as a means of philosophical confusion and clarification. A remark of Cardinal's suggests that a methodological ambivalence lies at the very heart of 'Factual Conversation': 'it nags at the mind as a demonstration as much of the admirable rigour as of the ultimate lunacy of systematic intellectual procedures' (Cardinal, 1995, p. 91). Much the same could be said of Wittgenstein's *Philosophical Investigations*. Given this ambivalence, how are we to read *Dimensions of Dialogue*?

There are, of course, a host of possible readings, none of them definitive:

> Philosophically speaking, ... *Dimensions of Dialogue* [makes] a case for supposing that contingent reality can never really keep pace with man's alternative readings and constructions, his hypotheses and ultimately his illusions. (Cardinal, p. 92)

Yet it is possible to go further than this. Nowhere more clearly than in the destructive climaxes of the three episodes can it be seen that Švankmajer is concerned as much as anything with the *limits* of language, dialogue, and communication. This concern once more aligns him alongside Wittgenstein, yet Švankmajer, by consciously rejecting language and using wordless visual metaphors instead, is able to gesture far more effectively towards these limits (and what lies beyond them) than could ever be achieved in any form of philosophical writing. In philosophy, as Wittgenstein regularly reminds us, we are constantly running up against the limits of what can be said. Švankmajer, instead, explores these limits through what can be shown.

That is why, in philosophical terms, Švankmajer's films are 'irreducible to a set of principles' (Hames 1995, p. 63). Yet nevertheless, 'In *Dimensions of Dialogue*, ... the overriding tendency is towards the abstraction of meaning' (*Ibid.*, p. 123), even if that meaning is ultimately withheld. Accordingly, Švankmajer's films are films that 'do' philosophy. They inevitably tempt us towards philosophical insight. Yet, just as inevitably, they frustrate us in our attempts to apprehend it. Perhaps, ultimately, this is what makes the invitation to read them philosophically so tempting.

Notes

1. Jan Švankmajer, *Švankmajer* (2 Vols), Argos Films/British Film Institute/ Connoisseur Video, 1991.
2. *Dark Alchemy: the Films of Jan Švankmajer*, ed. Peter Hames, 1995. Hereafter *DA*.
3. Roger Cardinal has made a similar claim about viewing Švankmajer's films as philosophical argumentation: 'Seen in terms of a signifying practice or expressive discourse, ... [t]he completed film is a sequence of visual para- graphs composed of sentences whose often irrational content is (as in Surrealist poetry) held tight within the syntax of the rhythmic exposures of the camera. It is in this sense that ... Švankmajer's films constitute a visual argument, a way of thinking, in which ideas are articulated through objects instead of words.' See his 'Thinking through things: the presence of objects in the early films of Jan Švankmajer', pp. 78–95 in *DA*.
4. Emmanuel Levinas, *Totality and Infinity: An Essay on Exteriority* (1969), p. 295. Hereafter *TI*.
5. To describe Levinas's thought as dialogical might invite controversy: certainly, its most important aspects are conceived of as prior to, and tran- scendent of, the medium of language. However, for a convincing 'dialogical' reading of Levinas, see Michael Eskin 2000.
6. 'The way in which the other presents himself, exceeding *the idea of the other in me*, we here name face.' (*TI*, p. 50).
7. For this assertion, see Levinas, 1990.
8. 'The face is present in its refusal to be contained. In this sense it cannot be comprehended, that is, encompassed.' (*TI*, p. 194)
9. Jill Robbins, 1999, pp. 67–8.
10. According to Michael Eskin, Levinas's use of the word 'face' ('*visage*') derives from the verb *viser*, the French translation of Husserl's 'to intend'. Not that I intend the face of the Other: rather, the face is what does the intending. The face intends me. Whether I can intend the destruction of the face of the Other without intending my own self-destruction is thus an important question. See Eskin, 2000, pp. 48–9.
11. See 'Interview with Jan Švankmajer', pp. 96–118 in *DA*, p. 109.
12. The problematics of violence within the economy of the Same and the Other are brilliantly discussed by Jacques Derrida in his 'Violence and Metaphysics: An Essay on the Thought of Emmanuel Levinas', pp. 79–153 in Derrida (1978).
13. Derrida, 1978, p. 128.
14. *DA*, p. 122, p. 147.
15. Some may object that Bakhtin's work is literary/cultural criticism or theory rather than philosophy. However, as we shall see, this is not true of his early philosophical work, and his later work resists such disciplinary bound- aries. In Bakhtin, 'criticism and theory become the pursuit of philosophy by other means', Gary Saul Morson and Caryl Emerson 1990, p. 32.
16. Mikhail Bakhtin, *The Dialogic Imagination: Four Essays*, 1981, p. 279. Hereafter *DI*.
17. Bakhtin, *Problems of Dostoevsky's Poetics*, 1984, p. 237. Hereafter *PDP*.
18. Bakhtin, *Towards a Philosophy of the Act*, 1994, p. 6.
19. For this argument, see Katerina Clark and Michael Holquist, 'The Influence of Kant in the Early Work of M.M. Bakhtin', pp. 299–313 in J.P. Strelka,

1984. See also their *Mikhail Bakhtin*, 1984. For a different view, see Michael Bernard-Donals, *Mikhail Bakhtin: Between Phenomenology and Marxism*, 1994, and his 'Bakhtin and Phenomenology: A Reply to Gary Saul Morson', 1995.

20. See Bakhtin, *Art and Answerability: Early Philosophical Essays*, 1990. Hereafter *AA*.

21. Caryl Emerson, 1988, p. 514.

22. Emerson, 1988, p. 517. I am aware that this characterisation of Bakhtinian theory is contentious, since his valorisation of the linguistic 'struggle' carried on in dialogue is central to many critical theorists' readings of his thought. Yet the 'struggle' he envisions still involves mutual participation and inter-illumination. For discussions of Bakhtin's thought as less discordant than it appears, see Andrew Gibson, 1996, pp. 151–6, and Chapter Four of my unpublished PhD thesis, *Wittgenstein and the Theory of Narrative*, University of London, 2000.

23. Quoted in Gary Saul Morson and Caryl Emerson (eds), 1989, p. 155 Michael Bernard-Donals even argues that for Bakhtin, such a state of fusion is impossible. See Bernard-Donals, 1994, p. 30.

24. Bernard-Donals, 1994, p. 25.

25. *DA*, p. 150. 'Whether a film by Švankmajer contains black farce, blasphemy or tragedy, the erotic meaning is always shown in its negative aspect ... The destructive obsession which permeates all Švankmajer's films is ... the destruction of the object of love and, at the same time, self-destruction as a defining, dominant feature of the erotic relationship. In 'Dialogue Passionate' the couple ... go through the motions of love in which passion devours and penetrates, but also aggressively devours the loved creature.' *DA*, p. 147.

26. Švankmajer 'creates a kind of unity between the world and ideas ... in the abstract form of the parable ... in the third episode of the film' *DA*, p. 122.

27. Roger Cardinal, 'Thinking through things: the presence of objects in the early films of Jan Švankmajer' in *DA*, pp. 89–90.

28. Wittgenstein, 1953.

29. Wittgenstein, 1980, p. 83, p. 74.

30. Wittgenstein, 1988, §430.

31. Wittgenstein 1953, §345.

32. 'Interview with Jan Švankmajer', in *DA*, p. 100. For Švankmajer's fascinating reflections on his clashes with authority and censorship, see *DA*, pp. 115–6.

33. See Cardinal, 1995, p. 91.

Calm: On Terrence Malick's *The Thin Red Line*[1]

Simon Critchley

Life contracts and death is expected,
As in a season of autumn.
The soldier falls.

He does not become a three-days personage,
Imposing his separation,
Calling for pomp.

Death is absolute and without memorial,
As in a season of autumn,
When the wind stops,

When the wind stops and, over the heavens,
The clouds go, nevertheless,
In their direction.

Wallace Stevens, 'The Death of a Soldier'

Wittgenstein asks a question, which sounds like the first line of a joke: How does one philosopher address another? To which the unfunny and perplexing riposte is, 'Take your time'.[2] Terrence Malick is evidently someone who takes his time. Since his first movie, *Badlands,* was premiered at the New York Film Festival in 1973, he has directed just two more: *Days of Heaven,* in 1979, and then nearly a 20 year gap until the long-awaited 1998 movie, *The Thin Red Line,* which is the topic of this essay.

It is a war film. It deals with the events surrounding the battle for Guadalcanal in November 1942, as the US Army fought its bloody way north across the islands of the South Pacific against ferocious Japanese resistance. But it is a war film in the same way that Homer's *Iliad* is a war poem. The viewer seeking verisimilitude and documentation of historical fact will be disappointed. Rather, Malick's movie is a story of what we might call 'heroic fact': of death, of fate, of pointed and pointless sacrifice. Finally, it is a tale of love, both erotic love and, more importantly, the love of compassion whose cradle is military combat and whose greatest fear is dishonour. In one night-time scene, we see Captain Starros in close-up praying, 'Let me not betray my men'.

The ambition of *The Thin Red Line* is unapologetically epic, the scale is not historical but mythical, and the language is lyrical, even at times metaphysical. At one point in the film, Colonel Tall, the commanding officer of the campaign, cites a Homeric epithet about 'rosy-fingered dawn', and confesses to the Greek-American Starros that he read the *Iliad* in Greek whilst a student at West Point military academy – Starros himself speaks Greek on two occasions. Like the *Iliad*, Malick deals with the huge human themes by focussing not on a whole war, and not even with an overview of a whole battle, but on the lives of a group of individuals – C-for-Charlie company – in a specific aspect of a battle over the period of a couple of weeks.

To non-Americans – and perhaps to many contemporary Americans as well – the significance of Guadalcanal might not be familiar. It was the key battle in the war against Japan, in a campaign that led from the attack on Pearl Harbor in 1941 to American victory and post-war imperial hegemony. If we cast the Japanese in the role of the Trojans, and Guadalcanal in the place of Troy, then *The Thin Red Line* might be said to recount the pre-history of American empire in the same way as Homer recites the pre-history of Hellenic supremacy. It might be viewed as a founding myth, and like all such myths, from Homer to Virgil to Milton, it shows both the necessity for an enemy in the act of founding and the often uncanny intimacy with that enemy. Some of the most haunting images of the film are those in which members of Charlie company sit face-to-face with captured Japanese soldiers surrounded by corpses, mud, and the dehumanising detritus of battle.

Malick based his screenplay on James Jones' 500 page, 1963 novel, *The Thin Red Line*.[3] Jones served as an infantryman in the US Army in the South Pacific, and *The Thin Red Line,* though fictional, is extensively based on Jones' wartime experiences. Jones was following the formula he established in his first book, the 900 page, 1952 raw blockbuster, *From Here to Eternity*, which deals with events surrounding the bombing of Pearl Harbor.[4] A highly expurgated version of *From Here to Eternity,* starring Burt Lancaster, Deborah Kerr, Montgomery Clift and

Frank Sinatra, won the Academy Award for Best Motion Picture in 1953. Malick's movie won just one Oscar, to Hans Zimmer, for best original score.

A curious fact to note about Malick's *The Thin Red Line* is that it is a remake. Jones' book was turned into a movie directed by Andrew Marton and starring Keir Dullea and Jack Warden in 1964. This is a low budget, technically clumsy, averagely acted, and indeed slightly saucy movie, where the jungles of the South Pacific have been replanted in Spain, where the picture was shot. But it is a good honest picture, and there are many analogues with Malick's version, particularly the dialogues between Colonel Tall and Captain Stein.

The narrative focus of the 1964 picture is on Private Doll who is an independently-minded existentialist rebel, closer to a young Brando than Albert Camus, who discovers himself in the heat of battle through killing 'Japs'. The guiding theme is the insanity of war, the thin red line between the sane and the mad, and we are offered a series of more or less trite reflections on the meaninglessness of war. Yet, in this respect, the 1964 film is much more faithful to James Jones's 1963 novel than Malick's treatment, with its more metaphysical intimations. In the 1964 movie, the existential hero finds himself through the act of killing. War is radical meaninglessness, but it is that in relation to which meaning can be given to an individual life. Doll eventually crosses the thin red line and goes crazy, killing everyone in sight, including his own comrades.

The novel is a piece of tough-minded and earnest Americana, somewhere between fiction and reportage, that at times brilliantly evokes the exhausting and dehumanising pointlessness of war. The book's great virtue is its evocation of camaraderie, the physical and emotional intensity of the relations between the men in C-for-Charlie company. Some of the characters are finely and fully drawn, in particular Fife, Doll and Bell, but I don't think it is too severe to say that James Jones is not James Joyce. Yet, in this regard, the novel serves Malick's purposes extremely well because it provides him with the raw narrative prime matter from which to form his screenplay. For example, the central protagonist of Malick's version, Witt, brilliantly played by Jim Caviezel, is a more marginal figure in Jones' novel. He drifts repeatedly in and out of the action, having been transferred from Charlie company to Cannon company, which is a collection of brigands and reprobates, but he is eventually readmitted to Charlie company because of his exceptional valour in battle. He is depicted as a stubborn, single-minded, half-educated troublemaker from Breathitt County, Kentucky, motivated by racism, a powerful devotion to his comrades, and an obscure ideal of honour. Although there is an essential solitude to Witt's character that must have appealed to Malick, the latter transforms him into a much more angelic, self-questioning, philosophical figure. Indeed, the culminating action of Malick's film is Witt's death, which does not even occur in the novel, where he is shown at the end of the book finally reconciled with Fife, his former buddy. Fife is the central driving character of Jones' novel, together with Doll, Bell and Welsh. I have been informed that Malick shot about seven hours of film, but had to cut it to three hours to meet his contract. Therefore, the whole story of Fife – and doubtless much else – was cut out. Other of Malick's characters are inventions, like Captain Starros, the Greek who takes the place of the Jewish Captain Stein. And, interestingly, there are themes in the novel that Malick does not take up, such as the homosexual relations between comrades, in particular Doll's emerging acknowledgement of his gay sexuality.

It would appear that Malick has a very free relation to his material. But appearances can be deceptive. For Jones, there was a clear thematic and historical continuity between *From Here to Eternity* and *The Thin Red Line* and Malick respects that continuity by integrating passages and characters from the former book into his screenplay. For example, the character of Colonel Tall is lifted from the earlier novel and, more importantly, Prewitt in *From Here To Eternity* becomes fused with Witt, becoming literally pre-Witt. As Jimmie E. Cain has shown in an invaluable article, Prewitt's speculations about his mother's death and the question of immortality are spoken by Witt in the important opening scenes of *The Thin Red Line*. After having repeatedly consulted Gloria Jones, the late novelist's wife, about the slightest changes from novel to screenplay, she apparently remarked, 'Terry, you have my husband's voice, you're writing in his musical key; now what you must do is improvise. Play riffs on this'.[5]

Malick crafts the matter of Jones' work into a lyrical, economical and highly wrought screenplay. Whilst there are many memorable passages of dialogue, and some extraordinarily photographed extended action sequences, the core of the film is carried by Malick's favourite cinematic technique, the voiceover. This is worth considering in some detail, for, as Michael Filippidis has argued, the voiceover provides the entry point for all three of Malick's films.[6] In *Badlands*, the voiceovers are provided by Holly (Sissy Spacek), and in *Days of Heaven* by the child Linda (Linda Manz). The technique of the voiceover allows the character to assume a distance from the cinematic action and a complicity with the audience, an intimate distance that is meditative, ruminative, at times speculative. It is like watching a movie with someone whispering into your ear.

If the technique of the voiceover is common to all three films, then what changes in *The Thin Red Line,* is the subject of the narration. *Badlands* and *Days of Heaven* are narrated from a female perspective and it is through the eyes of two young, poorly-educated women that we are invited to view the world. In *The Thin Red Line*, the voiceovers are male and plural. The only female characters are the wife of Bell who appears in dream sequences and whose only words are 'Come out. Come out where I am'; the young Melanesian mother that Witt meets at the beginning of the film; and the recollected scene of Witt's mother's death-bed. Although it is usually possible to identify the speaker of the voiceover, their voices sometimes seem to blend into one another, particularly during the closing scenes of the film when the soldiers are leaving Guadalcanal on board a landing craft. As the camera roams from face to face, almost drunkenly, the voices become one voice, one soul, 'as if all men got one big soul' – but we will come back to this.

The Thin Red Line is words with music. The powerful effect of the voiceovers cannot be distinguished from that of the music which accompanies them. The score, which bears sustained listening on its own account, was composed by Hans Zimmer, who collaborated extensively with Malick. The latter's use of music in his movies is at times breathtaking, and the structure of his films bears a close relation to musical composition, where leitmotifs function as both punctuation and recapitulation of the action – a technique Malick employed to great effect in *Days of Heaven*. In all three of his movies, there is a persistent presence of natural sounds, particularly flowing water and birdsong. The sound of the breeze in the vast fields of ripening wheat in *Days of Heaven* finds a visual echo in what was the most powerful memory I had from my first viewing of *The Thin Red Line*: the sound of the wind and soldiers' bodies moving through the Kunai grass as Charlie company ascend the hill towards the enemy position. Nature appears as an impassive and constant presence that frames human conflict.

Three hermeneutic banana skins

There are a number of hermeneutic banana skins that any study of Malick's art can slip up on, particularly when the critic is a professional philosopher. Before turning more directly to the film, let me take my time to discuss three of them.

First, there is what we might call the paradox of privacy. Malick is clearly a very private person who shuns publicity. This is obviously no easy matter in the movie business, and in this regard Malick invites comparison with Kubrick who, by contrast, appears a paragon of productivity. Of course, the relative paucity of biographical data on Malick simply feeds a curiosity of the most trivial and quotidian kind. I must confess to this curiosity myself, but I do not think it should be sated. There should be no speculation, then, on 'the enigmatic Mr Malick', or whatever.

But if one restricts oneself to the biographical information that I have been able to find out, then a second banana skin appears in one's path, namely the intriguing issue of Malick and philosophy. He studied philosophy at Harvard University between 1961 and 1965, graduating with Phi Beta Kappa honours. He worked closely with Stanley Cavell, who supervised Malick's undergraduate honours thesis. Against the deeply-ingrained prejudices about Continental thought that prevailed at that time, Malick courageously attempted to show how Heidegger's thoughts about (and against) epistemology in *Being and Time* could be seen in relation to the analysis of perception in Russell, Moore and, at Harvard, C.I. Lewis. Malick then went, as a Rhodes scholar, to Magdalen College, Oxford, to study for the B.Phil in philosophy. He left Oxford because he wanted to write a D.Phil thesis on the concept of world in Kierkegaard, Heidegger and Wittgenstein, and was told by Gilbert Ryle that he should try and write on something more 'philosophical'. He then worked as a philosophy teacher at MIT, teaching Hubert Dreyfus's course on Heidegger when he was away on study leave in France, and wrote journalism for *The New Yorker* and *Life* magazine. In 1969, he published his bilingual edition of Heidegger's *Vom Wesen des Grundes* as *The Essence of Reasons*.[7] Also in 1969 he was accepted into the inaugural class of the Center for Advanced Film Studies at the American Film Institute, in Los Angeles, and his career in cinema began to take shape.

Clearly, then, Malick's is a highly sophisticated, philosophically trained intellect. Yet the young philosopher decided not to pursue an academic career, but to pass from philosophy to film, for reasons that remain obscure. Given these facts, it is extremely tempting – almost overwhelmingly so – to read through his films to some philosophical pre-text or meta-text, to interpret the action of his characters in Heideggerian, Wittgensteinian or, indeed, Cavellian terms. To make matters worse, Malick's movies seem to make philosophical statements and present philosophical positions. Nonetheless, to read through the cinematic image to some identifiable philosophical master text would be a mistake, for it would be not to read at all.

So, what is the professional philosopher to do when faced with Malick's films? This leads me to a third hermeneutic banana skin. To read from cinematic language to some philosophical meta-language is both to miss what is specific to the medium of film and usually to engage in some sort of cod-philosophy deliberately designed to intimidate the uninitiated. I think this move has to be avoided on philosophical grounds, indeed the very best Heideggerian grounds. Any philosophical reading of film has to be a reading *of* film, of what Heidegger would call *der Sache selbst,* the thing itself. A philosophical reading of film should not be concerned with ideas about the thing, but with the thing itself, the cinematic *Sache.* It seems to me that a consideration of Malick's art demands that we take seriously the idea that film is less an illustration of philosophical ideas and theories – let's call that a *philoso-fugal* reading–and more a form of philosophising, of reflection, reasoning and argument.[8]

Loyalty, love, and truth

Let me now turn to the film itself. The narrative of *The Thin Red Line* is organised around three relationships, each composed of a conflict between two characters. The first relationship is that between Colonel Tall, played by Nick Nolte, and Captain Starros, played by Elias Koteas. At the core of this relationship is the question of loyalty, a conflict between loyalty to the commands of one's superiors and loyalty to the men under one's command. This relationship comes to a crisis when Starros refuses a direct order from Tall to lead an attack on a machine-gun position of the Japanese. Starros says that 'I've lived with these men for two and a half years, and I will not order them to their deaths' – for the carnage that the Japanese are causing from their superior hill-top vantage point and the scenes of slaughter are truly awful. Suppressing his fury, Tall goes up the line to join Charlie company and skilfully organises a flanking assault on the Japanese position. After the successful assault, he gives Starros a humiliating lecture about the necessity of allowing one's men to die in battle. He decides that Starros is not tough-minded enough to lead his men and, after recommending him for the silver star and the purple heart, immediately relieves him of his commission and orders him back to a desk job in Washington D.C.

Loyalty to the men under one's command must be subservient to the pragmatics of the battlefield.

The second relationship, based on love, is that between Private Bell (Ben Chaplin), and his wife Marty (Miranda Otto), and is dealt with rather abstractly by Malick. It is much more central to the 1964 version of the film, where it is transposed into the relationship between Private Doll and one 'Judy'. In Jones's novel, Bell is a former army officer who had been a First Lieutenant in the Philippines. He and his wife had an extraordinarily close, intense relationship ('We were always very sexual together', he confesses to Fife), and after spending four months separated from his wife in the jungle, he decided that he'd had enough and resigned his commission. As retribution, the US Army said that they would make sure he was drafted, and, moreover, drafted into the infantry as a private. All that we see of the relationship in the film, however, are a series of dream images of Bell with Marty, what Jones calls 'weird transcendental images of Marty's presence'. Then, after the battle, we hear Bell reading a letter from his wife saying that she has left him for an Air Force captain.

After the failures of loyalty and love, the theme of truth is treated in the third relationship, and this is what I would like to concentrate on. The characters here are Sergeant Welsh, played with consummate craft by Sean Penn, and Private Witt. The question at issue here is metaphysical truth; or, more precisely, whether there is such a thing as metaphysical truth. Baldly stated: is this the only world, or is there another world? The conflict is established in the first dialogue between the two soldiers, after Witt has been incarcerated for going AWOL in a Melanesian village, in the scenes of somewhat cloying communal harmony that open the film. Welsh says, 'in this world, a man himself is nothing...and there ain't no world but this one'. To which Witt replies, 'You're wrong there, I seen another world. Sometimes I think it's just my imagination'. And Welsh completes the thought: 'Well, you're seeing something I never will'.

Welsh is a sort of physicalist egoist who is contemptuous of everything. Jones writes,

> Everything amused Welsh...Politics amused him, religion amused him, particularly ideals and integrity amused him; but most of all human virtue amused him. He did not believe in it and did not believe in any of those other words. (p. 24)

Behind this complete moral nihilism, the only thing in which Welsh believes is property. He refuses to let Starros commend him for a silver star after an act of extraordinary valour in which he dodged hails of bullets to give morphine to a buddy dying on the battlefield, and quips, 'Property, the whole fucking thing's about property'. War is fought for property, one nation against another nation. The war is taking place in service of a lie, the lie of property. You either believe the lie or you die, like Witt. Welsh says – and it is a sentiment emphasised in the book and both versions of the film – 'Everything is a lie. Only one thing a man can do, find something that's his, make an island for himself'. It is only by believing that, and shutting his eyes to the bloody lie of war, that he can survive. Welsh's physicalism is summarised in the phrase that in many ways guides the 1964 version of the film and which appears briefly in Malick: 'It's only meat'. The human being is meat and only this belief both exposes the lie and allows one to survive – and Welsh survives.

Facing Welsh's nihilistic physicalism is what we might call Witt's Emersonian metaphysical panpsychism, caught in the question, 'Maybe all men got one big soul, that everybody's a part of – all faces are the same man, one big self'. Witt is the questioner, the contemplator, the mystic, perhaps even the holy fool. Much of what he says is in the form of questions – the very piety of thinking for Heidegger – and not the assertions propounded by Welsh. Unflinchingly brave in combat, with absolutely no thought of his own safety and prepared to sacrifice himself for his comrades, Witt views all things and persons with an impassive constancy, and sees beauty and goodness in all things. Where Welsh sees only the pain caused by human selfishness, Witt looks at the same scenes and feels the glory. He is like a redemptive angel looking into the souls of soldiers and seizing hold of their spark. It is this metaphysical commitment which fuels both Witt's selfless courage in combat and his compassion for the enemy. In one of the most moving scenes of the film, he looks into the face of a dead Japanese soldier, half-buried in the dirt – which speaks to him with a prophecy of his own fate – 'Are you loved by all? Know that I was. Do you imagine that your sufferings will be less because you loved goodness, truth?' In their final dialogue, Witt says that he still sees a spark in Sergeant Welsh. The truth is, I think, that Welsh is half in love with Witt, and behind his nihilism there is a grudging but total respect for Witt's commitment. Welsh cannot believe what Witt believes, he cannot behold the glory. And yet, he is also unable to feel nothing, to feel numb to the suffering that surrounds him. As a consequence, he is in profound pain. In tears, at the foot of Witt's grave, Welsh asks, 'Where's your spark now?', which might as well be a question to himself.

As in the two other relationships, there seems to be a clear winner and loser. As Welsh predicts in their second dialogue, the reward for Witt's metaphysical commitment will be death. Loyalty to one's men leads to dismissal from one's position, loyalty in love leads to betrayal, and loyalty to a truth greater than oneself leads to death. Yet, Malick is too intelligent to make didactic art. Truth consists in the conflict, or series of conflicts, between positions; and in watching those conflicts unravel, we are instructed, deepened. This conflict is particularly clear in the depiction of war itself. For this is not simply an anti-war film and has none of the post-adolescent bombast of Francis Ford Coppola's *Apocalypse Now* (1979), the cloying self-righteousness of Oliver Stone's *Platoon* (1986), or the gnawing, sentimental nationalism of *Saving Private Ryan* (1998). One of the voiceovers states, 'War don't ennoble men. It turns them into dogs. Poisons the soul.' But this view has to be balanced with a central message of the film: namely, that there is a total risk of the self in battle, an utter emptying of the self, that does not produce egoism, but rather a powerful bond of compassionate love for one's comrades and even for one's enemy. The inhumanity of war lets one see through the fictions of a people, a tribe or a nation towards a common humanity. The imponderable question is why it should require such suffering to bring us to this recognition.

Immortality

I would like to stay a little longer with the character of Witt and con-sider in detail one scene from the movie, namely the instant of his death. Witt, like all the male protagonists from Malick's previous movies, goes to his death with a sense of acceptance, willingness even. In *Badlands*, Kit (Martin Sheen), desires nothing more than the glorious notoriety of death and we assume at the end of the picture that he is going to be electrocuted. In *Days of Heaven*, the Farmer (Sam Shepherd) is told by his doctor that he is going to die, and it is this overheard conversation that prompts Bill (Richard Gere), into planning the deception of a marriage with his partner, Abby (Brooke Adams). After Gere stabs Shepherd to death in a smouldering wheat field, one has the sense that this is exactly what the Farmer desired. Similarly, when Bill is gunned down at the end of *Days of Heaven* – in an amazing shot photographed from underwater as his face hits the river – one has a powerful intimation of an ineluctable fate working itself out. In short, Malick's male protagonists seem to foresee their appointment with death and endeavour to make sure they arrive on time. Defined by a fatalistic presentiment of their demise, they are all somehow in love with death. Yet, such foreknowledge does not provoke fear and trembling; on the contrary, it brings, I will suggest, a kind of *calm*.

There is an utter recklessness to Witt and he repeatedly puts himself in situations of extreme danger. He is amongst the first to volunteer for the small unit that makes the highly dangerous flanking move to destroy the Japanese machine gun position, and the action that leads to his eventual death at the end of the film is very much of his own making. So, to this extent, Witt fits the death-bound pattern of Malick's male protagonists. Yet, what is distinctive about the character of Witt is that at the core of his sense of mortality lies the metaphysical question of immortality. This is established in the opening scenes of the movie in the Melanesian village, when he is shown talking to an unnamed comrade who has also gone AWOL. Against the recollected image of his mother's death-bed, he says,

> I remember my mother when she was dying, all shrunken and grey. I asked if she was afraid. She just shook her head. I was afraid to touch the death that I seen in her. I couldn't find anything beautiful or uplifting about her going back to God. I heard people talk about immortality, but I ain't never seen it.

The point here is that Witt is afraid of the death that descends over his mother, he can't touch it, find any comfort in it, or believe that it is the passage to her immortal home in bliss. Witt is then profiled standing on the beach, and he continues, less sceptically, and this time in a voiceover,

> I wondered how it'd be when I died. What it'd be like to know that this breath now was the last one you was ever gonna draw. I just hope I can meet it the same way she did, with the same...calm. Because that's where it's hidden, the immortality that I hadn't seen.

It is this pause between 'same' and 'calm' that I want to focus on, this breathing space for a last breath. For I think this calm is the key to the film and, more widely, to Malick's art. The metaphysical issue of the reality or otherwise of immortality obviously cannot be settled and that is not the point. The thought here is that the only immortality imaginable is found in a calm that can descend at the moment of death. The eternal life can only be imagined as inhabiting the instant of one's death, of knowing that this is the last breath that you are going to draw and not being afraid.[9]

With this in mind, let's look at the instant of Witt's death. Charlie Company are making their way, very precariously, up a river, and the whole scene, as elsewhere in Malick, is saturated with the sound of flowing river water. Phone lines back to HQ have been cut, enemy artillery fire is falling all around them and is getting steadily closer. The company is under the command of the peculiarly incompetent Lieutenant Band, who is leading them into an extremely exposed position where they will be sitting ducks for an enemy attack. Rather than retreating, as he should have done, Bard hurriedly decides to send a small scouting party up the river to judge the proximity of the enemy. He chooses the terrified Fife and the adolescent Coombs, and then Witt quickly volunteers himself. After progressing a little way up the river, they are seen by the enemy and Coombs is shot, but not fatally wounded. Witt sends Fife back to the company and the wounded Coombs floats back downstream. In an act of complete selflessness, Witt allows himself to be used as a decoy and leads off a squad of Japanese soldiers into the jungle. Witt then suddenly finds himself in a small clearing surrounded on all sides by some twenty Japanese troops. Breathless and motionless, he stands still whilst the Japanese squad leader screams at him, presumably demanding that he defend himself. Witt remains stock still, recovers his breath and then realises that he is going to die. The scene seems agonisingly long, the music slowly builds and there is a slow zoom into Witt's face. He is...calm. Then the camera slowly zooms out and there is a brief cutting shot of him half-heartedly raising his gun as he is gunned down. Malick then cuts to images of nature, of trees, water and birds.

What is one to make of this? Obvious philosophical parallels can be drawn here. For example, Heidegger's notion of *Angst* or anxiety is experienced with the presentiment of my mortality, what he calls *being-towards-death*. In one famous passage from the 1929 lecture, 'What is Metaphysics?', a text that Malick surely knows as it is directly contemporary with *The Essence of Reasons*, Heidegger is anxious to distinguish *Angst* from all sorts of fear and trembling. He says that the experience of *Angst* is a kind of *Ruhe*, peace or calm.[10] Similarly, in Blanchot's tantalisingly brief memoir, *L'instant de ma mort*, the seemingly autobiographical protagonist is described at the point of being executed by German soldiers, a fate from which he eventually escapes. He describes the feeling as 'un sentiment de légèreté extraordinaire, une sorte de béatitude'.[11] One also thinks of Wittgenstein's remark from the *Tractatus*, 'the eternal life belongs to those who live in the present'.[12] One could go on amassing examples. To interpret Malick's treatment of death in line with such thoughts is extremely tempting, but it would be to slip up on one or more of those hermeneutic banana skins discussed above. It would be to offer ideas about the thing rather than *der Sache Selbst*.

At the core of *The Thin Red Line*, then, is this experience of calm in the face of death, of a kind of peace at the moment of one's extinction that is the only place one may speak of immortality. This experience of calm frames the film and paradoxically provides the context for the bloody and cruel action of war. In particular, it frames the character of Welsh, who cares for Witt and his 'beautiful light' much more than he can admit, but persists to the end of the film in his belief that everything is a lie. His final words are, 'You're in a box, a moving box. They want you dead or in their lie'.

All things shining – the place of nature in Malick

Why do I claim that calm is the key to Malick's art? To try and tease this out, I would like to turn to the theme of nature, whose massive presence is the constant backdrop to Malick's movies. If calm in the face of mortality is the frame for the human drama of *The Thin Red Line*, then nature is the frame for this frame, a power that at times completely overshadows the human drama.

The Thin Red Line opens with the image of a huge crocodile slowly submerging into a weed-covered pond – the crocodile who makes a brief return appearance towards the end of the film, when he is shown captured by some men from Charlie company, who prod it abstractedly with a stick. Against images of jungle trees densely wrapped in suffocating vines, we hear the first words of the movie, spoken by an unidentified voice,

> What's this war in the heart of nature? Why does nature vie with itself, the land contend with the sea? Is there an avenging power in nature? Not one power, but two.

Obviously, the war in the heart of nature has a double meaning, suggesting both a war internal to nature, and the human war that is being fought out amid such immense natural beauty. These two meanings are brought together later in the film by Colonel Tall, when he is in the process of dismissing Starros from his commission and justifying the brutality of war,

> Look at this jungle, look at those vines, the way they twine around the trees, swallowing everything. Nature is cruel, Starros.

Images of trees wrapped in vines punctuate *The Thin Red Line*, together with countless images of birds, in particular owls and parrots. These images are combined with the almost constant presence of natural sounds, of birdsong, of the wind in the Kunai grass, of animals moving in the undergrowth and the sound of water, both waves lapping on the beach and the flowing of the river.

Nature might be viewed as a kind of *fatum* for Malick, an ineluctable power, a warring force that both frames human war but is utterly indifferent to human purposes and intentions. This beautiful indifference of nature can be linked to the depiction of nature elsewhere in Malick's work. For example, *Badlands* is teeming with natural sounds and images: with birds, dogs, flowing water, the vast flatness of South Dakota and the badlands of Montana, with its mountains in the distance – and always remaining in the distance. *Days of Heaven* is also heavily marked with natural sounds and exquisitely photographed images, with flowing river water, the wind moving in fields of ripening wheat and silhouetted human figures working in vast fields. Nature also possesses here an avenging power, when a plague of locusts descend on the fields and Sam Shepherd sets fire to the entire wheat-crop – nature is indeed cruel.

Although it is difficult not to grant that nature is playing a symbolic role for Malick, his is not an animistic conception of nature, of the kind that one finds lamented in Coleridge's 1802 'Dejection: An Ode': 'Oh Lady! We receive but what we give/And in our life alone does nature live'. Rather, in my opinion, nature's indifference to human purposes follows on from a broadly naturalistic conception of nature. Things are not enchanted in Malick's universe, they simply *are*, and we are things too. They are remote from us and continue on regardless of our strivings. This is what is suggested by the Wallace Stevens poem cited in epigraph to this essay. A soldier falls in battle, but his death does not invite pomp or transient glory. Rather, death has an absolute character, which Stevens likens to a moment in autumn when the wind stops. Yet, when the wind stops, above in the high heavens the clouds continue on their course, 'nevertheless,/In their direction'. What is central to Malick, I think, is this 'nevertheless'-ness of nature, of the fact that human death is absorbed into the relentlessness of nature, the eternal war in nature into which the death of a soldier is indifferently ingested. That's where Witt's spark lies.

There is a calm at the heart of Malick's art, a calmness to his cinematic eye, a calmness that is also communicated by his films, that becomes the mood of his audience: after watching *The Thin Red Line* we feel calm. As Charlie company leave Guadalcanal and are taken back to their ship on a landing craft, we hear the final voiceover from Witt, this time from beyond the grave,

> Oh my soul, let me be in you now. Look out through my eyes, look out at the things you made, all things shining.

In each of his movies, one has the sense of things simply being looked at, just being what they are – trees, water, birds, dogs, crocodiles or whatever. Things simply are, and are not moulded to a human purpose. We watch things shining calmly, being as they are, in all the intricate evasions of 'as'. The camera can be pointed at those things to try and capture some grain or affluence of their reality. The closing shot of *The Thin Red Line* presents the viewer with a coconut fallen onto the beach, against which a little water laps and out of which has sprouted a long green shoot, connoting life, one imagines. The coconut simply is, it merely lies there remote from us and our intentions. This suggests to me Stevens' final poem, 'The Palm at the End of the Mind', the palm that simply persists regardless of the makings of 'human meaning'. Stevens concludes, 'The palm stands on the edge of space. The wind moves slowly in its branches'. In my fancy at least, I see Malick concurring with this sentiment.

Notes

1. This text was originally prepared to introduce a screening of *The Thin Red Line* at Tate Modern, London, May 2002. An earlier version appeared in *Film-Philosophy*. I would like to thank Keith Ansell-Pearson, Nick Bunnin, Stanley Cavell, Jim Conant, Hubert Dreyfus, Jim Hopkins and Anne Latto for confirming and providing facts about Malick and also for helpful comments on my line of argument. I would also like to thank Espen Hammer for discussing *The Thin Red Line* with me, and Robert Lang for pointing out a number of infelicities in my first draft.
2. Wittgenstein (1980), p. 80.
3. Hodder & Stoughton, London, 1998 edition.
4. *Ibid.*
5. Cited in Jimmie E. Cain, Jr. (2000).
6. 'On Malick's Subjects', in *Senses of Cinema*, www.sensesofcinema.com, 2000.
7. Northwestern University Press, Evanston, 1969.

8. For a similar line of argument on the relation of philosophy to film, see Stephen Mulhall, 2002.
9. What is particularly intriguing is that the passages quoted above are lifted from a speech by Prewitt in *From Here to Eternity*. Jones writes,

> It was hard to accept that that he, who was the hub of this known universe, would cease to exist, but it was an inevitability and he did not shun it. He only hoped that he would meet it with the same magnificent indifference with which she who had been his mother met it. Because it was there, he felt, that the immortality he had not seen was hidden.

The question is why Malick replaces 'magnificent indifference' with 'calm'. This passage was brought to my attention by Cain's '"Writing in his Musical Key"', op. cit. p. 6.
10. Heidegger, 'What is Metaphysics?', in (1978), p. 102.
11. Blanchot, 1994.
12. Wittgenstein (1921), Proposition 6.4311.

Habitual Remarriage: The Ends of Happiness in *The Palm Beach Story*

Stuart Klawans

I begin with an observation that any number of readers must have made, that a thought is left dangling in Stanley Cavell's magisterial *Pursuits of Happiness: The Hollywood Comedy of Remarriage*. After Cavell drops an aside about Preston Sturges's *The Palm Beach Story* (1942), he at once passes on, never again to mention that remarkable film. I can't know what Cavell might have written about *The Palm Beach Story* had he not dismissed it so quickly – so suspiciously, one might say. But I now propose to tug on the loose end he left, to discover whether it will unravel part of his argument or instead lead through a labyrinth.

If I say that the all-too-casual mention of *The Palm Beach Story* is suspect, it's because no other film would seem more appropriate to a study of 'the comedy of remarriage.' Just on the level of plot, the film meets Cavell's elaborate and elastic criteria for the genre he has invented.

Very early in the picture, the airily self-confident Gerry (Claudette Colbert) announces that she no longer wants to be married to angry, failure-haunted Tom (Joel McCrea). Or perhaps she doesn't need to be married to him, or feels she shouldn't be. Her stated reasons for leaving are open to interpretation – but while Tom and the audience are busy interpreting, she takes off. What moral and social obstacles must Tom overcome to win her again? What experiences will convince her to give herself back to him? The plot's chief work is to answer these questions, once Tom gets past his helpless indecision and resolves to run after Gerry.

Already we're dealing with themes and situations that Cavell identifies as characteristic of the genre, primary among which is the explicit posing of the question: What constitutes a marriage? Is the glue merely the habit that two people form for one another? If so, and if the habits are bad (as Gerry says), then it's plausible to define marriage as something to be broken. But perhaps a true marriage is something more. Maybe it's something that Gerry and Tom will discover in one another through the course of the movie.

We know this something more must have to do with happiness, since Sturges refers to that condition explicitly, at the beginning of the picture. During the opening credits, he shows us a chaotic, as yet inexplicable affair, which turns out to be Gerry and Tom's wedding. Upon reaching the altar, the breathless pair are framed by a title, written in the script of a Valentine's Day card: 'And they lived happily ever after.' The camera then pulls back to reveal a second title: 'Or did they?' The soundtrack music imparts an aural sneer to this afterthought; but the question still demands an answer. We need to learn whether Gerry and Tom lived happily ever after: an 'ever' that covers not just the period beyond their marriage, but also the one after their break-up.

Now, the happiness that's at stake for Gerry and Tom has dimensions beyond the personal. Their circumstances suggest that it's a kind of Jeffersonian happiness, which America encourages them to pursue. So important is this theme to Cavell when it emerges in other comedies of remarriage that he writes it into the title of his book – another reason to be surprised that he neglects *The Palm Beach Story*.

Gerry's formal name is Mrs. Thomas Jeffers; and her husband, like the sage of Monticello, is a great improver. He knows that 'something is bound to come through' with his schemes, because he's got 'too many good ideas.' Nevertheless (as Gerry is not too delicate to mention), Thomas Jeffers has yet to achieve even one success – that is, a success in business – and for this shortcoming she blames herself, or at least claims to do so. She will therefore pursue happiness on her own, which to her means having it bestowed on her by men who have amassed wealth, or had it amassed for them by their grandfathers.

The first of her gift-givers, the Wienie King (Robert Dudley), is an elderly, brusquely candid little man, scarcely taller than his own black hat, who sets off the plot by handing Gerry seven hundred dollars and the impetus to abandon her husband. Having left, she will soon attract the attention of John D. Hackensacker 3rd (Rudy Vallee), who offers her far more costly presents, along with the prospect of remarriage as soon as her Palm Beach divorce is final. So Gerry's pursuit of happiness takes place within an America where people can enrich themselves, if they're canny enough. ('It's a good business,' says the Wienie King of his sausage-making, 'if you know where to buy the meat cheap.') This is also a society where the wealthy can spend freely – although they should do so within principled limits, as John D. Hackensacker firmly believes. He draws the line at tipping and the hiring of private railroad staterooms, both of which are 'un-American.'

As someone who knows herself to need money, and a lot of it, Gerry intends to make the most of the opportunities America provides. But, beyond that, she also needs to prove that she can create business opportunities for Tom. Her happiness depends upon his recognising that her good looks and ready wit are worth as much, in dollars, as his ideas. To be more precise: He must overcome his sexual jealousy and recognise that it's all right for her good looks and ready wit to have economic value.

Cavell's readers may now mark off another of his principal themes: the need for the man to acknowledge the woman's autonomy, and for her to see that he acknowledges it. Only by doing so will he make himself worthy of her, so that she may at last give herself to him. In the films discussed in *Pursuits of Happiness*, this mutual recognition requires a process of transformation, either in the woman or in the way the man views her, a process that Cavell sometimes calls 'the creation of a woman.' As in Genesis, this creation is accomplished through the word: the women in Cavell's comedies of remarriage are subjected to endless lectures. But in *The Palm Beach Story*, Gerry recognises her own value from the start – and so does Tom, evidently, since he chafes at it. What's more, Gerry is the one to do the lecturing, giving Tom several minutes of practical advice about the duties of helpmates and the role of sex in the business world.

Here, *The Palm Beach Story* diverges from the other films Cavell discusses. I intend to track that divergence – but before I do, I want to point out one more way in which this movie conforms to his model.

Cavell believes that movies are inherently self-referential; that they often toy with their own movieness by alluding to earlier films; that their stars are more vivid to us than the characters they portray. (We watch an adventure of Claudette Colbert, more than of Gerry Jeffers.) In its relationship to the Frank Capra-Robert Riskin movie *It Happened One Night* (1935), *The Palm Beach Story* confirms Cavell's ideas so strikingly that I wonder, why didn't he say so and take credit?

You will recall that in *It Happened One Night*, Claudette Colbert escaped from her father's yacht, then made her way overland from Florida to New York, travelling most of the way without money or luggage. I doubt it's mere coincidence that in *The Palm Beach Story*, Colbert escapes from a Park Avenue duplex, then makes her way overland from New York to Florida, travelling most of the way without money or luggage. In *It Happened One Night*, Colbert needed considerable help from Clark Gable to make her trip; but in the mirror image of *The Palm Beach Story*, she announces in advance her plan to make her own way, then proves beyond doubt her ability to do so.

It would be hard to exaggerate the popularity of *It Happened One Night* or the degree to which it defined Colbert, who would from then on be known as the woman who hitch-hiked by baring her legs. Clearly, then, Sturges builds some of the pleasures of *The Palm Beach Story* upon his audience's familiarity with Colbert and her past adventures. In thinking about the film, I find that I want to think about *her*. The moment of this realisation marks the moment of my enforced departure from Cavell.

As often as he insists upon the importance of the star, never once in *Pursuits of Happiness* does Cavell inquire into an actor's performance or looks. Faces, bodies, tones of voice, gestures, postures, tempos, inflections, attitudes – all suggestions of these are missing from *Pursuits of Happiness*, except for the meagre evidence of photographs and the repeated assertion that the story involves *this particular* actor. But what makes the actor particular? Cavell never tells us; and the omission is as troubling to me as the neglect of *The Palm Beach Story*.

So I begin my inquiry again, this time with Colbert.

*

She wore her hair short in *It Happened One Night*, sucked in her cheeks to produce a kewpie-doll pucker and often kept her face to the camera while peeking sideways at Clark Gable, so her big eyes looked bigger on their upward roll. All this made her seem juvenile – a 'brat,' as Gable called her – an impression strongly reinforced by the sight of her flopping around in his pyjamas.

Of course, her body contradicted the childish image. The celebrated legs were not so much long or sleek as propulsive, powering forward her rounded hips and automobile-figurehead bosom. Capra established this womanly presence first, before turning Colbert into a kid. For her introductory scene, on the yacht, he posed her in a clinging white robe with hands on hips, thereby demonstrating her defiance of her father's authority while giving the audience a good look at her figure. Capra then had her snarl, chase the crew from her stateroom and finally fling herself overboard.

Nothing about her lush, apparently luxury-bred person suggested athleticism; she was more likely to soak in a bath of asses' milk than to swim long distances in the open sea. But in *It Happened One Night*, it seemed plausible that she could swim fast enough to outpace a pursuing boat. If she was not an athlete, then Colbert at least had the vitality, and ferocity, of a healthy and mature animal.

How did she bring together these two aspects of the character she was playing, the marriageable young woman and the wayward brat? One obvious link was her quickness of gesture; Colbert moved more abruptly than anyone else in the picture. When she lifted an arm, crossed a yard, hitched a hem, you might have imagined you were seeing not only the action but also, at its onset, the decision to act. Impatience and impulsiveness merged in her performance with alertness, when the character was at her best.

If this description is accurate, then the circumstances where languor overtook her demand special attention. I can think of two such moments.

The first happened when she and Gable were preparing to sleep in the open, on beds of hay. Gable had slipped off without her realising it, to scrounge for food. When she saw that he was gone, she became frightened – so frightened that, upon his return, she threw herself into his arms. In the aftermath of this first embrace, in the stillness as the two settled down on the hay, there was a pause when it seemed as if Gable would kiss her. She looked like she wanted to be kissed. Then, with the camera hovering over her in close-up, she asked what he was thinking. Her voice was suddenly pitched much lower than at any previous moment. All trace of childishness was gone; the sound was that of a woman's invitation. And yet Colbert still was alert. Newly sensual but without any of the somnambulism of desire, she asked what Gable was thinking in a tone that made it clear: She knew.

The second and last time Colbert used her chest tones, she was playing the scene where she began to reconcile with her father. By this point, she had abandoned Gable; she had resolved, unwisely, to make official her marriage to a high-society aeronaut. (By around this point in the picture, she also had resumed her hands-on-hips stance – no more a child, but a woman again.) When her father, at long last grown sympathetic toward her, asked why she would marry a man she didn't love, Colbert slowed down and made her voice husky: 'I'm tired, Dad. Tired of running around in circles....I've got to settle down. It really doesn't matter how – or where – or with whom.'

Perhaps it seems paradoxical that the voice Colbert had used to convey sexual arousal, and an attunement to Gable's thoughts, should also serve for fatigue and resignation. But this was only the start of the contradiction, which soon broke into the dialogue as well. When her groom came in, and Colbert forced herself to be lively, she told him she wanted their marriage to be 'full of excitement... We'll get on a merry-go-round and never get off....We don't want to stop to think, do we? Just want to keep going.'

So this was what it meant to settle down, once you had accepted the proposition that any mate was acceptable: It meant living on a merry-go-round. A funny way to stop 'running around in circles.'

Of course, Colbert wasn't entirely wrong. You may become dizzy on a merry-go-round, but you can't go anywhere. The film even illustrated this peculiar form of stasis, using two images – one seen, and one merely described. The unseen image was that of the groom's intended entrance to the wedding: He was said to be planning to land in a helicopter. (The spin of the rotor, the idiot whirl of self-regard.) The visible image was that of Colbert in a fancy gown, drink held high, standing on a platform amid a circle of bachelors – as if they were the carousel's horses, and she the centre pole.

This latter image was part of the scene of sterile, brainless revelry upon which Gable stumbled, to his disgust and Colbert's shame, when he visited her home just before the wedding. In judging his harsh reaction, the viewer does well to remember that Gable was playing not merely a newspaper reporter but a *writer*, someone who had been fired for submitting his copy in the form of blank verse. He, too, liked to take a drink – he was drunk in his introductory scene – but he didn't drink thoughtlessly. So it would be too simple to say that at this point, he was contemptuous of Colbert for being a spendthrift rich woman, lapping up cocktails while millions starved in the Depression. Nor was he angry with her solely because she was about to throw herself away on a worthless clubman. What she was squandering most grievously was her mind. As she herself had just said of life on a merry-go-round, 'We don't want to stop to think, do we? Just want to keep going.'

No wonder, then, that for the climax of the movie, Capra and Riskin showed us Colbert thinking about things. The wedding scene consisted almost entirely of the sight of her struggling in silence to come to a decision. Her womanliness had returned; so now did her mindfulness (a mindfulness first achieved on the road, during her childlike period). And her vigour returned: Having thought, she ran, much as she'd swum away at the beginning of the picture. Perhaps feminists will object that Colbert thought only about which man to marry. True enough. But considering the range of new experiences she'd had with Gable, I would suggest there was more than a little substance to her decision.

We never got to see her marry Gable; we didn't even see her give him a kiss. Our last sight of Colbert, in this definitive role, was of a woman in a wedding dress, dashing flat-out for a future in which she wouldn't go around in circles.

*

You will understand why I have narrated all this in the past tense when I turn to *The Palm Beach Story* and the first glimpses it offers of Claudette Colbert. She is in a wedding dress, dashing flat-out for a future in which she and Joel McCrea will live happily ever after – or will they?

This brief but eventful opening-credits sequence plays like a complete screwball comedy in itself, run at forty times the normal speed. It's all fainting housemaids, disrupted phone calls, careening vehicles, disarrayed costumes and mysteriously trussed-up women, as if Sturges were beginning *The Palm Beach Story* by giving us the high points (and only the high points) of some story about Colbert's progress toward marriage with a large, handsome man.

The movie that follows this prelude will show us, in effect, how Colbert and her husband were getting on, several years after *It Happened One Night*.[1] It's impossible, of course, to imagine Gable himself performing in this update; he never would have made himself glower through an entire film, as Joel McCrea does here. But then, it's the unrelieved grumpiness of McCrea's performance that underscores the basic conceit. Once upon a time, Colbert married for love. As she herself says in *The Palm Beach Story*, she chose a man who looked like a movie star. (And no wonder – he *was* a movie star.) But what was likely to have followed her wedding to that dashing lug? Endless nights in motor courts, innumerable benders, perpetual unemployment, an inexhaustible store of indignation: That's what Colbert had coming as Mrs. Gable. Now, at the start of this new picture, she's stuck with the stone-faced Mr. McCrea. Her movie-star husband still looks good, but he seems to be no fun at all.

And yet, as *The Palm Beach Story* starts in earnest, we discover that fun is what Colbert still wants. She proves it by playing hide-and-seek with the little Wienie King.

On the surface, she has no reason to make sport of their meeting. The plot has her facing eviction from her apartment, into which potential renters have been invited to pry; and her physical presence now is unsuited to children's games. No longer an actress who might be addressed as 'brat,' Colbert wears her hair and eyelashes long and comes onto the screen in a form-defining wrapper, looking very like the beautiful and mature woman you think you might encounter in a Park Avenue boudoir. She also sounds like Park Avenue. She keeps her pitch to a rich middle register, and her smooth-flowing vowels declare their origins in her stage training.

A lovely clear voice, like a bell – so says the Wienie King, after he discovers Colbert behind the shower curtain. She pretends, momentarily, to be offended. But why did this mature, sophisticated woman hide in the first place? What made her hop from room to room, sneaking looks at the Wienie King and trying to stay out of his sight? As Gerry, she's still a woman in her own home – and as Colbert, she towers over the intruder, both physically and as a leading player. Neither the character nor the star has anything to fear; so I conclude that they must both be amusing themselves, indulging an aptitude for games and a willingness to plunge ahead experimentally.

To sum up: At the beginning of *The Palm Beach Story*, Colbert is trying to hold onto a girlishness that may already have slipped away. Once she enjoyed life on the road with a raffish adventurer. Now she's stranded on Park Avenue, unwilling to leave but too broke to stay. Evidently she wants to go on playing, but her opportunities to do so would seem to be vanishing. For these reasons, I take to heart the worldview articulated in this scene by the Wienie King. Given the setting, I'd have to call it a philosophy of the bathroom, more than of the boudoir; but it's a philosophy all the same: 'Cold are the hands of time that creep along relentlessly destroying slowly but without pity that which yesterday was young. Alone our memories resist this disintegration and grow more lovely with the passing years.'

Do I laugh at this pronouncement? Yes, every time. And I especially love the kicker: 'That's hard to say with false teeth.' But then, the funniest thing about the punch line is its justice. Once the cold hands of time have pitilessly wrenched out your teeth, you bet it's hard to talk. It seems the Wienie King is not only a philosopher, but an elegant one. He knows how to deflate his own solemnity while pointedly confirming its message.

If you've responded to the way Sturges uses Colbert – if you've allowed the Wienie King's words to register – then you'll feel what a terrible mistake McCrea makes in the scene that follows. Colbert phones him in high spirits, meaning to share the news that the rent is paid and they're going out on the town; and McCrea cuts her off. He's too busy at the office, trying to sell an airport scheme to a potential investor. It seems a grim business, the way he goes about it; and yet it needn't be. What's he doing, if not playing with model airplanes? He, too, might make a game out of his encounter with a rich older man. (The investor, in his own words, is retired and has plenty of time.) But to McCrea, the occasion is a burden, which prevents him from responding to his wife, or even listening to her.

No wonder she demands a divorce, as soon as he gets home.

She says she's holding him back in his career; she implies he can't make enough money for her. Though slightly incompatible, these twin reasons for wanting a divorce seem equally valid – but the viewer may guess that neither is as important to this 'long-legged gal' as the possibility of becoming 'an adventuress,' and neither speaks to her unhappiness in marriage so much as her husband's display of sexual jealousy. To put the matter crudely, she wants some fun – now, before time claims her teeth (and her legs); and she's hurt that he reduces fun to sex. If her body is truly hers to enjoy, then his body needn't be the limit of enjoyment. Why shouldn't she also get physical pleasure from, say, a 300-foot yacht?

By proposing this line of argument, *The Palm Beach Story* again makes itself the mirror image of *It Happened One Night*. Once, Colbert had abandoned her yacht for the simple life with Clark Gable; now Colbert abandons Joel McCrea, and a life that threatens to become simple, for the prospect of a yacht. Or, to phrase the issue in terms of communication: In the earlier film, Colbert felt she made contact with the world through her man. In this film, she feels her man blocks out the world.

But the problem that Sturges poses for Colbert is more complex than that. Very soon after we learn of her dissatisfaction, we find that she wriggles uncontrollably when McCrea sits her in his lap. 'Hold still,' McCrea orders; but even in movies made after Hollywood abandoned the Production Code, no one has acted out more vividly than Colbert the excitement of buttocks rubbing groin. Momentarily, McCrea's stolidity seems attractive. He enjoys giving her this order that he knows she can't obey. She wouldn't squirm so helplessly, if he weren't so proudly and completely a stiff.

At last we get to Topic A, as McCrea will later call it with disdain. He provides her with only one kind of fun, but one that's so powerful that she might give up the world for it. Sex keeps Colbert in her marriage, or threatens to. It's more than a habit, bad or otherwise. It's an irrational bond, whose absurd power she later acknowledges when she gives McCrea the pseudonym of 'Captain McGlue.' When Colbert flees her marriage, running so precipitously that she asks a taxi driver where to get a divorce, she is in effect struggling to change her relationship to her own sexual desires. Until now, she has been their agent. From this time on, she hopes, they will be her instrument.

This isn't a bad problem for an American movie to address, in its capacity either as American or as a movie. One of the ways in which Americans have not only pursued happiness but also changed the meaning of that pursuit is to have turned against such considerations as economics and clan solidarity as overt reasons for marriage. To a degree that is uncommon in history, Americans believe themselves to marry for love – which translates, in the movies, into marriage for sex. Outside of the movies, most people know that they must strike a balance between their sexual dreams and other needs: companionship, empathy, clan solidarity, economics. This balance is 'love.' But for cases in which a person has given up too much of the sexual ideal, Americans have coined an unlovely term: 'settling.'

Movie stars generally do not settle. They attain their sexual ideals, on big screens set up in public places, so that the rest of us may find it easier to believe in our compromised version of marriage for love. But in *The Palm Beach Story*, Colbert gives up her sexual ideal, precisely with the aim of settling. She does so in the expectation of embodying the dream of some wealthy man. (To amend my earlier formulation: She hopes to make *someone else's* sexual desire into her instrument.) And the first thing she learns is that it's not easy to lower her sexual expectations.

When she boards the train to Palm Beach with the 'rich millionaires' of the Ale and Quail Club, she proves that her charm is as potent as she imagines; but she also learns that wealthy suitors, as a class, are a trial. By the time they break into her sleeping compartment to serenade her, Colbert is smiling in a way that recalls her forced gaiety toward the end of *It Happened One Night*, with the difference that she and Sturges allow her misery to show through for a moment. She can't imagine providing sex to any of these men; she can't bear the thought of keeping one of them aroused while fending him off. And for what it's worth, she's not even in her own sleeping compartment. The members of the Ale and Quail Club may feel free to enter because the place belongs to them.

The humour of this sequence becomes hectic, until it's no longer humour but something almost frightening. How should I take the 'comic' mistreatment by the all-white Ale and Quail Club of their black bartender? Maybe audiences in 1942 – white audiences, at any rate – thought it unambiguously hilarious that these men should terrorise

Fred 'Snowflake' Toones. Or maybe some viewers, starting with Sturges himself, felt uneasy to see the rambunctiousness take this turn. It's impossible for an American of my generation to know with any certainty the full complexity of the first audience's response. But I do know that Sturges was capable of creating a black character as dignified as the preacher at the end of *Sullivan's Travels*. I also know that he had Colbert hide in fear from the pursuing mob, with their shotguns and baying dogs. Is it too far-fetched to think that the Ale and Quail Club turns into a lynch mob, once its collective sexual hopes have been frustrated? Is there no lesson in this for Colbert, as she starts her career as an adventuress?

From frustrated desire to little or no sexual urge: The next marital prospect Colbert meets is John D. Hackensacker 3rd, played by Rudy Vallee as if he had a zipper under his zipper. Vallee seems a perfect choice on whom to settle, especially when he's compared to the men Colbert has just escaped. He's younger and better looking than anyone in the Ale and Quail Club, and he has more money than the lot of them. It may also be a mark in his favour that he's so polite in his sexual interest, expressing it entirely in the subjunctive. If Colbert were to choose him, we understand, she could satisfy him with very little, and without having her sensibilities offended. After all, he's kind of cute. A woman could learn to call him Snoodles.

But then, 'Captain McGlue' shows up, and Colbert feels what it would mean to settle. To paraphrase Snoodles: It is one of the tragedies of this life that the men of whom Colbert is most in need are always enormous.

*

By now, through emulation, I hope to have demonstrated how highly I value Cavell's dual process of translation and exegesis. By carrying meanings across from one vocabulary to another – from the language of Hollywood comedy to that of American philosophy – and by leading the reader through his texts as if by a thread, Cavell has done more than endorse these films as works of art. His real achievement is to have shown how these movies may be understood as sustained arguments, carried out about subjects that continue to matter to people. I might compare his method of translation and exegesis in *Pursuits of Happiness* to the way Emanuel Levinas read excerpts from the Talmud. Though Cavell's source material is nothing sacred, I believe both writers shared the goal of making their texts speak to real human problems.

In *Pursuits of Happiness*, Cavell favours those films that speak convivially, optimistically, about these problems. But in carrying out my own reading of *The Palm Beach Story*, I have now reached the place in the film's argument where conviviality fails and optimism falters.

It might seem perverse to say such a thing about *The Palm Beach Story*, when *Pursuits of Happiness* so brilliantly discusses another Sturges film, *The Lady Eve*, in which the characters are richer and the surface far more troubled. (Where in *The Palm Beach Story* are Barbara Stanwyck's bitter tears?) But just as the uproariousness of the Ale and Quail Club turns ugly, so is there something desperate in the screwball lightness of the film as a whole.

To resume the reading: Captain McGlue returns, and Colbert understands at last that she must have him. In conventional translation, 'They were made for each other.' This formula may be applied to the couples in all the films discussed in *Pursuits of Happiness*, and in a great many lesser films, just as it is applied in life to the lead actors in the average wedding. Perhaps we acknowledge that marriage-for-love aspires through the movies to become marriage-for-sex; perhaps we admit that sexual energy is no respecter of persons. Even so, we are supposed to keep in place the fig leaf of individualism and imagine that only *this particular man* can provide satisfaction to *this particular woman*. If *this particular woman* goes by the name of Gerry Jeffers, we're to forget that she has tested as alternative mates only a small, symbolic sampling of men. If the particular woman is Colbert, we must ignore the satisfaction previously given her by Gable (and by others, too, in a rather larger sampling).

Yet in *The Palm Beach Story*, Sturges won't let us maintain our genteel fiction. It turns out, at the end, that there are *two* Colberts and *two* McCreas: enough to go around. And so, in the final shot, Snoodles attains his sexual ideal (though he might not know what to do with her); his too-much-married sister gets her ideal, too, in the extra McCrea (and will probably tire of him within the month); and the original, sexually compatible pair remain together.

That closing shot, of the three couples at the altar, resembles the conclusion of a fairy tale, in which life offers three neat possibilities: too cold, too hot and just right. But if the Colberts and McCreas are multiple and interchangeable, there can be no fairy-tale ending. This time, when we read 'And they lived happily ever after – or did they?' we know how to answer. They did not, because the story has turned out to be circular, and dissatisfaction must come around again; because sexual desire is a merry-go-round, which you may enjoy so long as you don't stop to think; because Colbert, doubled, gets to have both of her choices, which means that neither choice is uniquely right for her.

I know – I'm making a lot out of something that viewers may take simply as a surprise ending. The sudden production of twin Colberts and McCreas seems teasingly gratuitous, as if the author were showing us his hand at work. What's more, the device isn't even novel. In some of Cavell's other comedies of remarriage, the woman was also doubled or split, the most pertinent example being Stanwyck in *The Lady Eve*. First Stanwyck appeared to Henry Fonda as 'Jean'; then she came to him as Jean's fictional creation, 'Eve.' By showing up twice – thereby inciting Fonda to go twice through the same limp courtship speech – Stanwyck exposed the language of romance as being so much cardboard from Hallmark (a revelation that, for most viewers, is less than shocking). At the end of *The Lady Eve*, though, the fiction held. It still turned out that Stanwyck and Fonda were made for each other and no one else.

The finale of *The Palm Beach Story* makes nonsense of this notion of sexual exclusivity. It shows us that Colbert can make love to Joel McCrea and also to Rudy Vallee, that McCrea can make love to Colbert and to Mary Astor, too. We know it's in the nature of movies for stars to enjoy more than one partner; but it's not in the nature of movies to remind us of the fact. We observe a compact with the movies, a tacit agreement that allows us to enjoy a star's present adventure on condition that we pretend ignorance of the previous exploits. We pretend while knowing that we're pretending; that's a large part of the willing suspension of disbelief we practice at the movies. At the end of *The Palm Beach Story*, Sturges playfully violates this compact.

In so doing, he also violates his particular compact with the audience. His work appeals to moviegoers who like to think of themselves as wised-up. These are people who might identify with Gerry Jeffers as she appears in the early scenes of *The Palm Beach Story*, full of practical experience, fluent cynicism, and practiced sophistication. At the end, though, the worldly wisdom she mouthed is proved to have been so much hot air. She couldn't live by her principles; she succeeded in being an adventuress but wound up with her 'bad habit' anyway. Bright chatter is futile – a revelation that Sturges's core audience really *may* find shocking.

Finally, and most outrageously, Sturges violates the notion that our choices make a difference. The conclusion of *The Palm Beach Story* reminds me of that moment in *It Happened One Night* when Colbert claimed that 'It really doesn't matter how – or where – or with whom' she settled down; only here there's neither huskiness nor fatigue in her voice. There's no voice at all (words being nothing more than idle self-justification). Colbert, doubled, exercises both her choices simultaneously, and neither is likely to prove satisfactory.

As a philosopher other than the Wienie King might have said, 'Either you marry Rudy Vallee or you don't marry Rudy Vallee. Marry Rudy Vallee or don't marry Rudy Vallee, and you will be unhappy.'

There are also convivial, optimistic ways to phrase the same notion. As Molly Bloom put it at the end of *Ulysses*, 'I thought well as well him as another.' But for all the laughter it provides, the conclusion of *The Palm Beach Story* doesn't convey to me any of Molly's affirmation. The finale is jeering, discordant – a trick played on the characters and audience alike.

With that understood, I feel I know why Cavell omitted *The Palm Beach Story* from *Pursuits of Happiness*. Despite all its outward conformity to the genre, this picture is not a comedy of remarriage. It's a comedy of disillusionment. I also feel I know why, in *Pursuits of Happiness*, he dwelled so little on the actors' bodies and their ways of using them. Contingency, frailty, the creeping of the cold hands of time: These facts, which are so unavoidably bound up with our sense of someone's physical presence, have no role to play in his American commonwealth.

Now, Cavell does admit disillusionment into his philosophy and his film-going. Here, for example, is his reading of the final shot of another movie:

> ...the woman puts her hand on the man's shoulder not because she forgives his betrayal, or even his inability to offer tears and beg forgiveness, but because she accepts that there is nothing to forgive, to forgo, no new place to be won on the other side of this moment. There is no man different from any other, or she will seek none. Her faithfulness is to accept their juxtaposition in a world of uneventful adventure (one event is as adventurous or routine as another, one absence or presence as significant or unimportant as another, change as unthinkable as permanence, the many as the one) and to move into that world with him. (1971, p. 96)

This, of course, is the ending of *L'Avventura*. Would Cavell admit that an American woman, too, might feel that 'there is no man different from any other, or she will seek none'? Would he further admit that, given enough money, she might greet futility with laughter? Perhaps he would – but such a possibility lies outside the scheme of *Pursuits of Happiness*.

So I lay down my thread, having concluded that Cavell's argument holds up well against unravelling. It seems that the dropped thread of *The Palm Beach Story* does lead through a labyrinth. It's just a different maze from the one we've been exploring.

Note

1. The reader may reasonably wonder whether I'm imposing my way of thinking upon Sturges. For an answer, see his 1947 film *The Sin of Harold Diddlebock*, which opens with the final reel of Harold Lloyd's *The Freshman* and then shows us the same actor and character twenty years on.

Part II
Interview

'What Becomes of Thinking on Film?'

Stanley Cavell in conversation with Andrew Klevan

Andrew Klevan: How have Ludwig Wittgenstein and J.L. Austin been important to your work and, more specifically, why might their work, or your understanding of their work, be helpful to us when thinking about film? Why might it be beneficial for a film student to have a sense of these writers?

Stanley Cavell: The general fact about my encounter with them is that they convinced me, so to speak, to stay in the field of philosophy. I don't know whether I would have managed to leave, perhaps bought another saxophone and tried to make a living, but I was very dissatisfied with the work I was doing in graduate school. I didn't realise *how* dissatisfied until Austin visited Harvard in 1955, as a result of which I threw away what might have been half of a dissertation. I had read Austin, but it never hit me *hard* until we talked and I went to his various classes. So the question about Austin's importance to me, and Wittgenstein's several years later, is a question about philosophy's importance to me altogether. These two let me, encouraged me to, think about anything I was interested in, as very much opposed to almost all the rest of the philosophy that I was working at, where I felt to match the tone, the strictures, the agenda, the conventions of professional philosophy dictated a certain kind of response, a certain kind of research paper, a certain kind of sequence of chapters for a dissertation, that both gave me a subject but deprived me of having any say in the subject. I was rewarded for the work I was doing as a graduate student, but I didn't really believe what I was saying. I didn't feel that I was starting at fruitful places, or formulating topics that really moved me, nor leaving myself satisfied with my conclusions. Austin changed that, decisively but not completely. He allowed me to think about fascinating things all the time, but I was unsure whether this was philosophy.

Philosophy is a peculiar thing to want to do and I had to keep thinking that there was a motive in me, some fantasy in me, of what it was like to examine myself and be able to use this in some sort of scholarly rational way at a depth at which other subjects didn't permit. But Austin did directly inspire a substantial paper from me that is the first I am grateful for and still use, the title essay of my first book, *Must We Mean What We Say?* I knew that, whatever I was going to do, I could take that with me, let it guide me. An important effect of it was that it allowed me to read Wittgenstein for the first time with any sense of fruitfulness. (I'm still sometimes surprised by this, given their great differences of temperament and of ambition for philosophy.) I had tried reading *Philosophical Investigations* several years earlier and it meant essentially nothing to me. I thought it was interesting, inventive, but really nothing more than a kind of unsystematic pragmatism. A large number of philosophers still think that about Wittgenstein's *Investigations*. The step Wittgenstein took beyond Austin for me lay in his distrust of language as well as his trust in it and that began to open for me what it is I felt I needed from philosophy, that combination of absolute reliance and absolute questioning of every word that came out of me.

I might say that the promise of freedom I felt in these writers is epitomised in the surprise of their enabling me to think with some point and consecutiveness about film. Yet this did not happen at once. *The World Viewed* does not explicitly feature their work, but it was explicitly in preparation while the later essays in *Must We Mean What We Say?* were showing up and while the idea of writing a little book about Thoreau's *Walden* was forming. This means that I was gathering implications of Austin's and Wittgenstein's work in allowing contemporary philosophical access to the achievements of Beckett and Kierkegaard and Shakespeare and Thoreau, and this access I count as essential to the writing of *The World Viewed*.

I might specify three issues I recognise as exemplifying the kind of encouragement Austin and Wittgenstein lent to the progress of my thinking about film. One was allowing me to resist the idea that the relation of a photograph to what it is of is well thought of as representation; another is the role of the ordinary, or say the uneventful, in the motion picture camera's interests in things, especially in the human face and figure; the third, most general, issue is their enabling me to feel that I was at once philosophising and being responsive to, open to, the endless events (uneventful and eventful events, as it were) of film. Without that openness, I would not have achieved any conviction that I was talking about the unprecedented fact of film.

I might call this the conviction that film shares with the other great arts the proposal that everything matters – and you do not know what everything means.

AK: You've talked about the 'unsummarisable' examples of Wittgenstein and Austin, and how Austin would demonstrate distinctions with daunting, haunting dramas. Could there be a connection between your observation about Austin's examples and the process of describing films? When we describe films we are partly trying to find the best way to summarise them, but we also feel they are unsummarisable (and daunting), so how can we summarise them in ways that satisfy us?

SC: Here are a couple of immediate links that occur to me to follow up. One is to ask what it means to quote a film. Discussing a film differs from discussing a painting, where you can stand before an object, or sit with a slide on a screen indefinitely, and *that* is what you're thinking about. With music you can quote a passage, whistling or at the piano. But when the film is gone again it is again gone. But then we should look at quoting more closely. Even with literature, the home of quotation, you're saying words in your voice, in a particular moment, to some point. Professors of English used to be tempted to think of themselves as Shakespearean actors when they read speeches from the plays. Is this quoting or performing?

Paraphrase is another obvious device for bringing a moment of a work to the table for discussion. Paraphrase had been a target of literary instruction since what's called the New Criticism, and although the French onslaught of theory beginning in the late 1960s was importantly an attack on the New Criticism (it was for a while called the New New Criticism), it joined hands with its enemy in teaching contempt for paraphrase. This has produced generations of students who are mostly incapable of, anyway unpractised at, thinking about and executing the feat of putting a text in other words, which is like being unable to describe an object. In the world of Wittgenstein's *Investigations*, this amounts to depriving oneself of the capacity to think philosophically, since '[In philosophy] we must do away with all *explanation*, and description alone must take its place.'[1] This is one form in which Wittgenstein insists on the difference between philosophy and science – to the dismay of many philosophers. Part of its liberating effect on me was its permitting me to pay full attention to what struck me as the almost wantonly poor descriptions philosophers habitually give of their examples, in aesthetics and in moral philosophy no more than in epistemology. To understand this chronic condition can be said to be the task of the first three parts of my *Claim of Reason*.

AK: In the University where I teach we are encouraged to use a standardised form when we grade student essays. The form breaks down the assessment of the essay into different categories, and two of these categories are 'description' and 'analysis.' Description is presupposed to be separate from analysis, and often description is seen as a weakness, or at any rate, weaker than the thing we call 'analysis'. Therefore, if you've done a lot of analysis that is good, but if you merely seem to be describing then that's bad. Yet, I *want* my students to describe. I would like a whole essay of description, but it would have to be description of a certain type, or quality.

SC: That's good. Very hard to teach

AK: Yes absolutely. Like most of the best things, it can't be taught directly. One encourages seminar discussions, week after week, where the conversation hinges on the refinement of each other's descriptions of specific moments in films (rather than, say, around general thematic disputes). If the students get used to responding to each other (and the films) in this way then this process becomes habitual. Of course, it is another step for them to translate those skills into the more cogent form of an essay.

I wanted to return to what precisely was 'unsummarisable' in the examples of Austin and Wittgenstein. What do you think is being lost in summarising?

SC: I can't remember the context in which I said that they were 'unsummarisable'. There are two obvious things that I would mean now if I said that. One is that in order for the example to have its effect you have to *give* it. That is, you have to take one through the narrative of the example and see whether the effect of the example is there. I give you a favourite pair of mine as an instance of this from Austin's essay on excuses, one of his greatest essays.[2] If the subject of excuses had been thought of as a topic in philosophy on the continent of Europe Austin's material would have occupied a very large volume. In Austin it's twenty-three pages. But it is an enormous topic and he knows all he's doing is giving you notes for this topic (they were some of his notes for a seminar that he gave at Oxford over the years). The idea of excuses is of considerations that mitigate, extenuate, the slips or mishaps or lapses in actions so familiar in everyday life. The reticulation of terms of excuse reveals, I have wished to say, the inherent vulnerability of the human being, even, given the existence of the inexcusable, its openness to tragedy. I believe this description of Austin's work on excuses would offend many colleagues of mine. It makes Austin's work sound pretentious, something Austin was himself worried about. I think that his work on slips is as important to Austin as the idea of slips is to Freud, although they have completely different sensibilities and goals. It is, however, uncontroversial to say that the value of Austin's work is a function of his examples. Here is the pair of stories I had in mind, meant to show the difference between excusing oneself by claiming to have done something by mistake and claiming to have done it by accident.

First story. There are two donkeys, mine and my neighbour's, in a field there beyond the fence. I take a sudden dislike to my donkey and decide to shoot it. I take careful aim at one of the donkeys, fire, and the donkey that I aimed at drops. I walk over to the fence and discover to my horror that it's my neighbour's donkey. Have I done this by mistake or have I done this by accident? Wait before answering.

Second story. Same two donkeys; same sudden dislike. This time I take careful aim and just as I fire the donkeys shift and to my horror I realise I have shot my neighbour's donkey. I run up to it but it's dead. Now have I done that by mistake or by accident?

I have no doubt, going back over the thing, that when you have aimed and the donkey you aimed at drops dead and it turns out to be your neighbour's, what's happened is that you have *mistaken* yours for your neighbour's donkey. When they shift and you didn't intend to shoot the donkey that you aimed at, but he just got in the way of the bullet, something happened and you did it by accident. In my experience, telling the stories in a large class, if you ask beforehand whether people think there is a clear and distinct difference between doing something by mistake and doing it by accident there is a lot of disagreement, and if those who think there is a clear difference are asked to specify it, they understandably cannot manage it. Then when I have told the stories, the agreement is high, not perfect, but high enough to produce appreciative laughter. There are many reasons why agreement is not perfect – some weren't listening, some are not interested, some are suspicious or are imagining the examples differently from others.

Then what do I take myself to have learned from the examples, I who after the examples had absolutely no doubt in my mind which was which? There was nothing I failed to know that I have been informed of. I merely, let's say, could not articulate, or did not understand, what I knew. Does this mean that I go around saying things, allowing words to flow from me, without really knowing what I'm saying? That does not seem exactly to be a moral Austin wished to draw. On the contrary, what he says is that philosophers (or, say, any of us in a philosophical corner) are lazy, haven't done their work responsibly, are drunk with false profundity, and so on. I was not especially interested in these particular interpretations, matters I identify as chronic in philosophy and which I call the proposal of particular terms of criticism. But that I was unknown to my own language and contrariwise, that did sink in. And I still find myself every other day having to recognise that kind of blindness to myself. That one gets to oneself through an examination of one's language should be no surprise. What is in question is to what extent getting to oneself is philosophy's proper business.

AK: I was smiling through the example, and my amusement might have something to do with the 'unsummarisable.' I've got this vision of the fence and I am picturing the donkey suddenly moving in front of the other donkey and oh dear...The set-up and the development of the situation is amusing...I am also amused by the choice of using donkeys. If it had been horses, the example would have been different, or I might have felt differently.

SC: Yes. It would not have been different with the concepts of 'mistake' and 'accident' but the seriousness of horses would have pushed into flower the sadism or sadness of the dramas. Austin characteristically plays his examples for laughs. It is very important that many of his examples carry an air of whimsy. This raises the point of humour in his, and in Wittgenstein's, philosophising. Sometimes it resembles the laughter of Lewis Carroll with nonsense rhymes, language taking us for a ride. Various streaks in modern philosophy have been concerned with philosophy's mission to detect nonsense. The moral that I was drawing, of becoming unknown to my language, was more important to me than logical positivism's discovery of nonsense in classical metaphysics. What motivated me to philosophise was my own capacity for emptiness, or for rigidity, for inhabiting (I sometimes picture it to myself) a little shed, or outpost, of language, instead of reaching the open panoply of expression that my language offers as (potentially) *mine*. To show me differences as Austin does typically requires my recognising the humour of my mistakes, the humour of accidents, hair's breadths away from tragedy. I'm just agreeing with you that the humorousness of the donkeys is internal to Austin's teaching.

AK: Yes, but I hope we're not being anti-donkey! Of course, I might feel differently about the whole thing if it were a real life incident, or if my relationship to the incident was different and so on. I certainly don't think that horses would capture the neighbourliness in the story. It seems a real possibility that they would both own a donkey, and it evokes some sort of small community.

Your feelings about the importance of the humour in the examples of Austin prompts me to bring up something you have written about your father, and his propensity to tell jokes. Your father never told a joke without it having a telling pertinence to an immediate passage that had just occurred in a social context. This struck a chord with me because my father did something similar. It made me wonder what my own father was doing. I was wondering what the impulse to tell a joke in these contexts was. Why would he? What sort of offering was the joke?

SC: My father was uneducated, unentitled to intellectual authority, but had the ability to make others laugh, to make other's respond. That's power and that's authority. That's exercising some intellectual dominance, some emotional dominance that translates into some intellectual dominance in this moment. A point is made and a point that he could not have made intellectually or that he felt would have been lost. The human craving for narration is about as primitive a wish or form of interaction as exists. How early does a child want to hear a story? My father was not capable of intimacy with me when we were alone of anything like the intimacy he could create at a small gathering by telling a story. Intimacy, commonality, parabolic point and dominance are all achieved in these so-called jokes. But Yiddish jokes often require long narration; I remember a couple that seemed to last as long as ten or fifteen minutes. Perhaps I exaggerate.

AK: That is a *very* long time. That's a whole screenplay!

SC: What it means is you cannot always depend on a punch line. You have to be consumed in the telling of the thing. And then exhausted when it's over.

AK: Yes, *experiencing* the unfolding of the joke is important (like experiencing the 'unsummarisable' example). A good joke teller will be adept with rhythm and pace (knowing which bits to stretch and which bits to speed up). Jokes can be a communally shared short hand to express dynamics and consequences. They can transport you quickly to another place or position and speedily move you through various, sometimes extreme, events. We can easily go with the teller because it elides our usual fear of changes in perspective (these changes are offset by the humour) and we open up because the medium promises – gives us an anticipation of – a gain at the end. They are little fictional worlds that are described and narrated. There's an impulse to concreteness in a joke, but also to abstraction as well.

SC: Parable!

AK: Yes, like that, and like The Philosophical Example. Good jokes may be a popular form of giving philosophical examples. Your work has been eager to establish films as philosophical examples. My father was also a great lover of Hollywood movies and this love may be connected to his fondness for story jokes. I have just made a series of observations about jokes, for example, that they can transport you quickly to another place or position and speedily move you through various, sometimes extreme, events. These observations on jokes also sound like descriptions of films, especially those from Hollywood. Hollywood films and jokes both dramatise simple stories that are accessible. They may come from an impulse to please, and they are happy to be popular, but they need not be simplistic, and they may be *exemplary*.

SC: The ability to *tell* a story; it is *clear* that this is a talent. It is a talent that everybody has to some extent. I sense in myself, sometimes, a certain guilt in rewarding sheer talent, as if, if that's what we do, it's just too undemocratic to be in the university. In the sciences, somehow it's all right: We all understand that some people can do mathematics in a way that others can't, you accept that it is a form of virtuosity. But there's something that's against the grain for me in thinking that virtuosity is required in philosophy. It must be something that anyone can participate in. At the same time I feel I am looking for what Emerson calls genius – the thing just this person has it in himself or herself to do.

AK: You refer to Wittgenstein's claim that in philosophy we do not seek to learn anything new (distinguishing philosophy from science, since science is the unsurpassable source of paradigms for learning something new about the world. We want to understand what's already in plain view. The film criticism I admire most helps me to understand what is in plain view.

SC: Yes, I agree absolutely. What's the sense of something in front of your eyes that you do not see. Wittgenstein also says that what's hidden is of no philosophical interest to us, as though philosophy were a game of getting hot and getting cold – the object of its inquiry from the beginning a perfectly familiar object. But film dramatises 'all in front of your eyes' in a way painting does not. Film is *put* in front of your eyes and *persists* in saying something to you in front of your eyes. I suppose it is a source of film's popularity, as if we knew what this meant. Popularity is such a weak and misleading idea of what the power of film is to destroy false barriers within audiences, within individual viewers of film. This power is something that film in some way shares with music, in some way shares with drama, in some way shares with sports (evidently in some way with gladiators, inviting its popular critics to give individual films a thumbs up or thumbs down). But this power of, let's say, physical impression also makes possible a reticence that great film makers also have – the capacity of film to await your response, instead of tipping you off about how to respond. Of course all of these things can be abused.

The reverse, the absolute negation, of what one would mean by a film criticism that takes you to what is in plain view is, I judge, the familiar tendency to approach a film by producing an anecdote about it. This is familiar from the presentation of historical films on television, for example on the Turner Classics channel. The billionaire Turner has bought up an extraordinary, a priceless one would say, library of films, films it is on the whole a comfort to think are being preserved, and in good prints, in that place, and I hope in others. Invariably these films are introduced by way of anecdotes of casting or of some amusing misadventure during the shooting of the film. But what's interesting to me is that this can be done. You can in fact interest a certain large audience of a film by giving some tiny anecdote about its making. The equivalent would be hard to find with a painting or a novel or a piece of music. One could say there are no anecdotes about such things – beyond Proust's being oppressed by noise or Flaubert's looking for the precise word. Hardly very illuminating. It's tried of course: Mahler was saddened by one thing or another when he wrote this symphony; he always wrote in the morning, with strict orders that he not be disturbed until he appeared for lunch. So what is it about film that yields to this banal touch? Insipid and predictable in principle as many of these anecdotes are, what they are pointing to is something about film's fascination with, craving for, something like the accidental, the contingent, the subjection of human existence to indescribably many possibilities of catastrophe or joy. As in Austin's vision in excuses, in which we become conscious that for human actions to be what they are, for things to work out as they do, endless conditions have to be in place. Such thoughts reveal that film is about how things happen, or happen to happen, or happen just here and now, or happen to look. The anecdotes teach you nothing, yet they are not even boring, which is quite amazing. What difference does it make that this is the first film in which Tony Curtis appears and has no lines? This was the entire content on television the other night of the introduction to a really quite interesting film noir called *Criss Cross*, from just after World War II, and the way of introducing it was to alert the audience to notice this good looking young man who's dancing with Yvonne De Carlo (until Burt Lancaster comes along); this sixty seconds was the making of Curtis's career. But this film is about how people look and about the accidents of a career and about being able to appear and say nothing. All of these things are deeply part of the grain of film. The gossipy anecdote, about essentially nothing, of which nothing is made, nevertheless gives the audience a specific stake in the film. It breaks the smooth, hard, undifferentiated surface, like a dive. And the most serious criticism also needs to do that.

AK: I wonder why so many of the serious things we feel about films are mysteriously diverted when we speak or write about them. Why are our thoughts and words about film deflected? Anecdotes seem to be one of the many instances of diversion. I was just thinking of that anecdote about the Renoir film *Partie de Campagne*...

SC: ...Yes. 'It *rained* that day.'

AK: Actually that is not necessarily an unhelpful anecdote if it leads one, as it led me, to be even more astonished at how Renoir made use of the rain (on the water) in the film. Indeed, we are more alert to the complexity of its integration.

SC: Exactly, but instead I have heard the anecdote used as reductive, by saying 'Oh he didn't intend to film the scene in rain. He was just lucky.' In that case one might say that wonderful filmmakers are perpetually lucky. How can that be?

AK: In many places in your work you've explored or implied matters of avoidance and evasion: our capacity to avoid or evade the emotional particularities of what is before us. You've now given an example of one of these types of evasion in talking about film. Of course, it is not only true of film discussion, but it seems pervasive. Why is that?

SC: I don't know that I have wisdom about it. I suppose it is connected with the inherent emotionality of film. Austin and Wittgenstein, though they don't flaunt the matter, were the first philosophers whom I read who in their descriptions of cases included feeling, passion. As if philosophers believed implicitly that feeling and passion always interfere with reason, philosophy's aegis. The positivist revolution made this explicit – regarding all non-scientific assertions, that is to say religious, ethical, aesthetic assertions, as expressions of feeling and therefore not cognitive, not rational. Now if you just say that, you wonder how anyone could believe it; and in my years in graduate school, people tended to say *just that*, and other people, helplessly, tried to refute it. But the fear of nonsense, the fear of the irrational, is in some way pervasive in western philosophy, part of its origination. The idea that passion and reason are antithetical to one another seems to me a libel on human nature and conduct. As if passion were a form of superstition. But that was the avant-garde when I came into philosophy. A.J. Ayer's book *Language, Truth and Logic* preaches that doctrine, and it is the single most successful text-book of philosophy in modern times. There are more than a million copies of that book in print.

AK: It is one of the first texts encountered by first-year students at Oxford studying Philosophy, Politics and Economics.

SC: I am not answering your question about avoiding emotional particularity. Sometimes people say that we lack an adequate vocabulary of passion. What would it mean if that were actually true – that humankind has forever overlooked the need for exact expression in human speech? Or that, like the beasts we are incapable of much more articulation of expression than cries of rage, fear, pain, and hunger? And here we are to deal with the medium of film, in which feelings are not just the topic and the mode of interaction with these objects, but in which the possibility of having our feelings manipulated by them is incessantly present. Spencer Tracy's demonstration to Katharine Hepburn at the close of *Adam's Rib* that men can fake crying as well as women is a brilliant exposition of the truth that faking crying may cost producing real tears. The intimacy of this pair is expressed in her recognition that these tears of his, produced didactically, nevertheless betoken that she has hurt him. The denial of their importance is the male's way of calling attention to them, to one who can understand.

A good reason for evading emotionality is something that I lay at Pauline Kael's door – the incessant, seemingly exclusive insistence on nothing but the 'kiss, kiss, bang, bang' sense of what a film can do, the kick in American films as opposed to what she called European films. And that's done very heavy disservice to both professional and unprofessional views of writing about film, marring the good service she did in establishing film, among educated readers generally, as a body of work to be taken seriously.

I've just heard a lecture by a professional, indeed leading, scholar of film, who kept pressing upon the audience that film is a dramatic, an emotional, thing. And I wondered where I, or this scholar, have been all these decades? Why would anybody bother to say that now? I was just alluding to a male skittishness about feeling, but there is also a female, or feminist, distrust, women's distrust, not of feeling in general, but of film's feeling. I think of Laura Mulvey's tremendously influential paper, from 1975, on the male gaze.[3] What primarily is famous in that paper is its stress on the idea of the male gaze, and there are plenty of objections and exceptions to be taken to the stress, and I've taken some. But something much more interesting to me in that paper is Mulvey's direct advice or her fervent direction to destroy the pleasure of film. And that, I thought, was a really revolutionary, effective thing to say. The effect went beyond perhaps, or perhaps not, what was said. There she is saying beware of this pleasure that is poison, it's part of what's subjecting you to false views of yourself and of the world. That a certain kind of pleasure can be addictive or poisonous is certainly true. But I think Mulvey's view helped to cause a violent misreading of, especially, Hollywood film in particular. Many of these films contain the kind of poison she detects, but many – I think the best – are at least as opposed to that poison as she is. It is a task of criticism to explain how this can be the case. But something this means is that criticism has as an obligation to provide a criticism of false pleasure. Mulvey's indiscriminateness was, I thought, harmful. It hindered critical arguments about film from developing, anyway as I would have like to see them develop.

AK: You have written about interpretations that condescend (specifically in relation to the *Unknown Woman* films). You have made a distinction between interpretations of a work that do and those that do not allow the work a say in its interpretation.

SC: The idea of a film's having a stake in its own interpretation is meant to capture, and to refuse, the temptation to condescend to these works. I have had the impression in so much film criticism that it thinks it is better, higher-minded (which is what condescending says) than the objects of its attention. Perhaps instead of speaking of having a say in its interpretation, we might say that a serious film, like any work of art, *resists* interpretation, as it were insists upon being taken in its own terms. Resisting interpretation in these objects is another way of understanding what their stake in their interpretation is. They are no more transparent to criticism than persons are.

AK: I suppose I was also referring to the tendency in film writing to avoid particularity *per se*, not simply the particularity of a film's emotional effect: the particularity of what is before us. Film study seems to have gone to great lengths to avoid talking about what might be in plain view (and maybe the medium deviously encourages it). I should make a distinction here. Sometimes in our criticism, it's apt to be sensitive about avoidances because the film itself has been sensitive about them. We don't want to use words that betray the film's suggestiveness. I found this when writing about Joan Bennett in *The Woman in the Window*, Fritz Lang's film made in 1944. It seems that the woman, played by Joan Bennett, is some sort of prostitute, but the film remains ambiguous about the matter in a variety of ways. Initially, I used the word 'prostitute' in my writing. Then I decided that I shouldn't use the word because the film does not use the word (so to speak). I needed a way of implying aspects of her livelihood that would be sensitive to the film's handling.

SC: But there you're not avoiding anything. You were justly wary of being false to the experience.

AK: There is another way I want to put this. You have a rich and detailed film and then you will get an academic piece on that film that barely acknowledges any of that richness or detail (and richness is not necessarily caught in apparent close attention to the film; through, for example, shot breakdowns). I might announce that the piece is bad for failing to make an effort to acknowledge the film appropriately, but primarily my feelings are bewilderment and loss. When I'm studying a good film, it seems to demand of me that I give it attention and detail.

This is what I'm seeing and hearing. My eventual writing on the film will be woefully insufficient, partly necessarily so, partly because of my own problems with expression, but I'm never in doubt about the nature of the pursuit. This lack of doubt is not because of arrogance, but because good films won't let me doubt it. They take a hold of me. When I leave the screen, and go and do something else, the film follows me. Sometimes it rudely interrupts my enjoyment of other films, or it accompanies me into the shower: 'Hey there, don't forget me. I'm sure you're simplifying me to make it easy for your writing. Are you *really* doing me justice?' Oh, the inescapable responsibility, and the worry! Do others not similarly experience this intensity?

SC: That film is overwhelming is also a fact about it, the richness is overwhelming, 90 or 100 minutes and you have been taken through a larger span of passion and feeling than really 90 minutes of almost anything else. (Not more than Bach's *Saint Matthew Passion*. No indeed. But what kind of concession is that?) And you have the sense often about how terribly little of a film is articulated, as if, if you don't say anything about the film now, the experience of the film will vanish with the film. The density of stimulus is a fact about what's happened to you. Not to come to terms with it is to have something that has happened to you go unremarked, as if intellectually oppressive. Multiple re-screenings do not always help. They may confirm wordlessness. The sense of wanting to have something to say that matches the richness of experience is itself daunting. I think of Victor Perkins' response *just* to the Linz sequence in *Letter from an Unknown Woman* (Max Ophüls, 1948, US) [where the pair are isolated in a corner of the square and he proposes and she rejects him]. The intricacy of what Perkins can show of what is actually going on in that sequence is something that only a handful of people are capable of doing. So that cannot be an example of what you are asking of a decent non-evasive academic response.

AK: I find that after I've watched a film I normally have a few moments or maybe just one moment that really strikes me.

SC: Start there...

AK: Yes, I'll start there. I try to encourage my students to go with the moment that struck them.

SC: Absolutely. Another good exercise.

AK: Yes, although it wasn't an exercise for me. It feels intuitive. Anyway, I'll only have a dim sense of what it is about that moment. I'll just go 'hmmmm.'

SC: A moment you care about, however apparently trivial, can be productive. Why did the hand do that? Why did the camera turn just then?

AK: And why is this niggling me? Our direction of thought here reminds me that you have discussed Emerson's feeling that primary wisdom is intuition, whilst all later teachings are tuitions. The occurrence to us of an intuition places a demand on us for tuition. You call this wording, the willingness to subject one self to words, to make oneself intelligible. This tuition so conceived is what you understand criticism to be, to follow out in each case the complete tuition for a given intuition. There's a moment that really stuck me in Frank Capra's *Mr. Deeds Goes to Town* (Frank Capra, 1936, US). I read your piece on the film after re-watching it, and was pleased to see you mention this moment. It is when Mr Deeds (Gary Cooper) is lying on his back on his bed talking to Babe Bennett (Jean Arthur) on the phone. He has his right calf and ankle resting on the knee of the other leg, and he's playing with his foot while he's talking to her. The camera is behind his head so that most of his face is obscured (this shot is repeated a number of times). Then when the phone call is over you see him playing his trusty tuba and his face is even more hidden than in the previous version of the shot. Why did they think to execute it like that...*like that*?

SC: *Like that...*

AK: And *why* was I drawn to these shots? I suppose there *is* something unusual about seeing someone on their bed playing with their foot in a film, or with their tuba, and not seeing their face. Yet, I didn't only think the shots were unusual, or striking, I thought they were gently mysterious, and that they were significant. They asked questions of me. As the film continued, the memory of the shots kept returning. My intuition was that because these shots were *like that* they might give me a key to the whole film, and open it up in new and rewarding ways.

SC: I like it. I share it. It is always important that one is drawn, that a memory keeps returning. I'm inclined to say further that there is always a reason. But wordlessness may be as significant a response as an essay. You remind me of a little private concept of mine – 'the nothing shot'. Sometimes just rhetorically it makes a break in the narrative at certain times. In another Frank Capra film, *It Happened One Night* (Frank Capra, 1934, US), with the pair Clark Gable and Claudette Colbert, we find them walking together down a road *away* from us, an empty road, and that's a shot that over and over I came back to in my mind. I had nothing to say about it. I knew that it punctuated a moment in the film; it was the end of something and the beginning of something. It could have been months, maybe years, until I just stopped and asked myself, in the right mood, what is it about a couple together at dawn walking down a road together away from us? Where are they coming from (what is dawning), and going to; why are they – are they – silent? They direct brief words to each other, but what are they thinking about? And suddenly every word seemed to mean something and at that stage I could hardly keep up with thoughts that I was having about it. I then wrote a brief essay about simply that shot, *simply* that shot, which seemed to me to raise every issue in the whole film. *But as an exercise*, it is so hard – isn't it? – to characterise in such a way that a group of people each can follow it, get something out of it. It's not to be counted on.

AK: That's what's interesting about it. Yet, we both, I hope, would be reluctant to say it is some special privilege of our own to see these moments, or recognise them.

SC: Positively, I refuse to.

AK: Yes. And yet one knows from teaching...

SC: ...that anyone can draw a blank about anything. Especially with such a question as, '*What* does that sequence *mean*?' The question is why one is stopped. It is a question that marks something I think of as philosophical criticism, given the extent to which I think of philosophy as inherently a matter of stopping and turning and going back over (call this conversation rather than linear, monological argument). It is a portrait of philosophy I find stretching from the events in Plato's Myth of the Cave in *The Republic* to the practices recorded in Wittgenstein's *Investigations*, with their depictions of being lost, stopped, and the recurrent demand to turn and to return. It goes with a view I have advanced on a number of occasions, of philosophy as responsiveness, as not speaking first. There I am taking as exemplary Socrates' characteristically being drawn into conversation by being accosted, perhaps in the public street. I grew up with so many colleagues, fellow students and teachers, who seemed to me to hector and pester each other and strangers with their philosophy, demanding answers to questions about what exactly the other means when nothing turned on getting more precise at that moment. In Socrates' recounting of the opening events of *The Republic*, he depicts himself being accosted, stopped – his cloak is grabbed from behind – by the slave of a friend, to give him the message that his master urgently wants to speak with him, is eager to ask him something. Socrates tells the slave that he can release his cloak, implying that this is the sort of request that a philosopher will not willingly refuse, namely to attend to someone's need or desire for a response, sensing themselves at a loss.

What is wrong with criticism as appreciation (or diminishment) is not that the critic expresses his or her taste but that this taste is not allowed to be questioned by the work in question, and nor is the work declared as unworthy to be given this privilege. A rooted condescension toward film is encouraged by the (reasonable) assumption on the part of daily or weekly critics of film that their readers will view the film just once. So they present a sort of tiny travel guide of the film's events, with a tip or two of what to like or avoid. Nothing wrong with good tips; and some critics obligated to provide them observe and write memorably enough to elicit gratitude. But the short notice seems by its nature debarred from the project of getting viewers to stop, to consider, to check their own experience – to ask, for example, whether the reader shares the sense that the ending kiss in *Bringing Up Baby* (Howard Hawks, 1938, US) is awkward and to speculate about why that may be meant; or ask whether there may be an ulterior motive for Preston Sturges incorporating the opening strains of the Pilgrim's Chorus from *Tannhäuser* to accompany the sequence on the honeymoon train ride out of Connecticut in which Lady Eve (Barbara Stanwyck) wraps her pious bridegroom in tales of her lurid past, and ask further why virtually no one remembers those strains in remembering the film, lost among the thousand-and-one other conditions and decisions that have made this film the film it is (*The Lady Eve*, Preston Sturges, 1941, US). The harm of once-over film criticism is that it is the only sort of writing about film that most filmgoers will encounter.

AK: You seem to be drawing a distinction between viewing critically and viewing philosophically. This sense of being stopped underpins your idea of viewing philosophically. I am stopped by the shots of

Deeds on his back on the bed, and then my questioning or investigation of the shots is influenced by that sense of being stopped. If I then say to you, or to a class, look at this shot of Deeds on his back playing his tuba – 'Look at his leg' or 'Look at him on his back' – then I have already given illustrations. I've told you what to look at. We could then say all sorts of fine things about the shot, and, in your terms, we would be viewing the moment critically, rather than philosophically as such. In the classroom, I often find myself prompting critical questions of this sort, but I hope I also encourage situations where we start with only a dim idea of why we have stilled the frame in this place, and we all help each other discover why we have stopped.

We can contrast the sort of moment like the one of Deeds on the bed or the moment in *It Happened One Night* to another instance, and that is the moment that you don't realise at first, but later seems to be an important occurrence in the film. You mention a moment in *The Awful Truth* (Leo McCarey, 1937, US) where, at the beginning of the film, Irene Dunne throws an orange to Cary Grant. This orange is part of his gift to her. He has brought oranges back from Florida, where he was supposed to be visiting, but they're stamped with CALIFORNIA. They therefore reveal his deceit. You say something to the effect that initially you hadn't taken the action of her throwing the orange very seriously and then it became much more important to you. You say that she is not giving the fruit, but returning it. A train of questions then arose about what it is each wants the other to know, and who is to go first in trusting the other, and why each are perpetually tempted to test the other.

SC: It was only in the introduction to *Contesting Tears*, about the melodrama of the unknown woman, that it occurred to me that I wanted to say this about *The Awful Truth*, years after publishing my essay on that film. That's a reason to write more than one book or one sentence or to go to more than one film or to live more than one day. I sometimes wonder whether I am slower on average than others in being able to recognise with clarity and usefulness what's on my mind. I pride myself, in any case, on having a good memory for my inadequacies.

AK: It is a wonder to me how the great films keep pulling me back when they might appear to have exhausted themselves (other works of art pull one back, of course, but they don't appear exhausted in quite this way).

SC: Think how that goes with the ingrained habit of movie going, that lasted decades before someone broke it, and it still exists in many households, which is that you don't go to see a film that you've already seen. That is the idea that it doesn't matter how great or moving this film was; there is nothing to learn from seeing it again. And of course if the only reason to see it again is to learn something, maybe you don't learn what we're talking about. But the sense that a film is eaten up and the wrapper can be thrown away on one viewing is very deep.

AK: Although we should note that thousands of people do re-view films like *It's a Wonderful Life* (Frank Capra, 1946, US) every year and thousands of people buy videos of them. In fact films are often returned to more than books.

SC: Certain films are, and this is important. But isn't this apt not to happen because of a sense that one has not exhausted the issues of the film but rather because of something like the reverse, that one wants the sheer pleasure (or reassurance?) of finding it unchanged?

AK: The matter is importantly related to teaching because it must be true for me that these films are able to open up each year to different students. Every year a student will say or write something new about a film I've taught many times. This is why teaching is, or should be, continuous with our criticism. The fact that the films can be reinterpreted, provide new interpretations and new patterns, is intimately connected to the idea that you re-teach them. Students mustn't think that the object of study has a meaning that is fixed (and fixed by me, or you). Each cohort of students, each class, must feel they are participating in an ongoing, unfolding conversation.

SC: We expect this of every art but film. It would be impossible for me to go into a classroom and talk about any object, or text, if I didn't have some new suggestion to make about it. It can be the smallest detail, but if the compass needle just jogs, and you walk just a bit out of the way, everything can come out fresh, one's relation to the familiar is enlivened, the hard surface is broken. Yes, it's about teaching, about friendship, about marriage, about one's life, about taking an interest. If for a given class I draw a blank or find myself unhappy with my notes for an opening, I say so (I hope), and ask for someone else for a beginning response. This is placing trust in my view that philosophy does not speak first, but is responsive. Part of the sense of this is that on the whole it is easier to take an interest in another' response rather than to report and articulate a response of one's own. And without interest, philosophy as I care about it most cannot proceed.

AK: You've written the idea that films think, and further the idea of films thinking philosophically. One can imagine this sounding obscure. How can films *think*?

SC: Well, of course, that is to begin with just a somewhat provocative way of saying: Don't ask what the artist is thinking or intending, but ask why the work is as it is, why just *this* is *here* in just *that* way. The implication that the way the work is is a matter of its own thinking or intention may be brought out by noting that to ask 'Why has the artist done that?' (namely, modulated to the subdominant, held this shot longer than one would have expected, used a canvas whose vertical is many times longer than its horizontal span), and to ask 'Why does the work modulate, prolong the shot, employ this format?' are differently emphasised formulations of the same demand. Intending something (as in Anscombe's book on the subject[4]) is a function of wanting something. My formulation employing the work's thinking or intending or wanting something, is meant to emphasise the sense that the work wants something of us who behold or hear or read it. This is a function of our determining what we want of it, why or how we are present at it – what our relation to it is. It and I (each I present at it) are responsible to each other. As a music student, I was familiar early with thinking of a work as developing in response to itself. I shy away from the idea of a 'work of art'. But I do mean 'work of art', something made, if only made present, with reason, perhaps to defeat reason.

   Why is one so shy these days? 'Work of art' is a term almost never used in my hearing any more, what is used is 'artwork'. Artwork is spelled as one word and, unless it's just or simply or only a mispronunciation of the German word *Artwerk*, I find it an odd turn. (It is certainly not a translation of 'object d'art'.) It seems to me a mark of a significant shift in sensibility over the past several decades, in response to, let's call it, the end of modernism. The English word 'artwork' used to, and as far as I know still does, designate a sort of embroidery, and also the matter in a magazine layout that includes everything but the words, everything that requires a design decision. What is critical about what I called this recent shift of sensibility is that *artwork* is a different kind of noun from *work of art*. It's called, I believe, a mass noun. It's like the noun 'salt'; you wouldn't say, I'd like *a* salt, you'd ask for *some* or for *more* salt. And you wouldn't say you've got *an* artwork if what you have in mind is the design layout or the embroidery around the edge of a fabric, you would have *some* artwork and *more* artwork. So the shift from work of art to artwork seems a shift away from regarding a work as singular, as though nothing is (any longer) irreplaceable. I resist the idea.

I would not be inclined to ask about artwork what it is thinking about. That it is attractive, lucid, dramatic, is sufficient to justify its existence. (Though I might find that a given layout is thinking about, or say an homage to, Mondrian.) It's hard for me not to invoke here an idea I broach concerning *Mr. Deeds Goes to Town*, concerning Deeds' saying 'Everybody does something silly when he thinks.' This is said in a courtroom as Deeds begins to mount his defence against the charge that he does outlandish, incomprehensible things, like playing a tuba as he lies in bed, or feeding doughnuts to a horse. Taking its cue from Deeds the camera goes on to illustrate his examples as he picks out characters in the courtroom who are doodling, cracking their knuckles, drumming their fingers on a table, twitching their noses, and so forth. What we witness are human beings in various states of nervousness or restlessness, as if the human body and the human mind are not wholly at one with each other. Where Descartes says that nothing is more human than thinking, that thinking is the human essence that proves its existence to itself, this film is saying, 'Indeed. And what thinking looks like is *this*, namely a property provable upon the body.' (This is a perception congenial to Austin in the theory of excuses.) Descartes defines the human as a thing that thinks, and film retorts that it is an essentially restless body that thinks. I raise this not to argue it but to observe that in directing the camera to provide this proof by way of the body, Deeds is simultaneously showing that film is thinking about thinking, that is, about what it is to be human.

AK: I think it's fair to say that Hollywood films specialised in this sort of insight. How beguiling that the integrity of oneself, or the integrity of thinking, would be conceived, or proved, through silliness. It's charming, to put it mildly...and it is also profound.

SC: About silliness. I also have picked up that word reading so serious a critic as Paul de Man, who remarks that 'silliness is deeply associated with reference', that is, using language merely to say something that purports to be true or false. And I put that together with Wittgenstein's remark, collected in *Culture and Value*, 'Always climb from the heights of cleverness into the green valleys of silliness.' The valleys of silliness are part of the magnificence and the pity and the vulnerability and the waste and the beauty of human existence.

AK: The great clowns – Laurel and Hardy, Buster Keaton, Harold Lloyd, Charlie Chaplin – remind us of this repeatedly in endless creative variations.

SC: Endless. And they show that the highest and lowest moods may be separated by the thickness of a membrane. They join hands here with Shakespeare.

AK: With regard to *Mr Deeds Goes To Town* you have just discussed the expressiveness of the body while it thinks. You discuss the expressiveness of the human body in the *Unknown Woman* films, and how the self manifests itself in its embodiment. As you would say, film has found one of its important subjects. For you Garbo is the representation of absolute expressiveness, some extraordinary unity of body and mind. Charles Affron has written something instructive (and vivid) about Greta Garbo: 'Her acting is of a complexity that makes it difficult to assess in the context of standard technique. Yet she herself supplies the clue in the model of concentration that we must emulate if we are to perceive her properly. Lodged within the triteness of most of her vehicles, the glamour of a pristine shell, and the authentic image of solitude she projects are areas of sentiment that are attainable if we are prepared to pitch our tension of awareness as high as that of the actress. Garbo sheds the seductive veils of the love goddess, but only for those who are willing to share her intricacies. Punished with the numbness of adoration if we are lax, we visit the depths of her being if we can withstand the painful intimacy of her method. Garbo often seems lost in the labyrinth of her own privacy.'[5] In your own work on Garbo, you emphasise that Garbo's absolute expressiveness is impossible to acknowledge, but I take it that you don't mean that the viewer shouldn't try, or try to experience the detail of her behaviour. I like the way Affron brings *our* responsibility into the picture, and the way we have to rise to her, if she, and the film, is to be revealed.

SC: Learn from her how to think about her. I don't want to miss what's unique about Garbo, but to learn how to think about a character from the character is something like an ancient preoccupation of mine. I have said this about Cordelia in *King Lear* and said it in effect in comparing Garbo with Dietrich and, in all seriousness, with Mae West (in 'More of *The World Viewed*').[6] When Affron expresses the idea of Garbo's shedding the veils of the love goddess and promising intimacy, he also speaks, admirably, of her as lost in her privacy. So to withstand her intimacy is to find her – not to know her but perhaps to acknowledge her unknownness. To find her in her power of intimacy is to recognise the splendour, the reality, of the human other. That there are others is not something one recognises at just any time (much as philosophy would like independent assurance of their presence). Film joins the great arts in harbouring this fact in its own way – beginning perhaps with its insistence on mortality, on the permanence and transience of the past.

AK: You've illuminated what we might mean when we say that a work of art is thinking. We have an instance from *Mr Deeds Goes To Town* where thinking is one of the film's themes or subjects. You've also said that film is inherently self-reflexive. This is of course a very important topic in *The World Viewed*. What's our link here?

SC: What I wanted to capture by saying that film is inherently self-reflexive is simply the significance of the fact that what you're given in film is a view of a place or a person or an object that is from one place rather than any other, at this time and not another, for this interval rather than another, in this light and with this texture and not others, and so on. Choice – thought, reflection – is on the surface. Obviously there are homologous choices in the other arts, but with film the alternatives (of angle, distance, lighting, interval, etc.) are in principle so obvious as to be imponderable. The reason for emphasising this, even so brusquely, is that it is just the thing that is invisible about film. It's on the surface, you can't miss it, but you inveterately miss it. Film trades on this, on missing it; it is part of film's emotionality. Call it the false transparency of film. If we say that this transparency is achieved through film's power to induce trance-like states, then our next task is to uncover the sources of this power. Should we relate false transparency to a resistance to the recognition of reality's independence of us?

AK: Another way to associate philosophy with film is by the application of a philosophical thesis or a philosophical text to a film. This is another occasion where philosophy and film meet each other. For example, you associate Descartes with *Mr Deeds Goes to Town*. Can you take me through the process here? You are not simply applying Descartes...

SC: No, that's right.

AK: Ha!....Sorry to interrupt but I'm just thinking of Gary Cooper's simplistic answers during questioning by the House Committee on Un-American Activities...

SC: Yes. What we see there is that *this* is *Gary Cooper* thinking. Yet his uncensored embarrassment at his ignorance of the intellectual stakes in play (what does he confess to the House Committee he has never read? – not alone Marx) is so much more agreeable and illuminating than the self-presentations of Robert Montgomery and Adolf Menjou as deep thinkers. This goes with the revelation that on film Gary Cooper's portrayal of embarrassment can become a realisation of what philosophy calls self-consciousness, what Descartes specifies as my awareness that I think – that I cannot think that I do not think (for example, doubt it).

AK: Yes, look at the transformation in the film. Watching his silence at the end of *Mr Deeds Goes To Town* – he is astute about when one might speak or not speak or when one might want to show what one knows (or what one doesn't know). Anyway I'm sorry, you were talking about Descartes...

SC: I was agreeing with you that I do not invoke Descartes in my discussion of *Mr. Deeds Goes To Town* as something the film illustrates. It is rather that the film rediscovers what it is that Descartes changed philosophy by discovering. It's a rediscovery of philosophy. It is important to me to show that film can do this, important both about film and about philosophy. It's important to me to say that philosophy can be discovered. Indeed what I want to say is that there *is* no philosophy *unless* it is discovered. Otherwise, it's just something that takes place in a classroom. The sense of film's intervention in human culture as an unprecedented event in the history of the arts is something recapturable in the experience of a significant film, for example in an unprecedented revelation of the body's restlessness as an expression of the essence of mind. It presents thinking itself as an embarrassment as well as a glory.

AK: The danger is when all this becomes institutionalised: this week I'm teaching *Mr Deeds Goes To Town* and this week the accompanying reading is Descartes, and, oh dear, you get some strange things happening, and it is not at all like the 'discovery' you're describing. After the class, every poor student tries to write an essay contriving the connection, and both Descartes and the film are mauled. The question therefore is: how does one keep the spirit of discovery within a more formalised teaching environment?

SC: This sounds again like the problem of naming the prostitute. You want Descartes to be there, but if you just say 'This is Descartes' you've killed it. Can one teach tact? Think of it as learning what constitutes the right to speak. Wittgenstein in the *Tractatus* is concerned about what *can* be said, when silence *must* not be broken.[7] Nietzsche opens Book II of *Human, All Too Human* by declaring: 'One should speak only where one *may* not be silent.'[8] In the *Investigations*, Wittgenstein is more explicitly concerned with one's standing toward the object of one's speech. He keeps coming upon the moment at which the teacher has to recognise that the one being instructed or informed has to go on alone. To allow the other the freedom for her or his own discoveries is then the mark of a good teacher.

AK: I have a Laurel and Hardy example. *The Music Box* (James Parrott, 1932, US) is the film where they take the piano all the way up the stairs and it keeps falling back down again. The critic Raymond Durgnat says the film is the myth of Sisyphus in comic terms. One significant difference from the myth of Sisyphus is that there is not one person but two, and the acknowledgement of this is important to the appreciation of the aspect of togetherness in Laurel and Hardy. Yet, it is still a fascinating insight and an example of how the film seems to have discovered the myth itself, or rediscovered it, and reframed it.

SC: Yes. Although in general film's discovery of myth seems somewhat better recognised than its discovery of philosophy. The register of the mythic in film is part, perhaps, of what Thomas Mann distrusted in it. He found film too drastic, and too easily manipulative in its effects, to count as an art. For the author of *Joseph and his Brothers*, and with Joyce's *Ulysses* in mind, the achievement of the mythic can seem too easy to achieve when, for example, Sean Penn at the end of *Dead Man Walking* (Tim Robbins, 1995, US) looms up virtually bound to a cross before the witnesses of his execution. To achieve the discovery of tragedy in the myth of Cinderella took the novelistic genius of Dickens

in *Great Expectations*. To achieve the discovery of its comedy cinematically takes no more than the talents that went into the making of
Pretty Woman (Garry Marshall, 1990, US) in which Julia Roberts keeps
having trouble with one of her shoes.

AK: In *The World Viewed* you write: 'Given the feeling that a certain
obscurity of prompting is not external to what I wished most fervently
to say about film...I felt called upon to voice my responses with their
privacy, their argumentativeness, even their intellectual perverseness,
on their face; often to avoid voicing a thought awaiting its voice, to
refuse that thought, to break into the thought, as if our standing responses to film are themselves standing between us and the responses
that film is made to elicit and to satisfy.'[9] I think there is something
very suggestive in all this and I think it does fit with some of the things
we've been discussing. Could you unpack it for me?

SC: My first response to it is just to realise how early *The World Viewed*
is in the effort to write about film in some sustained way. The book
was published in 1971 and the writing had started in the late sixties,
some thirty-five years ago. There were already some wonderful things
to read about film, but not, as now, a sense of a body of significant
work from which to look for companionship. I am expressing in the
citation you read there a sense of isolation from my intellectual and
aesthetic worlds, in which taking film with whatever philosophical
seriousness one might bring to the subject was an eccentric thing to
do, measured either by lovers of film or by professors of philosophy. (I
won't attempt to characterise the state of my moral and political
worlds, marked by the Vietnam War and the Civil Rights Movement
begun in the earlier 1960s, but the ambience of these events is also to
be felt in such a passage as the one you cited from.) I was just completing the essays that make up *Must We Mean What We Say?*, which continues, even anticipates, the defence of Austin and Wittgenstein
worked at in my doctoral dissertation completed in 1961. Since they
seemed to show me a path into the present of philosophy, and at the
same time caused alarmingly hard feelings in much, most, of the philosophical community I inhabited, I had already been forced to some
recognition of my eccentricity. There were ample opportunities for me
to feel a mystery to myself as much as to others.

AK: Would it be fair to say that 'avoid voicing a thought awaiting its
voice' is associated with the idea of being torn between wanting to

evoke as precisely as we can, as truthfully as we can, but also wanting to maintain a vagueness, a sense of the incomplete, or the uncertain? We don't want to articulate in such a way that runs away from the inexact nature of our feelings. We want words that are more precise because we know they're a good way of rendering the experience, but we also don't want to go too far. Yet, moreover, we also know that feelings which feel justifiably inexact at one time, become less inexact with further observation and thought, or by seeking help from others, and then we no longer want to express them inexactly...You can see the problem here?

SC: Positively. And we owe an explanation of what *too far* is.

AK: Maybe another way of opening this out – 'avoid voicing a thought awaiting its voice' – is that good films prompt mysterious thoughts and feelings in us, amorphous, latent thoughts and feelings, and this is one of their achievements. All the arts can do this, but film seems to have a particular talent for it, and is drawn to it. The films are not simply prompting clear thoughts in us, or even clear ambiguities. They encourage us to take notice of those feelings that have yet to be voiced, which are 'awaiting' their 'voice.' They encourage us to keep a hold of that sense, not to lose it, or forget it; to keep a hold of the murmurings, the rumblings, that are the route into discovery, not simply the discovery in itself.

SC: Another clause in the sentence you read says something about voicing a thought in its confusion.

AK: You say, 'to voice my responses with their privacy, their argumentativeness, even their intellectual perverseness.'

SC: All of that. I'm not worried about going too far in conveying the perverseness but just about going exactly right up to the perverseness and getting that out. That would set the table for assessing whether it is I or the aspects of the world I was drawn to write in opposition to that is the perverse party. Take the thought expressed as 'avoid voicing a thought awaiting its voice'. Don't we all have the sense sometimes of being vulgar about our experience, loud mouths, cowardly in expressing ourselves, hence losing forever experiences that are, or might have been, of extreme value to us? This is something Nietzsche warns about in *The Birth of Tragedy*. This strikes me as something I was particularly aware of in writing *The World Viewed*. I wondered – oftener than usual even for me – whether anyone would ever stop over such a formulation to ask whether its oddness was worth understanding, that it is meant to say something other than that I should for some reason not say what is on my mind; it is meant rather to say that my impatient expressions do not allow me to know what is on my mind, that a standing formula is ready to take over thinking for us, that what is of distinct importance to us is masked by us.

AK: The subtitle to *The World Viewed* is *Reflections on the Ontology of Film*. Why do you think considerations of ontology are helpful to our readings of films, and how are they helpful to the critical process?

SC: Two things. No doubt I used ontology in part to be somewhat provocative and mysterious. But there are two immediate interests that I was hoping would be served by the term. One interest is to ask what makes film the specific thing it is, like – as I believe I said earlier – nothing else on earth; but to ask this without asking, at least too soon, 'What is the medium of film?', which inspires, or dictates, answers such as that it is essentially a visual medium or a dramatic medium, or more portentously, that it is a medium of light and shadow. Let's avoid these voices awaiting to be voiced. Let's do something about saying concretely and in detail what its differences from everything else on earth are. Shall we ask what the conditions are that a thing has to satisfy to count as a film? Does it help to add: what conditions are essential to it?

The second interest I had in mind specifies the question by linking it with a remarkable formulation from Wittgenstein's *Investigations*: 'It is grammar that tells us what kind of object anything is.'[10] (This can be taken as the founding insight of what Wittgenstein means by the ordinary, of his characterising his philosophical procedures as meant to 'bring words back from their metaphysical to their everyday use'.) One of Wittgenstein's early examples of this theme opens the *Blue Book* from 1934, one of the main drafts of material recognisably preserved in *Philosophical Investigations*. He asks 'What is the meaning of a word?' and proposes to attack the question by asking what an explanation of the meaning is, for what that explains will *be* the meaning – a grammatically related expression will tell you what kind of thing the meaning of a word is. In *The Claim of Reason* I say that to know what faith is *is* to know, for instance, how faith is acquired, how weakened, how lost. Accordingly I am proposing that to answer the question 'what is (the ontology of) film?' we have to investigate such questions as, 'what is the audience of film?' (as opposed to audiences of plays), 'what is the director of a film?' (as opposed perhaps to the director of a bank), 'what does the film screen screen?' (in contrast with what the support of a painting supports), 'what role does the script of a film play?' (measured against what role the libretto of an opera plays), 'what counts as remembering a film?' (as compared with remembering a poem, or a novel, or an argument, or what happened yesterday), 'what is a remake of a film?' (as opposed to a new production of a play), etc. Wittgenstein says of grammar (a grammatical investigation, which his investigations are) that it expresses essence (a remark I believe that has not much attracted the attention of philosophers). He is there claiming to satisfy, by educating, an ancient intellectual craving.

AK: So in what ways do you think that our more specific thoughts about individual moments, individual films, and individual moments in films, are helped by our thoughts about what the medium is, that is to say the ontology of the medium?

SC: Well, part of the continuing claim in the book is that it is only in films – and in the evolving criticism of films – that you care about, that the medium reveals itself. There is no fixed, mysterious thing underlying all of these manifestations (individual moments). I should add that I distinguish the medium of film from the material basis of the medium or media.

AK: One knows that criticism, even good criticism, can make intelligent observations about a film without acknowledging the medium's ontology. On the other hand, am I wrong? This is exactly what it will be doing: one feature of intelligent criticism is that it *is* acknowledging the medium even though it may not explicitly refer to it? Will our criticism be better for it being an explicit concern? I suppose I am also wondering about whether ontology is something that students should be aware of.

SC: I guess my best answer is that it should come with experience. I suppose this means that I put criticism first, and distinguish this from theory, which has to consider such things as the role of the real in film (as opposed to painting, theatre, and writing); and why certain genres and types occupy the history of film; and why certain subjects tap the depth of film. This ordering goes with my claim that the films we care about most are those that most surprisingly and richly reveal their medium

AK: Thinking about the medium in more general terms may lead us to understand it in ways that enhance our appreciation of specific elements. So for instance, if we understand that characters in films are real, live human beings then this leads us, or should lead us, to talk about these characters differently, say, to characters in novels. I've written criticism where I make continuous references to the characters' names, which is sometimes fine for my purposes, but sometimes reveals that I'm not adequately acknowledging the ontological particularity of characters: a human being, a performer, is moving and talking and gesturing....

SC: Exactly.

AK: Or another example. You have an observation in *The World Viewed* about the way that objects can be equal to humans in films, and they are not the same as 'props.' You give the example that in the theatre, two brooms can also represent two trees, or they can represent a forest, but on film, they will simply be two brooms. You call this 'ontological equality' and that opens up the *particular* ways in which elements relate to each other in film: the medium's *particular* achievement of synthesis, the *particular* relationship between the performer, his décor, the camera and so on and so forth. An ontological insight may sharpen our critical responses.

SC: Sharpen as well as complete. It's so in my marrow by now that I may skip over a step in responding to your questions. But you've been catching me out, you've been taking me back to something. I don't want to skip over the fact that the eventual appeal to the medium also works back and alerts you to what there is for criticism to respond to, as well as provides a necessary and explicit depth.

If you think of film as drama then, unlike what happens on a stage, the drama is carried more by actor than character, and more by what the camera does than what the actor does. Which again means that acting on film is specific to film. A work for the stage like Beckett's *Endgame* is thinking about how far acting and plotting can be stripped from human character, so that our differences become sheer matters of separateness or isolation. A work for film like David Mamet's *House of Games* is thinking about how far acting and plot can take over human character, so that we lose interest in others and in ourselves (and in such a film). I seem to be veering back to my insistence that we need to talk about the essence of differences but that what counts as essential has to be reconsidered, in each case has to be discovered. Otherwise you repeat what you think you already know. As soon as somebody learns that I've written about film I immediately start getting a lecture about what film is. There is something about film that makes it unbearable for people not to consider themselves experts about it. At a reception the other evening I was told, 'It is important to define what film can do that no other art can do' I said I agreed. My informant went on: 'Film is visual.' But last year I attended a crowded lecture by a renowned scholar of film the burden of which was that film is a thing of the past, and that what is of interest now is the visual as such. I take this to indicate that experts about film find it unbearable not to be inexpert.

AK: We must not lose sight of the point you made earlier: specific films will reveal the medium. Once you start forgetting that and start simply positing or reflecting on the medium separate to specific instances of it, you are going down a bumpy road. I suppose it should be a virtuous circle: particular films prompt thoughts about the medium, and those thoughts in turn reveal more about the films, and so on...

You have written two books on specific genres: Remarriage Comedy and The Melodrama of the Unknown Woman. You also make relevant observations on genre in your piece *The Fact of Television*. How helpful is a conceptual understanding of genre to our appreciation of specific films?

SC: Let's see concretely what help it can be. *It Happened One Night* opens with a woman's father attempting to prevent his daughter from marrying a particular man by stranding her on his yacht and trying to force her out of her hunger strike. Compare this with the opening of *A Midsummer Night's Dream*, in which a father demands from his sovereign the enforcing of a law that requires a daughter to obey her father's wishes for her marriage or else be put to death. In remarriage comedy, the father, if he is present, is always on the side of his daughter's desire. I cannot but believe that so massive a difference betokens something about the medium of film revealed in the genre of remarriage comedy – something about what I have called film's infantilising of its viewers, and been led to call the maternal gaze of the screen, here something about the maternal possibilities of certain fathers. Genre is *one* way of articulating the endless invisible forces or conditions or laws that our actions and passions obey, for all our sense of singularity. Such are the divinities that shape our ends; or that rough hew them.

I suppose I am talking about an idea that is as old as Plato, that you know things by knowing the concepts they participate in. For example, I don't find it helps much to conceptualise what an Antonioni film is, or a Rohmer film, or an Ophuls film, by asking what genre their films belong to. You have to begin, if the question interests you, by considering each in the light of their other films. *It Happened One Night* is a Capra film; it is also a remarriage comedy; it is also a Clark Gable film. I have forgotten who the writer of the film is ...

AK: As we normally do... (In fact it is by Robert Riskin, based on the story *Night Bus* by Samuel Hopkins Adams).

SC: Yes. As we normally do, and inexcusably.

AK: Yes inexcusably. And we feel guilt about it...

SC: ...as we should.

AK: And then we repress it rather quickly, I find.

SC: Yes, it's a blunder. So perhaps this comes back to the fact that film studies is still just beginning to get straight about what its responsibilities may be. Then if these questions open up, further questions follow. How, for example, does allegiance to a genre or being conceptualisable by appealing to a genre, relate to a film's capacity for being popular? The genre of remarriage allows room for the expression of the commonest, most conventional, of human emotions, and between the most primitive or comprehensible of human actions, including moments of a slapstick loss of control. Yet their range of variation serves to align these common human themes or frailties with their most refined expressions.

AK: What fascinates me about both the genres that are most associated with you, Remarriage Comedy and The Unknown Woman, is that they are associated with *you*! We did not particularly use these labels until you wrote about them in this way. Yet, there *is* this generic relationship between the Remarriage Comedies and between the Unknown Woman films. The generic features must have existed before Stanley Cavell, and were presumably part of the way they related to each other when they were made, but Stanley Cavell has now discovered the features. Acknowledging this is to acknowledge an important strand in your work and to acknowledge something about the critical process. Your work on genre could profitably be linked with your writing on intention. Put briefly, we don't necessarily find out about intention by asking the filmmakers, or by researching the studio documents, or by conducting any other investigations outside the work itself. The viewer, or the critic, discovers intention in the work, by looking further *into the work*. Stanley Cavell discovers this genre, but the genre was intended in some sense, even if that is not how the people at the time talked about the films, or how the studio talked about them – maybe they talked about 'screwball comedies' or 'women's weepies.' There is something liberating here for the viewer and the critic. Am I making any sense?

SC: Yes. Well part of this goes with how perpetually under-analysed the concepts of intention and convention both are. Intention is both prized and despised with next to no analysis of what the concept of intention does, with next to no examples given about how we actually use the concept of intention. (Would it be stuffy to say that it has become irresponsible of a scholar who finds herself or himself putting a certain weight on the concept of intention, not to read Austin and Wittgenstein and Anscombe on the subject?) Derrida recognises it only as familiar grist, New Critics despise or parody it. I am so often asked in response to a claim of mine (often, perhaps less often in recent years, about the existence generally of the genre of remarriage) 'Did anybody really think that?' 'Did they mean that?' 'Directors like Frank Capra didn't have this in mind did they?', with no sense that the concept of intention or of meaning something needs analysis. One might ask, for example: What are you denying if you deny that in *Adam's Rib* Hepburn's response to the ending (and the beginning) question – What's the difference between men and women? – is meant to relate to the earlier implied question, What's (how can you tell) the difference between a slap and a slug?, a relation suggesting both that a small empirical difference can signal a difference of abysmal psychological significance, and that the 'signal' must be perceived by the intuitive faculty of each person for herself or himself – as though we have here a crossing of the ethical and the aesthetic? Does denying the relation suggest that the connection is accidental, inadvertent, distracting, far-fetched, etc.? Each of these suggestions requires its own justification.

What causes the distrust of intention – beyond, I mean, an opposition to an unguarded, or metaphysical, trust in it? I am particularly alerted to this issue because when I came into the philosophical picture, in the 1950s, intention was being attacked by the so-called New Criticism, headed by a once very famous article 'The Intentional Fallacy', co-authored by a professor of English, W.H. Wimsatt, and a professor of philosophy, Monroe Beardsley.[11] I take up their article in my paper 'A Matter of Meaning It', collected in *Must We Mean What We Say?*, where I claim that what they say about intention in the region of literature makes it unlike the concept of intention in other regions of interest, in law or morality or sports. A more persistent issue for me concerns the concept of convention. There is a considerable controversy at the moment, in which I am involved, about whether Wittgenstein's idea of grammar and criteria are grounded on ideas of convention, say of actions as rule-governed, or grounded in some other way. On my view, Wittgenstein serves to break down aspects of the distinction between what is conventional and what is natural.

AK: I'm particularly interested in the way your understanding of the concepts is useful for people studying films. For example, with genre, there is so much work telling us what constitutes this or that genre (e.g. shadows in Film Noir), and these lists of features become institutionalised, and are perfect for textbooks. This is what the genre is, and it can be learned. Similarly with intention: we might be told what happened on the set; or told that the studio did this and that; or told about the actor's life; or told that this was going on in America at the time... And this is why the films contain what they do. My problem with these observations is not necessarily that they are unhelpful, because we all know that they may offer us insights of many sorts. My problem with them is that they can be taken in the wrong way, and excuse us from our own responsibilities for finding out what a film is about, what we see and hear in a film, and what might be important in it. They can restrict us from seeing aspects at an early stage of viewing and that can close down the possibilities for interpretation, hence viewing, and this may restrict our capacity to discover where the achievement in a work may reside. Such observations need not necessarily have this effect, but I see it happening repeatedly, especially with students. They think they can learn what a film is about, from outside the film, that they can somehow have the film explained separately from their own involvement with it. When you have a paper to hand in or an exam to pass with pressures of time these *explanations* are seductive.

SC: I would like to teach students to be unafraid of their language. If they are moved to invoke large ideas such as intention or convention or philosophy or essence, they should remind themselves that these are their words, and that the meaning and the use of words is no more transparent than, say, the significance of a gesture in a film. They have to make themselves familiar both with what they want of a word and of the various ways the word works in our language. Wittgenstein's *Investigations* is a wonderful help in getting us to realise that we become estranged from our language, even frightened by it. So are certain papers of Austin – I recommend to begin with '*Other Minds*' and '*Excuses*', even before *How To Do Things With Words*, on performative utterance, despite the fact that this work is greatly influential now in cultural studies.

AK: I've been reading some of your more recent work on Moral Perfectionism. Can you explain what you understand it to be, and why it is a helpful concept for understanding films or appreciating films? It's been important, for example, in developing your ideas on remarriage comedy.

SC: It took me rather a long time to become conscious of its importance. The conversations in, for example, remarriage comedy, are cases in which one soul is examining another, cases of moral encounter. These people are rebuking one another, questioning one another about how they live, specifically about how they live *together*. At some point, after publishing my book on remarriage comedy, it dawned on me to ask: What moral theory actually describes the point of these conversations, conversations that I had already argued are a fundamental, paramount feature of the genre of remarriage, and that, moreover, are among the permanent glories of world cinema. The principal moral theories in professional philosophical pedagogy are Utilitarianism and Kantianism, and neither illuminates what draws these pairs to commit themselves to each other and to confront each other as they do. Most generally, the pair at the centre of a remarriage comedy are not asking themselves whether the consequences of their marrying are likely to be good measured by utilitarian standards of the greater promise of pleasure over pain. That seems more pertinent to whether a pair might choose to spend a weekend together or buy a new car. Or can we elicit a Kantian principle that explains why it is we marry? Do we wish to attest that all who can marry should marry? This sounds like an attempt to overcome single-parent families, which just might, but cannot in general be thought to, bear on our own decision to marry and perhaps eventually have children. What our pair are talking about is who they want to be and what they want to be together and what kind of world they want to live in, in short whether they are being true to themselves in seeking each other out. But such questions are exactly what moral perfectionism asks us to ask of ourselves. This realisation about perfectionism awaited on my part my late discovery, or rediscovery, of Emerson's thought. In sum, since the nature of the conversation is fundamental to the films of remarriage, and since perfectionism illuminates these conversations more fully and precisely than any other moral theory, perfectionist writing articulates these films more fully and precisely than any other moral theory. For example, one of the earliest features of moral perfectionism, as early as Plato's *Republic*, is that education is essential to it. Well, nothing could be clearer about remarriage comedy than that education is essential to it.

AK: Let me now put the emphasis slightly differently. How might an understanding of Moral Perfectionism in relation to these films help us to understand why they are good?

SC: I don't see is how you could possibly have a satisfying answer to whether these films are good without a developing sense of what they *are*. So am I saying that any film that contains conversations of a certain kind is therefore good? No, of course I don't say that, both because for this to be part of the goodness of the film the conversation itself has to be good, and also because conversation of a certain kind is not the only feature that contributes to the value of these films. I point to two ways in which thinking of the thematics of moral perfectionism may help to comprehend the force of film. First, it picks up the pertinence of such bluff and unedifying concepts as 'screwball' or 'madcap' as applied to remarriage comedies. Which is to say, these comedies really are about marriage, about the terrible risks there must be in two intelligent people committing their intelligence to a shared life. (Intelligence does not mean intellectual.) These films think better of democratic citizens, of their intelligence and imagination – adapting a rebuke Tracy Lord (Katharine Hepburn in *The Philadelphia Story* – George Cukor, 1940, US) levels at the man she had tried to convince herself she should marry – than they think of themselves. Second, it reveals *how* deep the comedic pitfalls of aspiration to a life better than one has so far achieved for oneself run in Western philosophical thought.

AK: My feeling is that Moral Perfectionism is a moral theory or a moral conceptualisation that is responsive to the style and tone of the films, to their detail, to their suggestiveness, and to their modesty (in not declaring their relevance). The application of some moral theories to films can lead to schematic understandings, or alternatively they are applied to schematic films. Your thoughts on Moral Perfectionism allow one to consider, for example, Cary Grant in his billowing night-shirt as the wind blows through the rooms in the final scene of *The Awful Truth*. There are few moral theories, or positions, that would find a way of handling it, or registering it, registering its significance. One of the reasons the Remarriage films might *not* be studied or thought to be important is because they don't obviously dramatise moral issues or deal with lofty matters (draughty, but not lofty). The nightgown might be seen as irrelevant or unimportant, which it is and it isn't (importantly unimportant). This is partly a matter of finding moral importance in the routines of the everyday, of which conversations are a part. Although a crude example, we might think a film about capital punishment has much to teach us, whereas Cary Grant revealing himself in a big nightshirt at a doorway...well...fun perhaps, but insubstantial.

SC: The Problem movie...

AK: The Problem movie, yes, would be an overt example. But it could apply to any film that appears Significant.

SC: An obvious difference of remarriage comedy is that *what* is a significant problem is not *given*. That abortion, capital punishment, euthanasia, whistle-blowing, etc. are significant problems is not news. The news in remarriage comedy is that we help and hurt and interest and bore each other in our everyday lives in countless unremarked and fateful ways, that while we have to learn to tolerate clumsiness in one another – say inadvertent, heedless, thoughtless, careless slaps in our ignorant or uneducated responses to frustration – we have also to learn not to tolerate slugs, meaning any one of a hundred ways we have of dealing out little deaths of rejection. Such things require not calculation or generalisation but perceptiveness and responsiveness. About your wonderful example of Cary Grant in the nightshirt, we should distinguish this from the negligee he wears in *Bringing Up Baby*. In *The Awful Truth*, the pair are both in nightclothes that are too big. They are in effect repeating childhood. It's a part of remarriage comedy that childhood plays a particular role in the pair's life together. They regard themselves as having known each other forever. The thought is capped when we are given these little figurines at the end, behaving abstractly but childishly, retreating into a clock, as if they owned time. In *Bringing Up Baby* what there is to think about, as part of the intimacy demanded of marriage, is not childhood but gender indeterminacy.

AK: At one moment in the final scene of *The Awful Truth*, the door opens and Grant, in his nightshirt, outspreads his arms, lifts his body slightly and takes one foot off the ground as if he were floating away in this draughty house. It is silly, it is playful, but it is also a suggestion to her, a tentative intervention in their ongoing negotiations over their remarriage. Among other things, it is, perhaps, a declaration of lightness. We might say that from the point of view of Moral Perfectionism, this moment, this scene, suggests that they have all sorts of wonderful ways of communicating, of holding a conversation, of making themselves intelligible to each other (without necessarily making themselves fully known). The related question here is: How did the filmmakers and performers come upon these particular wonderful ways?

SC: Yes, the scene is inspired. You really would like to know about the various sensibilities involved in it. Whoever thought to put Cary Grant in front of the door in that nightshirt needn't be the one who thought to have a wind effect here. Well, I call it a wind effect to relate the wind there to the wind effect in the nightclub, to Dixie Belle's dress blown up to her waist in her *'Gone With the Wind'* routine, climactically imitated by Irene Dunne when she poses as Grant's sister, crashing Grant's so-called fiancée's family's party. Being discovered by the door opening – discovered by the camera, and to the woman – Grant, perhaps without outside guidance, rescues the situation by offering an incipient ballet for both camera (that is, for us, revealing his self-awareness, equal to his self-consciousness) and for the woman. The gesture in effect continues their walk-away from the stuffy party earlier that evening. It acknowledges that she is the one person in the world capable of appreciating his integrity, his emotional aplomb, his inventiveness, his acceptance of the silliness and uniqueness of the world, his readiness for what happiness may happen. (Acknowledges this to her, and simultaneously, as it were publicly, to us; prepared to go public for anyone who needs, and has established the right, to know.) The rapidity, the lightning inspiration from talent to talent, is exploding I think.

And here again I feel like repeating an old tune of mine, that concepts applied to film that are not specifically invented for film (unlike close-up, jump cut, etc.) tend to transform themselves. Film came after lightening came, so to speak. Any traditional concept that you use, from the region of theatre, or from painting, or writing, is going to have a further edge – it will be turned differently – when you apply it to film. Actor does, director does, staging does, marriage does, improvisation does. You can use 'improvisation' lightly and think you know what you are saying if you say 'Well they just improvised that.' Meaning they didn't write it, it was a sort of an accident. But if you really take the idea of improvisation with some seriousness, think what it means for musicians to improvise or for actors to improvise a play. I am prepared to believe that Grant improvised his proto-dance, as I am prepared to believe that it rained unexpectedly on Renoir's day in the country. Another actor would have mugged differently, or assumed there would be a further take (maybe there was); another director would have waited until the rain passed.

AK: I want to bring our conversation to a finish by returning to *Mr Deeds Goes To Town*. We talked about the couple of shots where he lies on the bed with the camera behind the back of his head. Another shot might link with these. Before this scene, Deeds and Babe are on their second date, and they are standing at the top of a Skyscraper looking out over the city, as part of a little tour she is conducting. As they look out the camera is once again positioned behind them so that they have their backs to us. Deeds says, 'What puzzles me is why people seem to get so much pleasure out of hurting each other. Why don't they try liking each other once in a while?' and he's specifically referring to the scurrilous newspaper reporters, of which Babe is one, unbeknownst to him, writing hurtful things about people. It is one of those Capra moments that people dismiss as 'sentimental' or 'cornball,' and it could be taken as corn, but how do we account for the fact that their backs are to the camera, and that we're watching them from behind? How does this perspective effect how we should take his line of dialogue? I haven't developed an explanation of this perspective, but I was fascinated with the contrast between the openness of his sentiment and the hiding of his face (and her face). If the dialogue is straightforward and direct, why is it directed away from us?

There is a sequence in *Stella Dallas* (King Vidor, 1937, US), one that I always find painful to watch, and which you discuss in *Contesting Tears*. Stephen Dallas has come home to take Laurel, the daughter, away for Christmas, and Stephen suggests they might take a later train so they can all spend some time together. Unfortunately, just as he is thinking more highly of Stella, Ed Munn turns up to embarrass everyone and Stephen can't get away quickly enough. Stella stands in that smart black dress, her back to the camera, watching the closed door behind which Stephen and Laurel have disappeared. You write that the shot is held somewhat longer that one might expect, calling attention to itself. You go on to write that, as elsewhere, a figure on film turned away from us tends to signal a state of self-absorption, of self-assessment, a sense of thoughts under collection in privacy. I am taken with the way we are invited to consider – and be considerate of – Stella's thoughts even though we only see her from behind, indeed *because* we only see her from behind. It is often a profitable question to ask of film: how does it make us aware of interiority through various forms of externality, and adjust our sensitivity to characters accordingly?

SC: Otherwise there is no history of film. There is no assured, a priori, way. You just have to see and to think. You take some (or choose some you consider) geniuses, or genii, of the medium, and stir them together and look at what they do, and see how they make this medium come to life. With your prompting, I will add a thought about my wish to relate film with philosophy. I have harped on the fact that they are both preoccupied in their way with the everyday, the diurnal (in relation to something of course, to the fantastic, to the metaphysical). Something this means is that they are both preoccupied with ways in which we miss our lives, miss the density of significance passing by in a film, in our speech, in our lives. And we are allowed to, we survive because we can, remain oblivious to it, sometimes feign oblivion. Freud says as early as The Scientific Project that psychic survival is a function of our capacity to protect ourselves from overwhelmingly massive sensory information. The absolutely obvious, to which, at every moment, we are oblivious, is enacted in film in a way that is uniquely powerful, playing with consciousness and unconsciousness.

The oscillation of obliviousness and obviousness is something Austin and Wittgenstein make philosophy of. I am forever grateful to them for it. I see that I am finally getting around to answering something of your opening question to me. Maybe we should start over.

I have lost your question about *Mr. Deeds Goes To Town*. (Yes. Why are they turned away? Hasn't it to do with their discovering an intimacy with each other they are unprepared for? Together with the fact that Deeds here risks – am I remembering this accurately? – showing in an American way his intellectual tastes, quoting Thoreau and imagining the childhood of Ulysses Grant.)

AK: There's another sequence that occurs before the other two I mentioned, after their first date. The shot is of Babe and her editor in the newspaper office. The editor is sitting at his desk reading out her story about Mr. Deeds and laughing at it, and she is listening in the foreground of the shot. I should say she is *partly* listening because she is also absorbed in playing with a coin (she seems to be rehearsing a magic trick, where the coin vanishes behind her fingers). The scene does not openly acknowledge her activity here and neither character mentions it (she continues playing with the coin, in one way or another, as she gets up and walks around, and until the scene ends). We might take her playing with the coin broadly as a colourful bit of business. Yet, how strange this is: all this messing around is going on in this scene, but it doesn't seem to be part of the purpose of the scene. Considering your interpretation of the final scene where fidgeting represents thinking, or reveals something about thinking, we might want to be moved by her gestures. She may want to present herself in a certain a way...

SC: She's clever, she's manipulative, she's self-possessed, she wants to distinguish herself from the ruffians that she deals with, even from her editor...

AK: Yes, and these same gestures present more than Babe knows. During her playing, she drops the coin, gets off the chair, and starts feeling around on the floor; she finds it eventually, down the side of the armchair, and gets back in her chair again. She is engaged in doing her trick (on Deeds), which she is not quite proficient at, not quite suited to, not quite in complete control of and not quite able to bring to completion. Although she doesn't know it, she's just starting to fall in love with Mr. Deeds. She doesn't know who this man is and she's not yet come around to thinking that her intrusive story on him for the newspaper is necessarily a bad thing. Like the coin, which she has to search for, she has not yet found her thoughts on these matters. We are watching fiddling and fumbling, but we are also watching the early murmurings of an extraordinary change of heart (and mind)...

SC: Another inspiration isn't it? It is not hard to imagine hitting on the idea of associating Babe with doing magic tricks. She could easily have been directed, or thought, to sit through the editor's recitation while practicing a coin trick. But in the moment of filming for somebody to have thought to have her drop the coin, that's a new inspiration.

AK: Or the performer dropped the coin by accident.

SC: Of course. It happened to rain that day. Filming is perhaps particularly subject to this kind of rain; some directors seem to cultivate it. Then the inspiration comes in welcoming it.

AK: You say that one of the interesting things about the final scene is that as Deeds points out the different silly actions people do when they think, the camera very overtly picks them out for us in a series of close-ups. The coin example is from much earlier in the film, and one might say that the theme is still only latent (like Babe's thoughts of love), and so the camera is not *pointing*, not pointing out (or up) her fiddling with a close-up. One might say that this instance is a more subtle variation, whereas the later examples are in a spirit of declaration.

SC: Just the last time I saw *Mr. Deeds Goes To Town* I recognised for the first time a blatant gag that may have no depth beyond signalling what else one might be missing. When Deeds first encounters the lawyers who come to see him, he opens a package and declares, 'I've just got a new mouthpiece', and he inserts it into his tuba. But of course lawyers, in American slang, are called mouthpieces. The term is all over movies from the 1930s and 40s. My laughter this time was magnified by the amazement and ruefulness in not having seen this ten or twenty or thirty years ago – however familiar I am with the phenomenon of blankness. You don't need the connection (but seeing it reveals from his opening words, Deeds' quickness, his privacy, his attention, being a writer of verse, to words). Thank heavens for it.

AK: And important to the court scene. Who will be, who should be, his mouthpiece? Other people speak for him, including, most significantly, Babe – his new mouthpiece perhaps? The film explores whether other people's words should speak louder than *Deeds*...

SC: In a film a trivial thing easily becomes a mythical object, probing its own significance. I won't mention a sled or a fake falcon, but in the past days I happened to have encountered again the cigar box containing a child's collection of objects successfully sentimentalised in *To Kill a Mockingbird* (Robert Mulligan, 1962, US) and the presenting and re-presenting of a hat in *Adam's Rib* (George Cukor, 1949, US). You can say of course that these objects are not trivial but that they are about triviality, about juxtapositions in human existence that either are fateful or are meaningless, and that you cannot know beforehand which any will prove to be.

Well I wouldn't have missed this life, and I'm glad it has incorporated film – it might not have.

AK: I'm very glad too that your life incorporated film. Thank you, so much, for having this conversation with me.

Notes

1. Wittgenstein (1953), §109.
2. 'A Plea For Excuses', in Austin (1961).
3. Mulvey (1975).
4. Anscombe (1957).
5. Affron (1977), p. 8.
6. In Cavell (1971), pp. 206–7.
7. Wittgenstein (1961) 6.53, 7.
8. Nietzsche (1996), p. 215.
9. Cavell (1971), pp. 162–3.
10. Wittgenstein (1953), §373.
11. To be found as a chapter in their (1954).

Bibliography

Books and Articles

C. Affron, *Star Acting: Gish, Garbo, Davis* (NY: EP Dutton, 1977)

R. Allen & M. Smith (eds) *Film Theory and Philosophy* (Oxford: Oxford University Press, 1999)

N. Andersen, 'Is Film the Alien Other in Philosophy?', *Film-Philosophy* VII No. 23 (August 2003)

G.E.M. Anscombe, *Intention* (Oxford: Blackwell, 1957)

J.L. Austin, *Philosophical Papers* (Oxford: Clarendon Press, 1961)

J. Baggini, 'Alien Ways of Thinking: Mulhall's *On Film*', *Film-Philosophy* VII No. 24 (August 2003)

G.P. Baker, *Wittgenstein's Method*, (Oxford: Blackwell, 2004)

G.P. Baker (ed.) *The Voices of Wittgenstein: Preliminaries to the Vienna Circle Project* (London: Routledge, 2003)

G.P. Baker & P.M.S. Hacker, *Wittgenstein, Understanding and Meaning* (*Analytical Commentary on* Philosophical Investigations, *Vol. 1*) (Oxford: Blackwell, 1980)

G.P. Baker & P.M.S. Hacker, *Wittgenstein, Rules, Grammar and Necessity* (*Analytical Commentary on* Philosophical Investigations, *Vol. 2*) (Oxford: Blackwell, 1985)

G.P. Baker & K. Morris, *Descartes' Dualism* (London: Routledge, 1995)

M. Bakhtin, *The Dialogic Imagination: Four Essays*, ed. Michael Holquist, trans. Caryl Emerson & Michael Holquist (Austin: University of Texas Press, 1981)

M. Bakhtin, *Problems of Dostoevsky's Poetics*, ed. & trans. Caryl Emerson (Minneapolis: University of Minnesota Press, 1984)

M. Bakhtin, *Art and Answerability: Early Philosophical Essays*, ed. Michael Holquist & Vadim Liapunov, trans. & notes Vadim Liapunov, supplement trans. Kenneth Bostrum (Austin: University of Texas Press, 1990)

M. Bakhtin, *Towards a Philosophy of the Act*, ed. Michael Holquist & Vadim Liapunov, trans. Vadim Liapunov (Austin: University of Texas Press, 1994)

M. Bernard-Donals, *Mikhail Bakhtin: Between Phenomenology and Marxism* (Cambridge: University Press, 1994)

M. Bernard-Donals, 'Bakhtin and Phenomenology: A Reply to Gary Saul Morson', *South Central Review*, Vol. 12, No. 2, 1995, pp. 41–55

M. Blanchot, *L'instant de ma mort* (Montpellier: Fata Morgana, 1994)

G. Button, *Computers, Mind and Conduct* (Cambridge: Polity Press, 1995)

J.E. Cain, Jr. '"Writing in his musical key": Terrence Malick's vision of *The Thin Red Line*', *Film Criticism*, Vol. xxv, 2000, pp. 2–24

R. Cardinal 'Thinking through things: the presence of objects in the early films of Jan Švankmajer', in Hames (ed.) 1995, pp. 78–95

H. Carel and D. Gamez (eds) *What Philosophy Is* (London: Continuum, 2004)

S. Cavell, *Must We Mean What We Say?* (New York: Scribners, 1969)

S. Cavell, *The World Viewed: Reflections on the Ontology of Film*, enlarged edition (Cambridge, MA: Harvard University Press, 1971; new edition 1979)

S. Cavell, *The Claim of Reason: Wittgenstein, Skepticism, Morality and Tragedy*, (Oxford: Clarendon Press, 1979)

S. Cavell, *Pursuits of Happiness: The Hollywood Comedy of Remarriage* (Cambridge, MA: Harvard University Press, 1981)

S. Cavell, *Themes Out of School: Effect and Causes* (Chicago: University of Chicago Press, 1984)

S. Cavell, 'A Capra Moment', *Humanities* 6:4 (August 1985): 3–7

S. Cavell, 'Psychoanalysis and Cinema', in Smith & Kerrigan (eds), 1987

S. Cavell, 'Two Cheers For Romance', in Gaylin & Person (eds), 1987

S. Cavell, 'Who Disappoints Whom?', *Critical Inquiry* 15:3 (Spring 1989): 606–610

S. Cavell, *Conditions Handsome and Unhandsome: The Constitution of Emersonian Perfectionism* (Chicago: University of Chicago Press, 1991)

S. Cavell, *Contesting Tears: The Melodrama of the Unknown Woman* (Chicago: University of Chicago Press, 1996)

S. Cavell, *The Cavell Reader* (ed. S. Mulhall) (Oxford: Blackwell, 1996)

S. Cavell, 'The *Investigations*' Everyday Aesthetics of Itself', in Cavell (1996) and McCarthy & Stidd (2001)

S. Cavell, 'An Interview with Stanley Cavell', *Harvard Journal of Philosophy*, VII (1999): 19–28

S. Cavell, *Cities of Words: Pedagogical Letters on a Register of the Moral Life* (Cambridge, MA: Harvard University Press, 2004)

D.R. Cerbone, 'Don't Look But Think: Imaginary Scenarios in Wittgenstein's Later Philosophy', *Inquiry*, Vol. 37 (1994): 159–83

D. Charles & W. Childs, *Wittgensteinian Themes: Essays in Honour of David Pears* (Oxford: University Press, 2001)

K. Clark & M. Holquist, 'The Influence of Kant in the Early Work of M.M. Bakhtin', in J.P. Strelka (ed.), pp. 299–313

K. Clark & M. Holquist, *Mikhail Bakhtin* (Cambridge, MA: Belknap Press, 1984)

S. Connor, *Dumbstruck: A Cultural History of Ventriloquism* (Oxford: University Press, 2001)

A. Crary & R. Read (eds) *The New Wittgenstein* (London: Routledge, 2000)

D.C. Dennett, 'Conditions of Personhood', in *Brainstorms* (Brighton: Harvester Press, 1981)

J. Derrida, *Writing and Difference*, trans. Alan Bass (London: Routledge, 1978)

C. Diamond, 'The Difficulty of Reality and the Difficulty of Philosophy', unpublished manuscript.

C. Emerson, 'Problems with Baxtin's Poetics', *Slavic and East European Journal*, Vol. 32, No. 4, 1988, pp. 503–25

M. Eskin, *Ethics and Dialogue in the works of Levinas, Bakhtin, Mandel'shtam, and Celan* (Oxford: University Press, 2000)

C. Falzon, *Philosophy Goes To The Movies* (London: Routledge, 2002)

M. Filippidis, 'On Malick's Subjects', *Senses of Cinema* on-line at: http://www.sensesofcinema.com/contents/00/8/malick.html

C.A. Freeland & T.E. Wartenburg (eds) *Philosophy and Film* (London: Routledge, 1995)

C.A. Freeland, *The Naked and the Undead: Evil and the Appeal to Horror* (Boulder, CO: Westview Press, 1999)

Willard Gaylin and Ethel Person (eds) *Passionate Attachments: Thinking About Love* (New York: Free Press, 1987)

A. Gibson, *Towards a Postmodern Theory of Narrative* (Edinburgh: Edinburgh University Press, 1996)

H-J. Glock, *A Wittgenstein Dictionary* (Oxford: Blackwell, 1989)

H-J. Glock, 'The Development of Wittgenstein's Philosophy' in Glock (ed.), 2001

H-J. Glock, 'Was Wittgenstein An Analytical Philosopher?', *Metaphilosophy* Vol. 35, No. 4, 419–44

H-J. Glock (ed.) *Wittgenstein: A Critical Reader* (Oxford: Blackwell, 2001)

P.M.S. Hacker, *Wittgenstein, Meaning and Mind* (*Analytical Commentary on Philosophical Investigations, Vol. 3*) (Oxford: Blackwell, 1990)

P.M.S. Hacker, *Wittgenstein, Mind and Will* (*Analytical Commentary on Philosophical Investigations, Vol. 4*) (Oxford: Blackwell, 1996)

P.M.S. Hacker, *Wittgenstein's Place in Twentieth Century Analytical Philosophy* (Oxford: Blackwell, 1996)

P.M.S. Hacker, 'Philosophy' in Glock (ed.) 2001

P.M.S. Hacker, *Wittgenstein; Connections and Controversies* (Oxford: University Press, 2001)

P. Hames (ed.) *Dark Alchemy: the Films of Jan Švankmajer* (Westport, CT: Praeger, 1995)

M. Heidegger, *Being and Time* (trans. J. Mcquarrie) (Oxford: Blackwell, 1962)

M. Heidegger, 'What is Metaphysics?', in *Martin Heidegger. Basic Writings*, ed. D.F. Krell (London & New York: Routledge, 1978)

P. Hutchinson & R. Read, 'The Fundamental Significance of *Philosophical Investigations* §122', in Moyal-Sharrock (ed.) (forthcoming)

D.D. Hutto, *Wittgenstein and the End of Philosophy: Neither Theory Nor Therapy* (Basingstoke: Palgrave, 2003)

P. Johnston, *Wittgenstein and Moral Philosophy* (London: Routledge, 1989)

J. Jones, *The Thin Red Line* (London: Hodder & Stoughton, 1998) (originally pub. 1962)

A. Kenny, *The Legacy of Wittgenstein* (Oxford: Blackwell, 1984)

A. Kenny, *The Metaphysics of Mind* (Oxford: Clarendon Press, 1989)

P. Kerr, *A Philosophical Investigation* (London: Vintage, 1996)

S. Kierkegaard, *Either/Or* (English translation of 1843 original Penguin Books, Harmondsworth 1992)

T.J. Kline, *Screening the Text* (Baltimore: Johns Hopkins Press, 1992)

M. Köbel & B. Weiss (eds) *Wittgenstein's Lasting Significance* (London: Routledge, 2004)

S. Kripke, *Wittgenstein on Rules and Private Language* (Oxford: Blackwell, 1982)

S. Laugier & M. Cerisuelo (eds) *Stanley Cavell: Cinema et philosophie* (Paris: Presse de la Sorbonne, 2001)

E. Levinas, *Totality and Infinity: An Essay on Exteriority*, trans. Alphonso Lingis (Pittsburgh: Duquesne University Press, 1969)

E. Levinas, *Difficult Freedom: Essays on Judaism*, trans. Sean Hand (Baltimore: Johns Hopkins University Press, 1990)

T. Malick, *The Essence of Reasons* (Evanston: Northwestern University Press, 1969)

T.G. McCarthy & S.C. Stidd, *Wittgenstein In America* (Oxford: University Press, 2001)

J. McDowell, *Mind Value and Reality* (Cambridge, MA: Harvard University Press, 1998)

J. McDowell, 'Non-cognitivism and Rule-following', in McDowell 1998, and in Crary & Read 1999

M. McGinn, *Wittgenstein and the* Philosophical Investigations (London: Routledge, 1997)

K. McKenna, 'An interview with Jacques Derrida', *LA Weekly*, 2002 (Available on-line)

D. McManus, *The Enchantment of Words* (forthcoming)

J. Medina, *The Unity of Wittgenstein's Philosophy: Necessity, Intelligibility and Normativity* (New York: Suny Press, 2002)

M. Merleau-Ponty, *Phenomenology of Perception* (Paris: Gallimard, 1945)(London: Routledge, 1962)

G.S. Morson & C. Emerson (eds) *Rethinking Bakhtin: Extensions and Challenges* (Evanston, IL: Northwestern University Press, 1989)

G.S. Morson & C. Emerson, *Mikhail Bakhtin: Creation of a Prosaics* (Stanford: Stanford University Press, 1990)

D. Moyal-Sharrock (ed.) *Perspicuous Presentations: Wittgenstein's Philosophy of Psychology* (forthcoming)

S. Mulhall, *On Being In The World* (London: Routledge, 1990)

S. Mulhall, *Inheritance and Originality: Wittgenstein, Heidegger, Kierkegaard* (Oxford: University Press, 2001).

S. Mulhall, *On Film* (London: Routledge, 2002)

L. Mulvey, 'Visual Pleasure and Narrative Cinema' *Screen* 16.3 (Autumn 1975) pp. 6–18, reprinted in Penley (ed.) 1988

L. Mulvey, *Visual and Other Pleasures* (Bloomington, IN: Indiana University Press, 1989)

F. Nietzsche, *Human, All Too Human* (ed. R.J. Hollingdale) (Cambridge: University Press, 1996) (Orig. pub. 1878)

C. Penley (ed.) *Feminism and film theory* (New York: Routledge, 1988)

W. Percy, *The Moviegoer* (New York: Alfred Knopf, 1960)

C. Plantinga & G.M. Smith (eds) *Passionate Views: Film, Cognition, and Emotion,* (Baltimore: Johns Hopkins University Press, 1999)

Plato, *The Republic* (trans. R. Waterfield, Oxford: University Press, 1998)

N. Pleasants, *Wittgenstein and the Idea of a Critical Social Theory* (London: Routledge, 1999)

K. Popper, *Conjectures and Refutations* (London: Routledge Kegan Paul, 1963).

A. Robbe-Grillet, *Last Year in Marienbad* (trans. R. Howard) (London: John Calder, 1961).

J. Robbins, *Altered Readings, Levinas and Literature* (Chicago: University of Chicago Press, 1999)

M. Rowlands, *The Philosopher at the End of the Universe* (London: Ebury Press, 2003).

O. Sacks, *The Man Who Mistook His Wife For A Hat* (Brighton: Duckworth, 1985).

L. Sass, *The Paradoxes of Delusion: Wittgenstein, Schreber and the schizophrenic mind* (New York: Cornell, 1994).

L. Sass, *Madness and Modernism: Insanity in the light of modern art, literature and thought* (Harvard: University Press, 1998).

S. Schroeder, 'Private Language and Private Experience' in Glock (ed.) 2001.

J. Searle, 'Minds, Brains and Programs', *Behavioural and Brain Sciences* 3 (1980), 417–58.

G.M. Smith, *Film Structure and the Emotion System* (New York: Cambridge University Press, 2003)

J.H. Smith and W. Kerrigan (eds) *Images in our Souls: Cavell, Psychoanalysis, and Cinema* (Baltimore: Johns Hopkins University Press, 1987)

J.P. Strelka (ed.) *Literary Theory and Criticism: Festschrift in Honor of Rene Wellek,* Vol. 1 (New York: Peter Lang, 1984)

J. Vitale, 'An Interview with America's Most Brilliant Science-Fiction Writer (Philip K. Dick)', *The Aquarian,* XI (October 1978) (available on-line)

G. Vlastos, *Socrates, Ironist and Moral Philosopher* (Cambridge: Cambridge University Press, 1991)

F. Waismann, 'How I See Philosophy', in his *How I See Philosophy* (London: Macmillan, 1969)

J. Ward, *Alain Resnais, or The Theme of Time* (London: Secker & Warburg, 1968).

B. Williams, *Truth and Truthfulness* (Princeton: University Press, 2002)

W.H. Wimsatt & M.C. Beardsley, *The Verbal Icon: studies in the meaning of poetry* (Lexington: Kentucky University Press, 1954)

L. Wittgenstein, *Tractatus Logico-Philosophicus* (trans. D.F. Pears & B.F. McGuinness) (London: Routledge, 1961) (Orig. pub. 1921)

L. Wittgenstein, *Philosophical Investigations* (Oxford: Blackwell, 1953).

L. Wittgenstein, *The Blue and Brown Books* (Oxford: Blackwell, 1958).

L. Wittgenstein, *Lectures & Conversations on Aesthetics, Psychology and Religious Belief* (ed. Cyril Barrett) (Oxford: Blackwell, 1966)

L. Wittgenstein, *Culture and Value* (ed. G.H. von Wright, trans. Peter Winch) (Oxford: Blackwell, 1980)

L. Wittgenstein, *Zettel* (ed. G.E.M. Anscombe & G.H. von Wright, trans. G.E.M. Anscombe) (Oxford: Blackwell, 1988)

L. Wittgenstein, 'Diktat für Schlick' in Baker (ed.) 2003

L. Wittgenstein & F. Waismann, *The Voices of Wittgenstein* (ed. G. Baker), (London: Routledge, 2003).

Websites

The Aquarian, http://www.philipkdick.com/media_aquarian.html
Film-Philosophy, http://www.film-philosophy.com/
LA Weekly Derrida Interview, http://www.hydra.umn.edu/derrida/laweekly.html
Philosophy and the Matrix, http://whatisthematrix.warnerbros.com/rl_cmp/phi.html
Quine Video Series, http://www.lse.ac.uk/Depts/cpnss/pi/quine_video_series.htm
Senses of Cinema, http://www.sensesofcinema.com/

Index